INDIA-SOUTH ASIA INTERFACE

India-South Asia Interface

Religion, Politics and the Wider World

PARTHA S. GHOSH

MANOHAR
2022

First published 2022

ISBN 978-93-90729-77-7

Published by
Ajay Kumar Jain *for*
Manohar Publishers & Distributors
4753/23 Ansari Road, Daryaganj
New Delhi 110 002

Typeset by
Kohli Print
Delhi 110 051

Printed at
Replika Press Pvt. Ltd.

To the common people of
South Asia

Contents

Preface

This is a collection of my short essays written over the last five years. They were essentially devoted to contemporary Indian affairs keeping the regional and global developments in mind. Most of them appeared as my monthly column in the *Dhaka Tribune* since December 2018 which, since August 2019, have also been simultaneously published by *Newsclick*, a Delhi-based news-portal. To supplement the overall picture, some other short publications of mine have also been incorporated, for example, the first chapter, which defines South Asia, is a reproduction of my 'Special Article' in *Economic and Political Weekly* (Mumbai) in its 6 August 2016 issue under the title, 'Region without Regionalism: Cooperation in South Asia'.

For the convenience of my readers I have not put these essays in chronological sequence of their publication but jacketed them in eight thematic chapters. The ninth one is of a different kind. It is largely autobiographical, telling the story of why and how I became a champion of South Asian regionalism, though not in the way the regional states want to approach it, which is the conventional wisdom. To my mind there is an undercurrent of South Asian consciousness running across the region but unfortunately it has been hijacked by the modern state systems and, in the process, completely messed up. In this chapter, which has been written from my heart, I have pleaded for more and more popular interaction across South Asia without which SAARC will always remain a dream never to be fulfilled.

At the end of the book is appended a list of my own writings specifically compiled keeping in view each country of the region or some overarching themes that are relevant for a better understanding of the region. In this connection one may think of the SAARC experiment, the issue of family laws (personal laws) and the discourse over the uniform civil codes, or, the important role that the refugees and migrants have been playing in shaping the destiny of South Asia.

In the making of this book, my thanks are due primarily to Mr Zafar Sobhan who has been regularly publishing my columns in his esteemed daily *Dhaka Tribune* without any interruption since December 2018. Their topical value was underlined when the Delhi-based e-portal *Newsclick* started publishing them simultaneously, for which I thank Dr Prabir Purakayastha, the managing editor of the portal. Besides, my thanks are also due to the *Economic and Political Weekly* (Mumbai), the *Mainstream* (New Delhi), the *Outlook* (New Delhi), *Scroll.in* (Mumbai), and *Policy Watch* (New Delhi) for allowing me to use my pieces published in them. A special word of thanks also to my son, Arunabh, who read many of these pieces and offered suggestions that invariably made them more readable. Last, but not the least, I thank my old friend Mr Ramesh Jain of the Manohar Publishers & Distributors, without whose encouragement this publication would not have seen the light of the day.

New Delhi PARTHA S. GHOSH

CHAPTER 1

In Search of a Region*

INTRODUCTION

The South Asian Association for Regional Cooperation (SAARC) consists of eight nations: Afghanistan, Bangladesh, Bhutan, India, Maldives, Nepal, Pakistan and Sri Lanka. They constitute the region of South Asia. Is this institutional definition enough to pass it as a region? Five elements foster regionalism; shared history and culture; political similitude; economic cooperation for mutual gain; power balance among member states; and non-conflicting strategic postures. South Asia fails on all these counts. Its so-called 'one civilization', or 'shared history', is always contested. The partitions of India (1947) and Pakistan (1971) were the results of that contestation. The common factor of democracy has barely reduced the danger of ethno-religious separatism. Intra-regional trade is not complementary, and therefore, very small, just 5 per cent of the region's global trade. There is a gross mismatch between India and the rest which also mars regional consciousness. The worst handicap for the region is the strategic divide between India and Pakistan, which is further complicated by the China factor. The weaker nations of the region utilize this triangular conflict to their advantage.

INSTITUTIONALIZATION OF SOUTH ASIA

South Asia qualifies as a region only in institutional terms. The eight SAARC members constitute it. Till 2007 when Afghanistan

* Published in *Economic and Political Weekly* (Mumbai), 51(32), 6 August 2016 as 'Region without Regionalism: Cooperation in South Asia'. Thanks to *EPW* for allowing me to reproduce it here.

was not in SAARC it was not considered South Asian. Logically, therefore, if a country quits the group it ceases to be South Asian. Already given Pakistan's alleged intransigence India has been promoting sub-regionalism. The high-profile 65-page *Non-Alignment 2.0: A Foreign and Strategic Policy for India in the Twenty First Century* ignores SAARC altogether though it says that 'within the Asian theatre no region is more vital for India than South Asia'.[1] The mere six pages that it devotes to South Asia is primarily a discussion on Pakistan. The latter ignores SAARC because it virtually means India. After Bangladesh (1971) when Pakistan's South Asian connection became tenuous it had developed the proclivity to come closer to its western Muslim neighbours. It may be noted that both India and Pakistan were unsupportive of the idea when Ziaur Rahman of Bangladesh mooted it in the late 1970s.

HISTORICITY OF SOUTH ASIA

Historically, there is no reference to South Asia. The references present are only to India. As early as in 326 BCE the Greek warrior Alexander had come to India. In 52 CE St. Thomas arrived in Kerala which marked the beginning of Christianity in India. In ancient and medieval times the Arabs traded in India's western ports. During Renaissance Christopher Columbus and Vasco da Gama searched for sea routes to India. In colonial India Indology thrived in a big way. All this contributed to making India the reference point for characterizing new areas. Ergo, we had the Indian Ocean, West Indies, East Indies, and Indo-China. The company that pioneered the British Empire in South and Southeast Asia was called the East India Company. Even the name Indonesia is derived from Indos Nesos, 'Indian Island'. That is why the Dutch company that traded in Indonesia was called the Dutch East India Company. In short, it was India that dictated the geographic names, rather than any abstract notion of South Asia.

SOUTH ASIA IN WESTERN CONCEPTION

In the United States the notion of South Asia developed in the aftermath of the Second World War as an offshoot of Oriental Studies, the backbone of which was Indology. It had a long tradition in American academia which in the interwar period (1919-39) got a boost because of American missionaries. Many such 'scholar missionaries' ended up in American universities. After the War, more particularly after India's Independence, interest in India grew faster. Still, India mattered less than China, Japan, Korea and the Soviet Union. On a similar pattern, depending upon their past connections or contemporary involvements, other Western nations concentrated more on region-specific studies. Thus, Britain focused on India; France on Indochina; and the Netherlands on Indonesia (Ludden 2003: 1059). In the 1960s many South Asia centres came up in American universities (Cohen 2006: 148-9). This interest in South Asia, however, meant interest in India. Academic conferences on South Asia were largely led by India specialists. For instance, the annual South Asian conference at Madison in Wisconsin, the largest one, which had its origin in 1973,[2] had sprung out of the 'Indian Studies Department' launched in the 1950s (ibid.: 159, Brown 1964: 54-62). The only other South Asian country that attracted attention was Pakistan but those involved were mostly strategic analysts.

India mattered also because of China. The two opposite models of development that India and China represented caught the imagination of the American academia. It was important for America to understand how the two distinct political and economic experiments would influence the future of Asia. All this led to the launching of the 'The India Project' at the Center for International Studies at MIT. Wilfred Malenbaum, the director of the project said;

> . . . countries, especially in Africa and Asia, will be influenced in their own programs by what seems to be happening in these two lands. However much India and China disavow a state of competition between alternative paths for the transformation to growth, comparisons will be made everywhere, and lessons put into practice. (Malenbaum 1958)

America's strategic thinking, however, was not Indo-centric. It was more Pakistan-centric. This was the time when the New Dealers were on their retreat and the Cold Warriors on ascendancy. The leading Cold Warriors were President Harry S. Truman and his Secretary of State, Dean Acheson, and their respective successors,

Dwight D. Eisenhower and John Foster Dulles. A 1949 document prepared by the Subcommittee for the Near and Middle East of the State-Army-Navy-Air Forces Coordinating Committee (SANACC) noted that 'our national interests require . . . the orientation of South Asia toward the US and other Western democracies, and away from the USSR'. The 'basic strategic objectives of the US' required, the report said,

> That Soviet encroachment or domination must be prevented; that the Soviets must be prevented from obtaining military support from these nations or given access to any of their facilities; that our side must endeavour to obtain the support and access to facilities denied to the other side; and that *Pakistan should be cultivated with a view to gaining access in emergency* to *base facilities in the Karachi-Lahore area.* (Gould 2008: 109) (emphasis is in the original)

It may be noted that while in the pre-Second World War period India was the referral point in the post-Second World War period Pakistan became the referral point to which India was appended.

Dulles was a pathological Cold Warrior for whom if one was not with the United States it amounted to immorality. American balance, therefore, had to tilt in favour of Pakistan. For the same reason, India's non-alignment, leave alone intellectually confusing for the Cold Warriors, was outrightly 'immoral'. One must not read too much into the fact that the then US Ambassador to India, Chester Bowles (1951-3), was appreciative of Nehru's foreign policy. His New Delhi posting itself was a White House ploy to keep him away from the Washington circuit so that he could not interfere with the US Cold War strategy (Gould 2008: 102-27). The Dullesian naïveté was exemplified in the following conversation he had with journalist Walter Lippmann in 1954:

> Look Walter . . . I've got some real fighting men into the south of Asia. The only Asians who can really fight are the Pakistanis. . . . We could never get along without the Gorkhas.' When Lippmann reminded him that the Gurkhas are Indian, not Pakistani, Dulles replied, 'Well, they may not be Pakistanis, but they're Moslems.' Lippman once more corrected Dulles, saying, 'No, I'm afraid they're not Moslems either, they're Hindus.' Dulles merely replied, 'No matter,' and proceeded to lecture Lippmann for half an hour on how SEATO would plug the dike against communism in Asia. (Gould 2008: 161)

From the above discussion it emerges that while for the US academia South Asia meant India, for the US strategic establishment it meant Pakistan. If at all the phrase South Asia figured in strategic discussions it was more for geographical reasons. It was as late as 1991 that the State Department had clubbed South Asia with 'Near East', which received the lion's share of attention although it had one-third of South Asia's population. A deputy assistant secretary four levels junior to the secretary of state handled relations with India. The same arrangement held good for the National Security Council and the Central Intelligence Agency. It was only with the creation of the National Intelligence Agency in 2005 that a separate South Asia Bureau was created which directly reported to a director of the intelligence (Rubinoff 2008: 171).

Outside of the United States the expression South Asia as an 'Area Studies' region was specifically used when the South Asia Institute (SAI) of the Heidelberg University (Germany) came into being in 1962. In early 1960s it was thought to establish an institute in Heidelberg to study the developing countries. Later South Asia was chosen as the focused region as Heidelberg University had the long tradition of Indology. The idea was to pool expertise from various disciplines to make the understanding of the region holistic. The result was the establishment of the 'Indo-Asia Institute' (Nuesser n.d.: 4). From 'Indo-Asia Institute' how it became the SAI is an interesting story which may be instructive for all those non-Indian South Asians who allege that India suffers from a big-brotherly superiority complex. Here is what German historian Dietmar Rothermund writes:

> At the time when the Rourkela plant was built, the shortage of specialised engineers was a pressing problem in India and with German aid one of the new Indian Institutes of Technology was established in Madras (Chennai) in 1959. This period of very active German interest in India also witnessed the establishment of several branches of the Goethe Institute which in India are called Max Mueller Bhavans (MMBs). . . . The South Asia Institute of Heidelberg University, opened in 1962 [23 May] in the presence of Nehru's sister, Vijayalakshmi Pandit, was another testimony to this German interest in India. *Originally it was to be named 'Indo-Asia Institute,' but President [S.] Radhakrishnan suggested the name South Asia Institute as he felt that 'Indo-Asia'*

was reminiscent of 'Greater India' and would be resented by India's neighbours. (Rothermund 2010: 5, emphasis added)[3]

SOUTH ASIA IN INDIAN CONSCIOUSNESS

If there was no clear concept of South Asia in Western academic and strategic thinking in the case of India it was not any better. India's consciousness about its pre-eminence in the region was so overpowering that it viewed an Indo-centric regionalism to be its destiny. Two years before India's Independence India's first prime minister, Pandit Jawaharlal Nehru, visualized a manifest destiny for India in which only four powers would have the strategic wherewithal to become major powers, namely, India, America, Russia, and China. In a sense, it was Curzonian. J.N. Dixit, India's former foreign secretary and author of many books on foreign policy and diplomacy, considered Curzon as one of 'the greatest of the Indian nationalists' (Raja Mohan 2006: 204).[4] Although the Partition of India made Nehru's vision anachronistic, still, India's quest for regional leadership did not die. It conceptualized its strategic doctrine in concentric circles in which India's defence perimeter lay not at its own borders but at the outer borders of its regional neighbours.

One is not sure when the idea of South Asia as a region took shape in India. For Nehru the world as a whole mattered in the Cold War in which India's neighbours were mere dices. The two pillars of India's foreign policy were non-alignment and treating Pakistan as an enemy as it was an active participant in the Cold War. India, however, made it clear that non-alignment was not neutrality but it was an input from the decolonized world to reduce the scourge of war inherent in the Cold War circumstances. No particular country or region was, therefore, to receive any special attention in India's Area Studies, not even Pakistan. For this, another explanation could be that Pakistan as a bad dream better be underemphasized lest it destabilize the delicate Hindu-Muslim relations already under severe strain following the Partition riots and displacements. Nehru's fortnightly 'Letters to the Chief Ministers' (compiled and edited in 4 volumes by G. Parthasarathi) reflected this concern. Also to be noted is that during his 17 years of rule (1947-64) the 1,742 documentaries that his government produced not for once mentioned the issue. Their emphasis was entirely on modernism as a tool of nation building (Taneja 2009: 1-4). India-Pakistan borders were not strictly enforced and it was common to have cross-border bridal processions, particularly in the Rajasthan sector (Ghosh 2016: 44).

It may not be just a coincidence that during Nehru's time, barring Kashmir, there was no other military confrontation with Pakistan. On the contrary, there were evidences of thaw, as seen in the co-ordinated refugee rehabilitation policies and the resolution of certain disputed border pockets (Nehru-Liaquat Agreement of 8 April 1950, and Nehru-Noon Agreement of 12 September 1958, respectively), Ayub Khan's personal invitation to Nehru to see the ongoing construction of Islamabad as Pakistan's new capital, and in his sending of Kashmiri leader Sheikh Abdullah to Pakistan as his emissary to discuss Kashmir (Nehru died during Abdullah's sojourn making him rush back to Delhi resulting in the collapse of the mission).[5] Curiously, or expectedly, within less than one year after Nehru's death, Pakistan started its second war on Kashmir in April 1965 and the post-Nehru period experienced a noticeable rise in Hindu-Muslim riots.[6] From the above discussion, one may surmise that probably Nehru's so-called lack of interest in South Asia was more dictated by his consideration that India be let to assume a low and humanistic profile in the region, lest it could be seen as a big brother, which it was any way (refer to our discussion earlier with regard to the establishment of SAI in Heidelberg).

During the Bangladesh crisis of 1971, Indira Gandhi saw to it that Pakistan was cut to size. Still, she ensured that her diplomatic offensive did not complicate the Hindu-Muslim relationship in India. She feared that if the news spread that more than 80 per cent of the refugees arriving from East Pakistan were Hindu it could cause serious communal strife leading even to riots. To preempt that danger she took the Jana Sangh (forerunner of the BJP) leader Atal Behari Vajpayee into confidence and requested him not to communalize the issue, which would give Pakistan the handle to portray the Bangladesh problem as a Hindu-Muslim one, thereby defeating the Indian plan (Raghavan 2013: 76, 120, 206; Bass 2013: 154, 236-7). It was not merely Pakistan, Indira Gandhi was equally determined to show India's other neighbours that India's capacity to destabilize them must be respected for their own political survival. The way India trained and financed the LTTE in the early 1980s to thwart Sri Lanka's alleged anti-India policy is a case in point.

So much is made out of the so-called Gujral Doctrine which is claimed to have ushered in some kind of South Asian regionalism. The five principles that constituted the doctrine, though, emphasized good neighbourly relations with India's smaller neighbours like Bangladesh, Bhutan, Maldives, Nepal and Sri Lanka (Afghanistan was not in South Asia then), even without expecting reciprocity from them, a policy that culminated in sub-regionalism in later years. It addressed neither the real question, relations with Pakistan, nor how to reorient SAARC to make it handle bilateral and contentious issues. The doctrine pontificated that all countries must respect each other's territorial integrity, but completely glossed over Kashmir which was the bone of contention between India and Pakistan. In his autobiography, I.K. Gujral himself confessed that much: 'The logic behind the Gujral Doctrine was that since we had to face two hostile neighbours in the north and the west, we had to be at "total peace" with all other immediate neighbours in order to contain Pakistan's and China's influence in the region' (2011: 406).

Nothing has changed till this day in substantive terms. Although following his victory in the 2014 elections Prime Minister Narendra Modi kickstarted his regime with a South Asian diplomatic blitzkrieg by inviting all SAARC leaders to his oath-taking ceremony and soon took steps to improve ties with Bangladesh,[7] Sri Lanka and Nepal, his ideological baggage continued to remain his liability. The BJP's Election Manifesto of 2014 had promised 'to establish friendly and cooperative relations with India's neighbours' but its underlying thrust on Hindutva (though the word was not used) blurred Modi's promise. Besides bragging about 'Brand India' the party highlighted India's traditional glory as *vishvaguru* (the knowledge-giver to the world). The foreign policy section of the manifesto read more like a propaganda statement on India's traditional greatness. Any student of South Asian affairs knows that there could not have been a worse neighbourhood diplomacy to start with than this. It could be actually viewed as offensive. For example, juxtapose this to how Pakistan recognizes its Indian past. It starts with the invasion of Muhammad Ghori on India (1202) and ends with the end of the Mughals (1857). Pakistani textbooks completely gloss over the country's pre-Muslim past when Hindus or Buddhists had ruled.

Modi's subsequent domestic record was potentially disruptive of South Asianism. Events surrounding such controversies as murder of liberal thinkers, general atmosphere of intolerance to freedom of thought, refusal to Pakistani cricket team or vocal artistes to play/perform in India, violence against alleged beef eaters, and so on, were bound to hamper confidence building in the region at the mass level. However much the BJP supporters might argue that Hinduism by nature is tolerant and that such controversies had taken place in the past as well, these issues became matters of popular debate all over the region in which Modi's India was not seen in positive light. This author's personal conversations spread over many years with liberal voices in India's neighbouhood have convinced him about how much they have put in store in India's secular/liberal future. They argue that India alone can show the region the way to encourage secular and scientific temper aimed at societal development. And if that India itself falters there is little hope for a liberal region to survive—and hence regionalism.

BEYOND HIGH POLITICS

In this section, let us show that beyond high politics South Asia as a region is on the whole on the periphery of India's consciousness. Our sample consists of the organizational set-up of the Ministry of External Affairs (MEA), the MEA'a cultural wing called the Indian Council for Cultural Relations (ICCR), the MEA-funded Indian Council of World Affairs (ICWA), the Ministry of Human Resource Development (MHRD)-funded Indian Council of Social Science Research (ICSSR), the Ministry of Defence (MOD)-funded

Institute for Defence Studies and Analyses (IDSA), the SAARC-sponsored South Asian University (SAU), and South Asian Studies as Area Studies.

MEA: In the MEA structure there is no concept of South Asia though there is one division, called the SB & BC Division, which deals with matters related to SAARC, BIMSTEC (Bay of Bengal Initiative for Multi-Sectoral Technical and Economic Cooperation), and border connectivity. Given India's growing interest in building relations with Southeast Asia and promoting sub-regionalism, SAARC receives relatively less attention. In any case, Myanmar and Thailand, both in Southeast Asia, are very significant in so far as BIMSTEC and border connectivity issues are concerned. In bilateral terms, the following (Table 1.1) will show how the South Asian states have been organized in the MEA Divisions. There is indeed geographical and strategic logic in this distribution but the point we are making is that it obfuscates the concept of South Asia.

ICCR: With respect to culture promotion in South Asia the activities of MEA's autonomous wing called the Indian Council for Cultural Relations (ICCR) may throw some light on India's commitment to South Asian regionalism. Besides organizing cultural events abroad and inviting cultural troupes from outside of India, ICCR has a massive scholarship programme meant for students

TABLE 1.1: DISTRIBUTION OF SOUTH ASIAN STATES AMONG MEA DIVISIONS

Name of the Country	Name of the Division	Other Countries Included
Afghanistan	PAI Division	Pakistan, Iran
Bangladesh	BM Division	Myanmar
Bhutan	Northern Division	Nepal
Maldives	Indian Ocean Region	Sri Lanka
Nepal	Northern Division	Bhutan
Pakistan	PAI Division	Afghanistan, Iran
Sri Lanka	Indian Ocean Region	Maldives

Source: Ministry of External Affairs Website.

from developing countries, which include South Asian nations. It distributes more than 6,000 scholarships besides managing 16 scholarships funded separately by the MEA and the Ministry of AYUSH.[8] Africa and Afghanistan each get 1,000 of them. The scheme for Afghanistan is called the Special Scholarship Scheme for Afghan Nationals which started in 2005, two years before Afghanistan joined the SAARC. Of the remaining South Asian countries, Bangladesh is supposed to get 100 scholarships, Bhutan 20, Maldives 20, Nepal 64, and Sri Lanka about 195.[9] There is none for Pakistan under the above scheme. Besides, there is the SAARC Chair/Fellowship/Scholarship Scheme, the record of which is dismal. The idea of the SAARC Chair was first mooted in 1987 but it hardly worked. In 1992-3, Shelton Kodikara, Professor of Political Science, Colombo University, was invited by the University of Delhi to become the first SAARC Professor. But neither was he given a salary which could take care of his stay (without any house or rent allowance) nor did he have a well-organized academic programme. He returned after his tenure, most dejected.[10] Many years later, in 2013-14, another professor from Sri Lanka held the Chair at the PUSA agricultural institute. Under the SAARC Fellowship/Scholarship scheme, India is supposed to bring 14 students, two each from Afghanistan, Bangladesh, Bhutan, Maldives, Nepal, Pakistan and Sri Lanka. This scheme was launched in 2013-14. But so far it has not recorded any activity. In 2015-16, the MEA discontinued it. If one goes into the details of the application procedures under all these schemes, one would be struck by the bureaucratic red tape. Inordinate delay in the processing of applications is structured in the system, a typical Third World phenomenon.[11]

ICWA: In the Indian Council of World Affairs (ICWA), South Asia is not a thrust area. Though several ICWA fellows are working on individual South Asian countries, yet if one goes by the ICWA's calendar of events during the last two years, which coincides with Modi's high-profile South Asian diplomatic push, one would be surprised to see how the region has been ignored. Between May 2014 and April 2016, mostly on its own but sometimes in collaboration with other organizations, ICWA has organized as many as 70 events of which South Asia related ones are just six including three lectures delivered by visiting South Asian leaders. In the activities scheduled for the coming months, too, South Asia does not figure.[12]

ICSSR: South Asia hardly figures in the International Collaboration (IR) programme of the Indian Council of Social Science Research (ICSSR). It has ongoing collaborative programmes with 14 countries that include exchange of scholars and joint projects. The active ones are with China, England, France, Germany, Japan, the Netherlands, Thailand, Russia, South Africa, Sweden, Switzerland and Vietnam. The one with the United States is non-functional though on paper since 2013. Among the collaborative partners, only one South Asian country figures, that is, Sri Lanka. An MOU was signed with it on 13 March 2014, which envisaged exchange of two scholars every year for 30 days each. So far no such exchange has taken place though a joint seminar has been held in Colombo in August 2015 and the next one is supposed to be held in India. The neglect of South Asia is reflected in ICSSR's fellowship programme as well. In the last decade only three or four Bangladeshi and Nepali scholars were granted these fellowships but none ever since.[13]

SAU: It is probably too early to comment on the South Asian University (SAU) as it is just in its sixth year. Still some preliminary remarks may be made. Its present 56-member faculty is virtually an all-Indian affair—49 Indian, 3 Bangladeshi, 3 Nepali and 1 Sri Lankan. Even by the measure that India is 75 per cent of the region, India's representation in the faculty is as large as 87.5 per cent. The absence of any Pakistani in the faculty shows that the university has not been able to break the diplomatic sound barrier. Efforts are now on to broadbase the faculty. So far as student intake is concerned it is more broadbased, still not ideal and there, too, Pakistani representation is small. Out of 490 students admitted in 2014 and 2015, 301 were Indian, 36 Afghan, 66 Bangladeshi, 3 Bhutanese, 3 Maldivian, 49 Nepali, 23 Pakistani and 9 Sri Lankan. The ratio is supposed to be 50 per cent Indian and

50 per cent from the remaining seven countries.[14] It appears that the SAU's Delhi location and its overwhelmingly Indian faculty have turned it virtually into an Indian university with a large student population from South Asia. It is hoped that when its campus shifts from its present building to its sprawling campus now under construction the university will pick up. Whether it would then be really South Asian and really world class only time will tell. The better, more ambitious and richer students probably would still prefer to study in Western universities for in any case India, too, is a foreign country to them.

South Asian Studies in India: Unlike in the West, South Asian studies developed in India in a disorganized way. Since Area Studies has a clear connection with a nation's foreign policy outlook the neglect of South Asian studies in India is explainable as we have seen how for Nehru the world, at large, mattered and not any particular region, including South Asia. This was evident in the formation of the Indian School of International Studies (ISIS) in 1955, first as an affiliated institute of University of Delhi and then from 1961 as a 'Deemed University'. After the establishment of the Jawaharlal Nehru University (JNU) in 1969, the ISIS merged into it as School of International Studies (SIS). Among the various divisions of SIS one was on South Asia. In the University of Rajasthan (Jaipur), too, a South Asian Studies department was started. In other universities, too, South Asian countries are studied. Unfortunately, however, one does not find enough scholarly knowledge on South Asian societies. In most places, barring JNU and a select other centres where domestic themes are also addressed, doctoral dissertations by and large are written on contemporary relational matters. On the whole, unlike the Area Studies programmes in the US, which emphasize on micro-research based on archival and anthropological sources, travelogues, diaries, etc., Indian researches are basically oriented towards macro foreign policy studies, which by nature are source-starved (Gangopadhyay 2008: 67-8). Two reasons for this are, one, resource crunch, for Area Studies is cost intensive, involving field trips, and two, difficulties involved in conducting fieldwork in the neighbouring countries. South Asian states are more welcoming to Western researchers than their regional counterparts. This deficiency can be compensated to some extent by exchange of scholars programmes, say, between India and Pakistan, but their mutual suspicions come in the way. That confirms our hypothesis that regionalism has little future in South Asia.

IDSA: The only silver lining in the above pattern is the Institute for Defence Studies and Analyses (IDSA). It gives adequate attention to South Asia. Its South Asia Centre is most prominent among its 14 centres (previously called 'clusters'). It has the largest number of researchers, 14 now, consisting of 1 Distinguished Fellow, 1 Senior Fellow, 1 Research Fellow, 1 Senior Research Associate, 4 Associate Fellows, 5 Research Assistants, 1 Visiting Fellow from Nepal, and one Intern. Ever since 2007, the Centre has been organizing an annual conference, the central theme of which is South Asian Regional Cooperation. Till date about 100 participants from the neighbouring countries (including Myanmar, though it is not in SAARC) have attended these conferences. Besides these activities, IDSA, too, has a specific project on Pakistan and another on Pakistan Occupied Kashmir (PoK). Under these projects IDSA organises conferences/workshops/seminars from time to time. The faculty members of the South Asia Centre keep visiting their countries of specialization which have led them to develop expertise on these countries. Besides writing scholarly monographs, they also actively participate in the print and electronic media of the region.

INDO-CENTRICITY OVERSHADOWS REGIONALISM

India is too big compared to other states of the region. It is more than two-thirds of the region's area and more than three-fourths of the region's population, GDP, and military. To illustrate its relative predominance, the following comparative chart will help (Table 1.2).

It may be seen in Table 1.2 that America, too, is dominant in NAFTA. But there is a difference. First, America is a superpower, and second, there is no China type challenge in the neighbourhood

TABLE 1.2: LEADING COUNTRY SHARES OF REGIONAL AGGREGATES (%)

Aggregates	SAARC (8) India	African Union (53) Nigeria	Agadir (4) Egypt	UNASUR (12) Brazil	NAFTA (3) United States	ASEAN (10) Indonesia
Area	66.22	3.40	58.69	48.02	44.40	42.71
Population	76.41	18.05	61.30	49.79	71.4	67.37
GDP	79.65	16.40	63.17	16.54	83.99	37.73
Military Spending	82.24	22.90	19.81	47.12	99.02	39.18

Note: Figures in the parentheses mean the number of constituent countries.
Sources: Computed from the country chapters of *The New Encyclopedia Britannica* 2011; GlobalSecurity.org. For the GDP and Military Spending figures of Nigeria it was difficult to compute the figures from the above sources as a result we depended on somewhat old data available in Rudolph and Rudolph 1987: 5.

which can make it vulnerable if Canada or Mexico wants to take advantage of that factor. Also, there is no substantive security disagreement among NAFTA members. In other words, neither Canada nor Mexico can afford the luxury of having conflicting security outlooks vis-à-vis the United States. Even though Mexico's presence in NAFTA is not appreciated by some of its Latin American neighbours like Venezuela, Bolivia, and Uruguay, economic advantages of a partnership with America trump those concerns. Even after 9/11 when border movements between the US and Canada and between the US and Mexico were restricted to prevent the entry of potential terrorists, the countries worked out the idea of 'smart borders' so as not to allow their trade to suffer (Andreas 2003: 93-6).

SUB-REGIONALISM DILUTES SAARC

In promoting intra-regional trade SAARC's record is dismal. It is as little as 5 per cent of the region's total international trade. Here are some comparisons: in NAFTA it is 40 per cent, in ASEAN it is 26 per cent, in EU it is 67 per cent (Jain and Singh 2009: 82). Since India-Pakistan conflict is at the core of this problem India has tried to find a way out: Go for sub-regionalism. Nepal had originally mooted the idea in December 1996 which had India's blessings. There is nothing wrong with sub-regionalism as complementary to regionalism. Many regional groupings have taken recourse to this method to supplement their cooperative efforts. Variously called as growth triangles, transnational economic zones, micro-regional organizations, natural economic territories, etc., these sub-regional formations have been there since 1980s (Kumar 2016). But the point being made here is that in the South Asian context it poaches into the notion of regionalism. Whether it is the South Asian Growth Quadrangle comprising Bangladesh, Bhutan, India and Nepal in the Ganga-Brahmaputra-Meghna basin or the 2001 Asian Development Bank (ADB)-mooted BIMSTEC (Bay of Bengal Initiative for Multi-Sectoral Technical and Economic Cooperation) and SAFTA (South Asia Free Trade Association) involving South Asia's neighbours in East and Southeast Asia, it gives Pakistan the impression that they are meant to marginalize its importance in the region, which is indeed one of India's mottos. Some economists have argued that probably through these processes the economic integration of South Asia could be possible (Batra 2015) but this author would take the logic with a pinch of salt given the region's complex politics and strategic differences. It may be noted that, besides Pakistan, sub-regionalism has not been well received in Sri Lanka and Maldives on the ground that it was at the cost of SAARC.

STRATEGIC DIVIDE AND THE CHINA FACTOR

Ever since the days of Cold War, the strategic divide between India and Pakistan is total. Thrice they have gone to war (1947, 1965 and 1971). In the 1950s, Pakistan was an active conduit for America's anti-Soviet strategy. And from the late 1960s onwards, against the background of a growing rift between the Soviets and the Chinese, Pakistan played a critical role in bringing rapprochement between the Americans and the Chinese. Bass's study shows that in graphic detail (Bass 2013: 303-10). In contrast, India was non-aligned, which, let alone America (discussed above), even Pakistan used to mock. Its first foreign minister, Chaudhry Sir

Muhammad Zafarullah Khan (1947-54), famously sneered at the idea by saying that it amounted to 0 + 0 + 0 + 0 = 0, each zero standing for a non-aligned country. Later the Indo-Pak divide became much wider when India moved further close to the Soviets. The strategic shift came in handy for India to dismember Pakistan and help create Bangladesh. In its aftermath, the Pakistan-China friendship became stronger.

To the above-mentioned three wars, one must add the 1999 Kargil (Jammu and Kashmir) conflict. Its potential escalation raised the spectre of a nuclear war as both belligerents had by then acquired nuclear weapons. The global community was so much alarmed that President Bill Clinton had to use his arm-twisting diplomacy to force Pakistan to withdraw its forces. India was convinced of Pakistan's complicity in the terror attacks of 1 October 2001, on the Jammu and Kashmir assembly and of 13 December 2001, on the Indian parliament. Once again, on 28 November 2008, the commercial capital of India, Mumbai, was massively attacked by Pakistan-sponsored terrorists. To draw global attention to these terror tactics, India twice had to indulge in brinkmanship, in 2002 and 2008, by amassing troops along Pakistan's borders. Expectedly, global anxiety went out of bounds. There was a flurry of diplomatic activities between Washington and Islamabad and between Washington and New Delhi. War was avoided, but peace remained elusive. Soon cross-LoC firings and shelling became routine keeping the countries constantly in war mode. Accusations of mutual interference also became routine, Pakistan's in Kashmir and India's in Balochistan. The most dramatic was the Pakistan-origin terrorists' attack of January 2016 on the Indian Air Force base in Pathankot which exposed India's vulnerability.[15]

India-Pakistan conflict apart, the entire web of South Asian relationships is complex in which China is a common denominator. Its proximity to the region and its growing power make it attractive to many of India's neighbours. The China card comes handy to them in bargaining with India. Bangladesh, Nepal, and Sri Lanka, and to some extent even Bhutan and Maldives, have played the card, and, at times even the Pakistan card, to neutralize India's predominance.[16] The hard reality is that China is far more powerful than India. For one of my earlier papers I had prepared a chart to show their comparative strength. The chart was revealing. India was way behind China in almost everything from electricity generation to vocational training to cement production to health care and in many other sectors (Ghosh 2013: 116). On the military-strategic front, too, the technological gap between India and China was expanding. Against the background of the systematic dulling of India's conventional military edge over Pakistan the spectre of Sino-Pak threat is much more than academic. According to recent reports, China and Pakistan are coordinating their strategies to block India's entry into the Nuclear Suppliers Group (NSG) (*Hindustan Times*, 13 May 2016).

The only advantage India has over China is its model of democratic development. Since all South Asian states have moved towards democracy, they all look upon India as their role model. But India's negative record in respect of health care, child mortality, illiteracy, and social strife dents that image. It is possible that if India-China relations improve, which actually are improving in terms of economic contacts, China may not encourage India's neighbours to play their China card. But India will have to be watchful on another front. Its growing proclivity to upgrade its relations with America and Southeast Asian nations, more so with Vietnam, could come in the way of China's interests in the Asia-Pacific region, more particularly in the South China Sea. In that scenario, it is possible that China is tempted to make things difficult for India in its north-east which it has a record of doing in the past.

CONCLUSION

Mark Twain once said: 'A person with a new idea is a crank until the idea succeeds.' The same is true of SAARC. It is a great idea but it has to succeed. The problem, however, is that India and Pakistan, the two dominant South Asian nations are indifferent towards it. The general impression in India is that for the failure of SAARC it is Pakistan which is responsible. But we have shown in this paper that India is equally to blame. The fact that India has larger ambitions which SAARC cannot fulfil and that its bilateral diplomacy serves it better are both well taken but that is another story which this paper is not addressing. Our argument is that India has done precious little to the building of regional consciousness in South Asia.

Still, everything is probably not lost. Notwithstanding so much of animosity between India and Pakistan, displayed through their public posturing, Indians and Pakistanis feel at home in each other's country. Anand Patwardhan's anti-nuke documentary/film *War and Peace* produced right after the back-to-back nuclear tests by India and Pakistan in May 1998, was hugely appreciated in both countries at the popular level in spite of all hurdles that the dominant political forces in the respective countries tried to put up (Patwardhan 2010: 95-102). The runaway success of Rajkumar Hirani's Bollywood flick *PK* (2014) and Kabir Khan's *Bajrangi Bhaijan* (2015), both of which portrayed India-Pakistan relationship in positive light yet again proved the point. The region displays an unusual sociocultural congruity. Bengali, Hindi, Nepali, Pashto, Punjabi, Sindhi, Tamil, and Urdu are widely spoken in at least two countries of the region. Most music and dance forms are a shared heritage of all South Asians. One single individual, Rabindranath Tagore, composed the national anthems of Bangladesh, India, and Sri Lanka. Mohammad Iqbal, Pakistan's national poet, is revered in India, whose poem *Saare Jahan se achchha Hindustan hamara* (meaning: best amongst all nations is my country, India) is sung as a patriotic song.

There is no doubt that if India and Pakistan loosen their mutually harsh visa regimes there will be a huge spurt in bilateral tourism, which has been on the rise. In 2013, there was a huge jump in the number of Pakistani tourists in India. Although the top ten tourist-sending countries remained, as always, the same, namely, the US, UK, Bangladesh, Sri Lanka, Russia, Canada, Germany, France, Malaysia and Japan, as many as 1,11,000 Pakistani tourists visited India in that year (*Times of India*, 5 July 2014). Since high diplomacy has failed, let us wait for the success of subaltern regionalism in South Asia.

NOTES

1. It is authored by Sunil Khilnani, Rajiv Kumar, Pratap Bhanu Mehta, Lt. Gen. (Retd.) Prakash Menon, Nandan Nilekani, Srinath Raghavan, Shyam Saran and Siddharth Varadarajan under the auspices of the National Defence College and the Centre for Policy Research, New Delhi, ostensibly with the support of the Government of India. The document is available online. The quotation is from page 15.
2. In 1968 the European Conference on Modern South Asian Studies was launched. It is held every two years. In 2016 it will be in Warsaw. [2018 conference was held in Paris, and 2020 conference in Vienna has been postponed to July 2021 due to COVID-19.]
3. In the beginning SAI had departments on Myanmar and New Zealand but after 1995 it became only South Asia-centric.
4. To know more about Curzon's vision of India's place in the world, see Lord Nathaniel Curzon, 'The Place of India in the Empire', London: J. Murray, 1909, 46 pages. Curzon's views were opposed by the Commander-in-Chief of the British Indian Army, Horatio Herbert Kitchener, who found India not so important for the overall British Empire. Curzon had to resign (details of the controversy in Cohen 1968).
5. India's defeat in the war with China (1962) made Nehru understand that there was no escape from adjusting with Pakistan and resolving the Kashmir tangle. India could ill afford two hostile neighbours. He seemed to be in favour of a confederation of India, Pakistan and Kashmir. See Guha 2014: 138-9.
6. Even before Nehru's death some riots took place which disturbed Nehru but he seemed to be helpless to prevent them. After his death such riots became frequent. See Engineer 1999: 264-5.
7. If Bangladesh today is one of India's most friendly neighbours the credit should not entirely go to the Modi government but to the way Indira Gandhi had supported the liberation warriors of Bangladesh against all odds and to the texture of West Bengal politics which has all along shunned communal intrigue. Even after Partition communalism could not play any role there (for more on this point, see Ghosh 2016: 62-9).
8. Ministry of AYUSH was formed on 9 November 2014. It was the upgrading of the Department of Indian Systems of Medicine and Homoeopathy (ISM&H) created in March 1995. The abbreviation AYUSH stands for Ayurveda, Yoga and Naturopathy, Unani, Siddha and Homoeopathy. The BJP in its election manifesto had said that it would increase public investment to promote AYUSH and start integrated courses for an Indian

system of medicines and modern science. Ayush is also a common Hindu given name, derived from Sanskrit, meaning 'life'.

9. Information available in public domain is very sketchy. It is not possible to know how many students have actually availed themselves of these scholarships. Presumably the slots are not filled as a matter of routine.
10. Personal knowledge.
11. http://saarc-sec.org/areaofcooperation/detail.php?activity_id=16: http://iccr.gov.in/content/many-other-schemes; http://SAARCChair Fellow shiScholarshipScheme 2007.doc; http://Scholarshipnotifications.pdf (all accessed on 5 May 2016).
12. Based on information collected from ICWA sources.
13. Information collected from various ICSSR sources.
14. Thanks to Professor Rajen Harshe of the SAU faculty for supplying me these data.
15. For a critical appraisal of the vulnerabilities of the elite National Security Guard (NSG) as compared to their American, British, French and German counterparts, see Ojha 2016.
16. In May 2016 when Nepal's K.P. Sharma Oli government was on the verge of collapse as the Maoist leader Prachanda threatened to withdraw his support to the government it was reportedly the Chinese 'intervention' that saved the day for Oli. The Chinese persuaded Prachanda to withdraw his threat. According to analysts this was the first time that China 'expressed a firm opinion on the domestic political situation' in the country. See the exclusive report by Nepal watcher Prashant Jha in *Hindustan Times* (New Delhi), 11 May 2016.

REFERENCES

Andreas, Peter, 2003, 'Redrawing the Line: Borders and Security in the Twenty-first Century', *International Security* (Cambridge, MA), 28(2), Fall: 78-111.

Bass, Gary J., 2013, *The Blood Telegram: Nixon, Kissinger and a Forgotten Genocide*, New York: Alfred A. Knopf.

Batra, Amita, 2014-15, 'SAARC and Economic Cooperation', *IIC Quarterly* (New Delhi), 41(3&4): 50-60.

Brown, W. Norman, 1964, 'South Asia Studies: A History', *Annals* (Philadelphia), vol. 356: 54-62.

Cohen, Benjamin B., 2006, 'The Study of Indian History in the US Academy', *India Review* (Bloomington, IN), 5(1): 144-72.

Cohen, Stephen P., 1968, 'Issue, Role, and Personality: The Kitchener-Curzon Dispute', *Comparative Studies in Society and History* (Cambridge), 10(3), April: 337-55.

Engineer, Asghar Ali, 1999, 'Muslim Views of Hindus since 1950', in Jacques Waardenburg (ed.), *Muslim Perceptions of Other Religions: A Historical Survey*, New York: Oxford University Press.

Gangopadhyay, Aparajita, 2008, 'Area Studies and the Challenge of Globalization: Issues and Concerns', *The Icfai University Journal of International Relations* (Goa), 2(4), October: 64-72.

Ghosh, Partha S., 2013, 'An Enigma that is South Asia: India versus the Region', *Asia Pacific Review* (Tokyo), 20 (1), May: 100-20.

——, 2016, *Migrants, Refugees and the Stateless in South Asia*, New Delhi: Sage.

Gould, Harold A., 2008, 'The Reasons why America's Half Century Struggle to Control the Political Agenda in South Asia', in Lloyd I. Rudolph and Susanne Hoeber Rudolph (eds.), *Making U.S. Foreign Policy toward South Asia: Regional Imperatives and the Imperial Presidency*, New Delhi: Concept: 101-68.

Guha, Ramachandra, 2014, 'Jawaharlal Nehru: A Romantic in Politics', in Ramachandra Guha (ed.), *Makers of Modern Asia*, Cambridge, MA: Belknap Press: 117-46.

Gujral, I.K., 2011, *Matters of Discretion: An Autobiography*, New Delhi: Hay House India.

Jain, Rajeev and J.B. Singh, 2009, 'Trade Pattern in SAARC Countries: Emerging Trends and Issues', *Reserve Bank of India Occasional Papers*, 30(3), Winter.

Kumar, Vikash, 2016, 'Sub-Regionalism as a Complementary Factor to Regionalism: The Case Study of Bangladesh, Bhutan, Nepal, India Motor Vehicle Agreement', unpublished manuscript.

Ludden, David, 2003, 'Presidential Address: Maps in the Mind and the Mobility of Asia', *The Journal of Asian Studies*, 62(4), November: 1057-78.

Malenbaum, Wilfred, 1958, 'East and West in India's Development: Preliminary Draft', Econ. Dev. Program, Project No. 7674, NPA Competitive Coexistence Study, Center for International Studies, MIT, Cambridge. Link: http://hdl.handle.net/1721.1/85144.

Nuesser, Marcus, n.d., 'The South Asia Institute', *The South Asia Institute: 50 Years of Looking Ahead.* (A booklet published by the University of Heidelberg.)

Ojha, Ranjit, 2016, 'Force Alarm: The Many Failings of the National Security Guard', *Caravan* (New Delhi), 8(2), February: 20-2.

Patwardhan, Anand, 2010, 'Reflecting Peace', in Smitu Kothari and Zia Mian (eds., with Kamla Bhasin, A.H. Nayyar and Mohammad Tahseen), *Bridging Partition: People's Initiatives for Peace between India and Pakistan*, Hyderabad: Orient BlackSwan: 95-102.

Raghavan, Srinath, 2013, *1971: A Global History of the Creation of Bangladesh*, Ranikhet: Permanent Black.

Raja Mohan, C., 2006, *Crossing the Rubicon: The Shaping of India's Foreign Policy*, New York: Palgrave Macmillan.

Rothermund, Dietmar, 2010, 'Indo-German Relations: From Cautious Beginning to Robust Partnership', *India Quarterly* (New Delhi), 66(1), January-March: 1-12.

Rubinoff, Arthur G., 2008, 'From Indifference to Engagement: The Role of the U.S. Congress in Making Foreign Policy for South Asia', in Lloyd I. Rudolph and Susanne Hoeber Rudolph (eds.), *Making U.S. Foreign Policy toward South Asia: Regional Imperatives and the Imperial Presidency*, New Delhi: Concept: 169-224.

Rudolph, Lloyd and Susanne Hoeber Rudolph, 1987, *In Pursuit of Lakshmi: The Political Economy of the Indian State*, Chicago: Chicago University Press.

Taneja, Anand Vivek, 2009, 'Muslimness in Indian Cinema', *Seminar* (New Delhi), http:www.india-seminar.com2009/598/598_anand_vivek_taneja.htm

CHAPTER 2

Religion and Politics

Essay 1: Bangladeshization of Indian Politics*

Now that India's secularism is degenerating into one of competitive Hindutva it is being seen as the Pakistanization of Indian politics. Even the liberal fringe of Pakistan, ever unhappy with all that has been happening in that country, looks at it that way. A musical video clip that went viral some time ago parodied: 'Alas, you too, turned out to be like us' (in Urdu: *Aap bhi hamare jaise nikle*). But this comparison is partially true. In reality the Indian politics more resembles that of Bangladesh. The essential point of similarity between them emanates from their nationalism which is rooted in history. For the same reason they can entertain the luxury of calling themselves secular in constitutional terms but cannot afford the total negation of their majoritarian personas. The result is an acrimonious coexistence of secularism and communalism. The existence of sizeable minorities in both counties, 15 per cent Muslims in India and nine per cent Hindus in Bangladesh, makes this balancing all the move imperative.

These realities are not valid for Pakistan. In terms of nationhood, Bangladesh any day has a better score. It is a textbook case in so far as the national language is concerned, almost all have Bangla as their mother tongue. Even in ethnic terms Bangladeshi Muslims and

* 'Bangladeshization of Indian Politics', *The Dhaka Tribune*, 17 December 2018. https://www.dhakatribune.com/opinion/op-ed/2018/12/17/the-bangladeshization-of-indian-politics, reproduced in *Mainstream* (New Delhi), 57(9), 16 February 2019: 3-4.

Hindus are less differentiated. Sociologist Ramakrishna Mukherjee had argued (1976) that if the British rule had not intervened a Bengali nation was almost formed by the end of the eighteenth century. Their easy-going religion, *sahajiya*, was a blend of Islam and Hinduism. The Prophet Mohammad was seen as an *avatar* of Allah who was addressed as *prabhu, gosain*, or *niranjan*, the Bengali words for the almighty or his incarnation. It was only in the aftermath of the combined Hindu-Muslim revolt of 1857 against the East India Company rule that such words were replaced by Arabic ones with the motive of dividing the Muslims and Hindus, a masterly political strategy of the imperial British. The rest is history. East Bengal became one of the major bases of the Muslim League, which, notably, was launched in 1906 in Dhaka under the auspices of the Nawab of Bengal. It was no surprise, therefore, that these same people would rise in revolt in 1971 against the hijacking of their politics by those sitting in West Pakistan who had little claim to that heritage.

Post-1947 India and post-1971 Bangladesh had marked similarities. If a critical element of the Congress-led freedom struggle of India was its intercommunal partnership so was it for the Awami League's in the Bangladesh liberation war. The way the British tried to disrupt the Hindu-Muslim unity, the Yahya Khan-led Pakistani junta did exactly the same. It advertised the liberation war as the handiwork of Hindu India and that the Bangladeshi Hindus were its active conduits. To underscore the point the Bengali Hindus were specifically repressed to start with forcing them to flee to India in droves. That explains why about 90 per cent of the refugees in the initial phases of the exodus were Hindu. Curiously, or, predictably, both the British and the Pakistani policies ended up in dividing the countries. But because of the respective heritages of the their liberation struggles India and Bangladesh both opted for secularism as their constitutional commitments.

In multi-religious Third World societies, where state formation tends to precede nation formation, secularism is a difficult ambition to achieve. Notwithstanding their constitutional commitments, therefore, both India and Bangladesh succeeded only partially to adhere to the principle, much less so for Bangladesh. It amended and re-amended its constitution to renege and restore its secularist position. Mercifully, India has not done anything like that so far, but one is not sure any more. The way the militantly ascendant Hindutva forces are asking for a Hindu *rashtra* the days of India's secularism may not be ever-lasting. The only saving grace for both India and Bangladesh is that because of historical reasons both the forces of secularism and communalism think that it is politically prudent for them to go slow, thereby reconciling themselves to coexist however antagonistically or competitively.

The cumulative effect of these processes is that both India and Bangladesh have become semi-secular/semi-communal. This is evident in the way the secular Congress or the secular Awami League have conceded to communal demands of the respective majority communities. Or, at another level, both the communal BJP and the communal BNP, have not shed their pro-minority pretensions. Thus while the memories of Jawaharlal Nehru and Mujibur Rehman have become necessary for political use of secularism for the grass-root vote bank requirements they have to be selectively shelved, too. Even Mujib had to make compromises with respect to secularism. In the case of Nehru, though he steadfastly stuck to his credo yet he appeared helpless when at the local levels the foot soldiers of his party had to ask for votes in the name of Hinduism. Nehru's lament in this regard is on record. His daughter Indira Gandhi, his grandson Rajiv Gandhi, and now his great-grandson Rahul Gandhi have all underscored this reality during their electoral campaigns. The same is true for Mujib's daughter Sheikh Hasina Wazed or her present challenger Dr Kamal Hossain, who had drafted the secular constitution of Bangladesh, to bring in his fold the communalist Bangladesh Nationalist Party (BNP) and the Jamaat-e-Islami.

In conclusion, let it be said that in both India and Bangladesh it is not only politics that is being communalized, alongside secularism, too, is being politicized. In India in response to BJP's pro-Hindu innovation in flagging off the Shri Ramayana Express which would transport Hindu pilgrims from Delhi to many Ram-related pilgrim places, namely, Sitamarhi, Janakpur (Nepal), Varanasi, Prayag, Chitrakoot, Hampi, Nasik, and Rameshwaram, the country's avowedly secular Aam Aadmi Party (AAP) government of Delhi has responded by a secular blitzkrieg. To placate all religions across the board, Delhi's Chief Minister Arvind Kejriwal, has launched the Mukhyamantri Tirth Yatra. The offer is open to senior citizens of all religions to visit the Golden Temple, Wagah Border, Anandpur Sahib, Vaishnodevi-Jammu, Mathura, Vrindavan, Haridwar, Rishikesh, Nilkanth, Pushkar and Ajmer. Bravo India's political ingenuity. Are Sheikh Hasina and Kamal Hossain listening?

Essay 2: Sheikh Hasina's Obtuse Parallelism with India*

Prime Minister Sheikh Hasina is exuberant. And she has reasons. By any standard her victory is extraordinary. Not only has she won 288 seats out of 299 (election for one seat is to be held later), she has also garnered 80 per cent of the votes, a rare feat in a first-past-the-post system. The Bharatiya Janata Party (BJP) of India which got absolute majority in the parliament after the 2014 election could achieve it by polling merely 31 per cent of the votes. What is even more dramatic is that in her own constituency she trounced her rivals by unbelievably massive margins. Against her tally of 2,29,539 votes, the BNP and the Islami Andolan Bangladesh could manage barely 123 and 71 votes, respectively. Notwithstanding all allegations of rigging and intimidation, since the election was more participatory than the previous one, her command on the administration will be unassailable. So much so that one may playfully say that she is not Mujib's daughter now. *Bangabandhu* Sheikh Mujib is Hasina's father.

But power begets challenge, and the more the power, the bigger the challenge. With her country's human development record better

* 'This Gain Should Not be Squandered', *The Dhaka Tribune*, 5 January 2019. https://www.dhakatribune.com/opinion/op-ed/2019/01/05/this-gain-should-not-be-squandered

than that of almost all other South Asian nations, coupled with her own credentials as a secular leader (Hefajat-e-Islam's presence in her coalition notwithstanding), she can well be seen as the beacon of hope for the region. South Asian polity is proverbially unstable, torn between the forces of secularism and communalism putting the former ever under constant threat of disruption. Since her victory over 'Bangladeshi nationalism', which translates into Islamic fundamentalism in the Bangladeshi context, is stunning, she is expected to behave more like a statesman because the region, more particularly India, which is increasingly becoming communally polarized, needs her more than the other way round. She should be aware of this onerous responsibility and, therefore, must utter every word with utmost care.

In response to questions by foreign journalists as to how come the opposition fared so miserably in the elections she made a superficial comparison with what happened in India. In making the remark, she sounded patronizing to the opposition, on the one hand, while on the other, explained away their lamentable performance as their mere failure to project a prime ministerial face. Notably, this last point is the most important poll strategy of the BJP for the forthcoming Indian election with which to beat the opposition.

Look at the BJP, which, Hasina said, 'had just two seats when Rajiv Gandhi won the election [in 1984] . . . [but] now they are in power. So there's a chance for other parties as well [like BNP] if they work properly.' Then, tongue in cheek, she compared the failure of the leaderless BNP+ opposition to that of the Congress+ in the Indian election of 2014. 'How many seats did they [the Congress] get in the last election? They could not focus on who would be their PM. Such an old and established party, but who will be the leader of the party? It was not clear. So people didn't vote for them,' she explained. It is the bane of all South Asian parliamentary democracies that all national elections are being converted into presidential ones, a mishmash most dangerous for plural societies, India being the most glaring example.

Evidently, Sheikh Hasina missed the critical point. Narendra Modi's victory in 2014 was not merely because the opposition could not put up a comparable leader. Had it been only that factor BJP would not have ended up with only 31 per cent votes. In the recently held state elections in Chhattisgarh, Madhya Pradesh (MP) and Rajasthan, where Congress won all the states, it had not projected a chief ministerial face anywhere. On the contrary, BJP did it everywhere. Modi's rise on the national scene in 2014 was the culmination of a well-honed strategy to Hinduize the Indian politics, which had its beginning in the early 1980s to which Modi's development model was cleverly tagged so as to broad-base the party's mass appeal. It was not at all meant to dilute its Hindutva ideology.

The BJP had internalized that the massive Congress victory under Rajiv Gandhi in 1984, and its own dismal show in contrast, was all because of the unprecedented Hindu backlash (barring the Partition riots) generated by the assassination of Indira Gandhi in the hands of her two Sikh (non-Hindu) bodyguards, which was immediately followed by wanton killings of thousands of Sikhs in Delhi and other places. The BJP read the situation perfectly well, that is, the Congress did indeed steal its patented Hindu vote bank for the time being but in the process it reconfirmed the potential electoral dividends that it was capable of providing if circumstances changed to the BJP's advantage anytime in the future. As such, to compare the Bangladeshi situation with that of India would amount to an invitation to the Bangladeshi Islamists to emulate India's Hindutva model in their own land by any name whatsoever. Of course, Sheikh Hasina would not want that.

It makes sense here to underscore that throughout the 1980s and 1990s BJP's one-point agenda was to consolidate the Hindu vote. Given the Hindu-Muslim binary of Indian politics an anti-Muslim tirade was BJP's most tested tool. Starting from the *Ekatmata Yajna* of the early 1980s through the Shah Bano controversy (1985-6), through the Ram Janmabhoomi movement that culminated in the demolition of the Babri Mosque in 1992, through the milk-drinking Lord Ganesh farce (1995), it was all well strategized to keep the Hindu communal pot boiling. In recent times its manifestations are to be found in the Hindutva brigade's cow protection vigilantism, its making ridiculous fuss over *love jihad* (Muslim men forcibly marrying Hindu women for the ostensible purpose of converting them into Islam), organizing *ghar wapsi* (meaning, returning home, that is, forcible re-conversion of Muslims to the Hindufold), and the beating and heckling of meat traders on false allegations of cow slaughter, etc.

Against this background Sheikh Hasina sounded rather unpremeditated, even if not naive, when she tried to reduce this complex phenomenon to a singular leadership variable. She should have been more aware than anybody else in Bangladesh that her country had a powerful undercurrent of Islamism which needed extremely cautious handling. Any wobbly analogy, devoid of deeper circumspection, could be potentially perilous. Giving all the brownie points to the BJP can be good diplomacy, but it is bad politics, and certainly not seasoned statesmanship.

The victory of secularism in Bangladesh is a cause for celebration for the entire region. This gain should not be squandered, least of all in Bangladesh itself.

Essay 3: A Predictable Unpredictability Looms Large*

The seventeenth parliamentary election of India is underway. This seven-phase exercise is spread between 11 April and 19 May (the fourth phase was over on 29 April). The results will be out on 23 May when one would know who the 543 new MPs are (two Anglo-Indian MPs to be added later through presidential nomination). The question is whether Narendra Modi will continue in power.

* 'The Election that is Predictably Unpredictable', *The Dhaka Tribune*, 2 May 2019. https://www.dhakatribune.com/opinion/op-ed/2019/05/02/the-election-that-is-predictably-unpredictable. Subsequently, BJP won 303 of the 543 seats and went on to form the government as NDA, with Narendra Modi returning as the prime minister.

Election is a routine matter in any democracy. But this Indian election assumes larger importance because Modi has introduced a new brand of politics which India was unfamiliar with. RSS-inspired BJP has ruled India earlier, too, when Atal Behari Vajpayee was the prime minister (1998-2004) but his was more a continuity of India's democratic journey. The Modi regime has marked a departure on several counts some of which have hit certain fundamentals of the Indian polity. In that sense this election represents India's search for its soul.

In 2014 Modi started off with a bang, as if a *new* India was just to kick off. An India that would be corruption-free, and prosperous. *Sab ka sath sab ka vikas* (together with all, progress for all) became his catchphrase. Although the votes in Modi's kitty were barely 31 per cent he boasted telling the world that 1.3 billion Indians were behind him. That his party got absolute majority in the parliament was misread as entire India's endorsement. The megalomaniac that he is it was expected of him.

It was this persona that was on display at his inauguration. Something that had never happened, he flung his foreign policy blitzkrieg by inviting all SAARC leaders to witness the event. Soon he started hopping from capital to capital warmly hugging the world leaders and addressing the local Indian communities. His foreign visits became so frequent that a stand-up comedian christened him as India's first 'multi-national prime minister'.

Two things became Modi's brand statements. One, condemning Pandit Nehru at every drop of the hat (Nehru regime had ended 55 years ago) for everything wrong in the country, which itself was extravagantly manufactured. And two, glorifying India's past with ludicrous bragging. Both belonged to the same narrative: how to de-emphasize the Nehruvian 'scientific temper', which was an anathema to all that BJP represented.

The first point that BJP's 2014 manifesto had said about the party's foreign policy outlook was that India was the *vishwaguru* (the leading light of the world). Soon after assuming power such boasts touched obnoxious heights with every passing day. The party bragged *ad nauseam* about ancient (Hindu) India's scientific exploits: India had plastic surgery, test-tube baby, aeroplane, spaceship and the

Internet. Even pen-drives were found in excavations, claimed Tripura's BJP chief minister. Ancient Indians also knew about the gravitational singularity theorems of the Stephen Hawking fame.

Such outlandish gibberish was heard earlier also but they were confined only to some self-styled 'intellectuals' or drawing room chats. More they were peddled by the ruling class their impact became vicious. A contempt for the intelligentsia became fashionable. Intellectuals and liberals, whether in academia or journalism, were ridiculed as *libtards* (liberal bastards), *sickular* (sick secularists), or *presstitutes* (prostitute female journalists). The latter were particularly hounded through social media trolls with unutterable sexual innuendoes.

Modi himself ridiculed Amartya Sen and his ilk on several occasions. He tauntingly rhymed Harvard versus hard work to cheering crowds. The only crime Sen committed was that he had doubted the efficacy of Modi's demonetization scheme. Now even a common man on the street knows that it was a gaffe, for which Modi alone was responsible, for it had the approval of neither the Reserve Bank, nor the Finance Ministry, nor even Modi's own economic adviser.

A ruling party seeking re-election generally advertises its achievements during the previous term. But for Modi's BJP (I deliberately chose not to say BJP's Modi because he and his hand-picked party president, Amit Shah, have effectively hijacked the party) it is no longer the development agenda which was the case in 2014. It is an about-turn to the time-tested Hindutva into which the bogey of national security has been cleverly interwoven.

Taking advantage of the recent face-off with Pakistan (see pp. 74-9) Modi has projected Islamic terrorism and Pakistan as his electoral talismans. They provide the subtexts of his larger narrative: Hindus of India have only one enemy and that enemy is India's Muslims. Never during the six hundred years of Muslim rule and the two hundred years of Christian rule were Hindus as insecure as they are now in Modi's India.

According to Ashis Nandy, India's leading political psychologist, Modi is 'a classic, clinical case of a fascist [who believes in] . . . a theory of cosmic conspiracy against India that painted every Muslim as a suspected traitor and a potential terrorist.' Many would argue that he has changed his stripes after being in power for so many years. But the way he has overlooked those who have lynched and terrorised the Muslims in the name of beef eating, *love jihad* (Muslim boys are forcibly marrying Hindu girls for the purpose of making them Muslim) and *ghar wapsi* (Indian Muslims must come back to their original Hindufold) it is difficult to agree with this proposition. Modi has shed tears at both the massacred Muslims in Christchurch and the massacred Christians in Sri Lanka but one who has carefully noted his statements knows that his tears had different thicknesses.

If all of the above is true then Modi's defeat must be unavoidable. But it is not so simple in any mass democracy. Much of his failings on the delivery fronts are compensated by his party's organizational strength. In the ultimate analysis what matters the most is how and in what numbers people vote. The RSS which has grown exponentially during the Modi rule would see to it that its foot soldiers throng the BJP election rallies and on the election days come in droves to vote for Modi and bring others likewise.

Also, thanks to his clever ploy of introducing the system of electoral bonds, Modi's party is flush with funds through corporate donations, much of which is laundered black money. Theoretically, all parties can take advantage of the scheme. But donors know where the maximum return of their investment will be. Of the thousands of crores of rupees so donated 95 per cent has gone to the BJP.

Any article on elections must end with a forecast. That is what the readers like to know the most. This piece may be a disappointment in that sense. In a mass democracy academic reasoning does not necessarily work. Given the fact that we are in an age of big money, fake news, manipulated social media, a castrated press and TV, and most importantly, bogus election issues, I would rather prefer to be woolly: it is a predictably unpredictable election.

Anything is possible: a BJP + rule with Modi as PM, a BJP + rule without Modi as PM, a Congress + rule with Rahul Gandhi as PM, or a non-BJP-non-Congress coalition rule with a 'dark-horse' as PM. Remember that I.K. Gujral was woken up from sleep at midnight to become India's twelfth prime minister (1997-8). He was a successful prime minister at that.

Essay 4: Hindutva's Heyday: Narendra Modi in his 'Divide, Distract and Rule' Avatar*

Nothing succeeds like success. In spite of failures on almost all development fronts India's Prime Minister Narendra Modi has massively won his second term. As against 282 seats in 2014, his BJP has won 303 seats in 2019. The party's vote share has jumped from 31 to 38 per cent, from 17 crore to 22 crore.

The question is, has India's democracy lost in the process, both in parliamentary and federal terms. In the vote, neither the candidate, nor state-specific, leave alone constituency-specific, issues, figured. People voted either for Modi, or against him. If not so, how can one explain that an alleged terrorist Sadhwi Pragya Singh, who thinks that cow urine cures cancer, cuddling cows reduces blood pressure, and that Mahatma Gandhi's killer Nathuram Godse was a patriot, can defeat by a massive margin a veteran Congress leader Digvijaya Singh, who is known for his secular credentials? Modi has promised not to forgive her ever for her anti-Gandhi remark. We will wait to see how Modi's anger is expressed in the parliament, or, who knows, in the cabinet.

The BJP's Hindutva is a clever region-specific ploy to craft a Hindu vote bank. For example, in UP, which has 20 per cent Muslims, beef eating, location of meat shops near temples, *love jihad* (Muslim boys forcibly marrying Hindu girls to convert them to Islam), and *ghar wapsi* (Indian Muslims should reconvert to Hinduism) are the veritable tools. For Assam and West Bengal, each of which has about 30 per cent Muslims, and which have meat-eating food

* 'Hindutva's Heyday: Narendra Modi in his "Divide, Distract, and Rule" Avatar', *Dhaka Tribune*, 28 May 2019. https://www.dhakatribune.com/opinion/op-ed/2019/05/28/hindutva-s-heyday

habits in general, beef is a non-issue. The issue there is Bangladeshi Muslim infiltrators; Hindu infiltrators are most welcome. In Goa, Kerala, or north-east, which have sizeable Christian populations, beef is not the issue. Conversion to Christianity or Hindu temple entry topics matter there.

On the national level, Hindutva is denoted by anti-Pakistanism and anti-(Islamic) terrorism. When in Christchurch Muslims are massacred Modi sends condolences to the New Zealand prime minister. But when Muslims massacre Christians in Sri Lanka it figures in Modi's campaign speeches. Only adolescents will fail to recognize the connection between Modi's reference to the Indian Air Force's Balakot attack and his tongue-in-cheek Hindutva message.

In the international context, who cares about beef eating or beef exports. When Indians beeline for visas to go to beef-eating America, Europe or the Middle East, I wish someone reminded them of their national credo against beef. Ironically, the stoutest section among Modi's NRI's support bases is comprised of vegetarian Gujaratis in beef-eating America and England. The same Amit Shah, a Gujarati, who ridicules Bangladeshis in India as 'termites' forgets to remember that his community had the biggest presence in America till recently (lately overtaken by people from Andhra Pradesh).

Indians are obsessed with religion and nationalism these days as never before. No drawing room conversation can be complete without it. I recall a German professor who used to frequently visit India and Pakistan telling me about twenty years ago that how, unlike Indians, Pakistanis were obsessed with Islam and India. Indians were so relaxed, he used to find. I think if the same professor visits India now he would see a mirror image of the then Pakistan in today's India—Indians' obsession with Hinduism and Pakistan. This is Modi's singular contribution, and he deserves credit for it.

For an academic like this writer, it is always a huge trial to analyse a vote. Should his tool be normative or explanatory? The latter is simpler because it is post-facto. TV anchors keep explaining to their viewers all of that which went wrong with the opposition. But if they are so omniscient why did they not say so before the results? To be normative is to take an unaltered position both before and after the election. A mandate has, therefore, to be dissected through that single prism.

Viewed from that perspective, it is being argued here that this pro-Modi mandate does not augur well for India. So much of Hindutva linctus has been injected into India's body politic that it needs courage for any political party to downright denounce it in the name of secularism or social inclusiveness. The chief challenger, the Indian National Congress, which always had a Hindu nationalistic undercurrent yet could boldly project its secularism (in the Indian parlance equi-proximity to all religions) as its brand platform, has increasingly diluted this time-tested duality in favour of completely avoiding any discussion on secularism or defending its position as an equal champion of all communities, particularly the Muslims.

Secularism as an ethos of Indian polity was seldom audible during the entire campaign. Rahul Gandhi, Modi's chief challenger, was busy projecting himself as a *Shivbhakt* with vermillion mark on his forehead and by hopping from temple to temple. His cronies even proudly talked about him as a *janeu* (the sacred thread, *poitey,* in Bengali) wearing Brahmin. The same was true of Priyanka Gandhi, Rahul's sister and the party's star campaigner in UP. No wonder that the BJP would score the point that even the Congress had to concede to their Hindutva thrust.

Even an avowedly liberal Congress leader like Shashi Tharoor, who wrote such a brilliant book as *Why I am a Hindu,* highlighting the syncretic nature of Hinduism and its doctrinal inclusiveness, thoroughly disillusioned his fans by taking a weird position with respect to the Sabarimala Temple in his home state Kerala, when he argued in favour of upholding the temple's tradition of disallowing menstruating women from worshipping there, even in defiance of a Supreme Court ruling. His political excuse was that the ruling Left Front government in Kerala was inciting the BJP there to carve out a space to poach into the Congress vote bank. That Tharoor's idea has politically worked is evident from the fact that while in the entire India, Congress has a lacklustre performance, in Kerala it has massively succeeded in defeating the Left and preventing the BJP from making any headway. But the fact remains that his political positioning has reduced his secular, liberal and modernist stature.

In the larger South Asian context, since the region is one political-cultural space, notwithstanding its inherent religious and societal contradictions, the rise of Hindutva in India, which is three-fourths of the region (barring Afghanistan), sends a wrong signal. The way Myanmar is dealing with its Rohingyas with tacit Indian support, or the way militant Buddhism is up in arms in Sri Lanka against the country's 6 per cent Muslims, once again having the clandestine blessings from India's Hindu nationalistic Rashtriya Swayamsevak Sangh (RSS), South Asia may be characterized as a sleeping volcano ready to erupt anytime. There is enough incendiary material in the neighbouring Muslim countries starting from Indonesia in the east to the Islamic State in the west to trigger the eruption. And thanks to Donald Trump's adventurism these fears are no longer sheer academic.

In all likelihood in the forthcoming Sri Lankan elections the Buddhist chauvinistic Mahinda Rajapaksa will sweep the polls. In the 2020 elections, the Rajapaksa brothers registered a thumping win, securing the people's mandate. Given his record, anti-Muslimism as his political platform is foreseeable. Remember his policy during the 2004 tsunami relief. The way he took care of Hambantota, his Sinhala-Buddhist majority constituency in the Southern Province, and the way he displayed at the same time stepmotherly treatment towards Tamil-speaking Muslim majority Ampara district in the Eastern Province, indicate which way the wind will blow once he becomes the president. According to the 2006 report of the National Reconstruction and Development Agency (NRDA), almost double the number of houses were reconstructed in Hambantota than what was actually required, while just 50 per cent of such houses were built in Ampara.

I have no doubt that if anti-Muslimism in India, Myanmar and Sri Lanka is not contained Pakistan and Bangladesh will not be able to withstand the heat for a long time. The challenge for Bangladesh is much bigger for it has a sizeable Hindu population and a strong Islamic political force ever ready to disrupt the democratic process. I pray that I am proved naive.

Now that Modi is comfortably ensconced in power with massive majority would his leopard stripes change? All humans love to hope. I, too, hope that Modi would shed his malicious language against the opposition leaders and would be more accommodative of minority interests, which is the essence of any democracy. One of Winston Churchill's dictums was: In victory, magnanimity. Should we expect some kind of magnanimity from the victorious Modi? If we go by his first post-victory tweet we seem to have reasons to hope. It said: Together we will build a strong and inclusive India. The word 'inclusive' is significant. It is a secular/Congress catchphrase. To the best of my memory it has never figured in BJP's lexicon. On the contrary secularism has become an abusive term in Modi's India.

Postscript: India, probably the entire South Asia, is a strange region. While, on the one hand, religious fanaticism is on the ascendancy everywhere, then, on the other, we keep hearing of extraordinary stories of intercommunal bonhomie, rather routinely. This latest one comes, of all the places, from Delhi's dreaded Tihar Jail. This year the number of Hindu criminals observing the Ramzaan *roza* to express solidarity with their Muslim counterparts has reached an all-time high of 150. Isn't India an incredible country?

Essay 5: *Epaar-Bangla-Opaar-Bangla* (Bengali on Either Side of the River): An Impending Crisis or an Inescapable Compromise?*

'What Bengal thinks today, India will think tomorrow.' This is how the first generation Indian nationalist Gopal Krishna Gokhale

* 'Epaar Bangla, Opaar Bangla: Bengalis on Both Sides of the River', *Dhaka Tribune*, 18 June 2019. https://www.dhakatribune.com/opinion/op-ed/2019/06/18/epaar-bangla-opaar-bangla, reproduced in *Mainstream* (New Delhi), 57(31), 10 July 2019: 17-19, also reproduced as 'Bangladesh too will to have to Pay Dearly for the Saffronisation of West Bengal', in *Scroll.in*, 21 June 2019, https://scroll.in/article/927714/the-saffronisation-of-west-bengal-will-push-bangladesh-further-to-the-right

had certified the political wisdom of Bengalis a hundred years ago. Today the slogan is better turned on its head: What the rest of India thought yesterday, West Bengal is thinking today.

Something that never happened is happening lately. The Hindu right is fast occupying the centre-stage of West Bengal politics. In the parliamentary election held last month, the Hindu nationalistic BJP won as many as 18 seats out of 42 in the state by reaping 40.25 per cent votes, which is massive in any multiparty democracy.

There is little doubt that the BJP will fare much better in the assembly polls scheduled for 2021, unless an intervening governor's rule advances the date. Chief Minister Mamata Banerjee is losing her grip over West Bengal politics leaving the ground virtually wide open for the BJP to ensure a thumping victory.

Situated next to Bangladesh, which has a record of playing hide and seek with Islamist regimes, this complex *epaar-bangla-opaar-bangla* space can pose serious communal challenges with their inevitable fallout on Assam. A 'saffron' West Bengal facing a 'green' Bangladesh is by any reckoning a jarring colour combination with potentially perilous security ramifications.

To speculate upon the impending probabilities two popular myths must be exploded at the outset: one, Bengalis are not communal; and, two, Bengalis are a less violent people.

Contrary to popular wisdom that Hindu nationalism originated in the 'cow belt' of north-central India, the first saplings of Hindutva were sown in Bengal. It was in 1858, just a year after the Hindu-Muslim joint revolt had rocked British rule in India, that Tarinicharan Chattopadhyay wrote his *Bharatbarsher Itihas*, the first virtual anti-Muslim manifesto. Everything wrong in India was attributed to the thousand years of Muslim domination, the book explained:

> The misfortunes and decline of this country began on the day the Yavana [Muslim] flag entered the territory of Bengal. . . . Ravaged by endless waves of oppression, the people of Bengal became disabled and timid. . . . The country was reduced to such a state that the wealth of the prosperous, the honour of the genteel and the chastity of the virtuous [Hindu women] were in grave peril. . . . The resumption of good fortune was initiated on the day the British flag was first planted on this land. . . . It must be loudly declared that it is to bless us that *isvara* [God] has brought the English to this country.

The mission Tarinicharan Chattopadhyay launched picked up momentum in no time. Rajnarain Bose founded the Nationality Promotion Society to inculcate nationalist sentiments among the Bengali *bhadralok* (genteel class). The Calcutta-based Hindu *mela* (fair) became a popular annual event and soon spread to Lahore and Madras.

The motto of the Hindu *mela* was to make the 'Hindu *jati*' nationalistically conscious. When questioned as to how Hindu *jati* and Indian nation could be synonymous it was clarified that 'certainly [Hindus] form a nation by themselves'. The popular Hindu *mela* song, penned by Hemchandra Banerjee, eulogised 'Hindu heroic pride'. The song lamented how it had tragically 'departed' after the advent of Muslims.

Even as these kinds of Hindu nationalistic sentiments were being roused in Bengal, similar tendencies were growing amongst the Bengali Muslims. They found expression in the replacement of Sanskritized Bengali words by Persianized ones. On the larger Muslim canvas, the National Mohammedan Association came into being in 1877 and soon submitted a list of Muslim grievances to the British government.

It is instructive to note how in the beginning of Indian nationalism both Hindus and Muslims looked upon the British as their respective saviours. We are simply fooling ourselves if we still think that the British were the crooked ones who manufactured the tool of 'divide and rule'.

In Muslim communal consciousness two strains were noticeable. While, on the one hand, the Muslim leadership was placatory to the Hindus in north India then, on the other, it had complete disdain for the Bengali *bhadralok*. Thus, while addressing the Hindus of Punjab, Sir Syed Ahmed Khan, the doyen of Muslim modernism, would complain as to why they did not regard him as a Hindu, with respect to Bengali *bhadralok* he would critizise the latter for their Hindu-accented upper caste politics.

He routinely referred to 'Mahomedans' and 'Bengalis' to emphasize the distinct motive of the Bengali Hindu elite to drive a wedge between them. For him the Indian National Congress was virtually a Hindu contraption in which the Bengali Hindus called the shots: 'It is incumbent on me to show what evils would befall my [Muslim] nation from joining in the opinions of the Bengalis.' That during this period there was a clear cleavage between *bhadralok* politics and *dalit* politics in Bengal in which the latter was in tune with the Muslims is well known.

On the question of Bengali violence, it was in Bengal where the maximum number of communal riots had occurred before Partition. Suranjan Das's *Communal Riots in Bengal 1905-47* (1991) discusses them in detail. In the corresponding period Punjab, which witnessed the worst Partition riots, did not have anything like the Mymensingh riots of 1906-7, Calcutta, Pabna, and Dacca riots of 1918-26, other riots in 1927-31, Dacca riots of 1941, and, finally, the Great Calcutta Killing and the Noakhali riots of 1946.

But unlike the Partition riots in Punjab, those in East Bengal lingered on for a long time, culminating in the massive anti-Hindu riots of 1964. Even otherwise, Hindus of East Pakistan/Bangladesh remained under the constant threat of eviction thanks to the communally motivated application of enemy property acts. The deteriorating Hindu-Muslim situation in India, say, during the 1992 Babri mosque demolition, contributed to Hindu Bengali plight vis-à-vis Muslim highhandedness.

In contrast, thanks to the dominance of the liberal/left in West Bengal politics, anti-Muslim riots in the state were virtually non-existent. But it did not mean that violence per se was non-existent. Towards the end of the sixties Naxalite terrorism had reduced Calcutta to a veritable war zone which cost many lives. The movement was quelled by the Indian state with an iron hand and matching brutality.

In West Bengal today political violence has engulfed the state as never before. During the recent parliamentary elections it witnessed the maximum number of murders. The apprehension is that the trend would continue till the next assembly elections. Given the ongoing political polarization on religious lines, large-scale Hindu-Muslim riots also cannot be ruled out.

If that happens, its impact on Bangladesh politics is elementary political science. Already Prime Minister Sheikh Hasina is under tremendous strain to maintain a precarious balance between the country's 'secularists' and 'Islamists'. The more she would be cornered by the latter, the more she would be forced to transfer the problem to her Indian counterparts. One foreseeable outcome would be the reopening of Bangladeshi territory for India's north-east insurgents to maintain their hideouts. Politics by definition is not a game for solving problems but a game to ensure the political longevity of leaders.

The BJP's Hindu card can make it win elections but it cannot make it solve either the inherent Assamese-Bengali rift or the caste dynamics of the Bengali Hindu refugee movements. Likewise, it may be fine to fan the hopes of millions of 'non-citizen' Hindus to dream of earning Indian nationality but to make them prove 'persecution in Bangladesh' as their legitimate ground for migration into India is extremely tricky, both diplomatically and administratively. Let us brace ourselves for another round of *Bongal Kheda* (oust the Bengalis) agitation in Assam, and the eruption of now-dormant SC politics in West Bengal.

These doomsday probabilities notwithstanding, let me conclude with an optimistic proposition. South Asia is an area of Hindu-Muslim experimentation, which no other region in the world can compare with. The world's maximum number of Hindus and Muslims live here and they are destined to continue as such. As Saadat Hasan Manto used to say, how many Hindus or Muslims would the rioters kill, maximum a thousand or two. But would that change their respective demographics. Per a rough count there are 1,100 million Hindus and 500 million Muslims in the region.

Let both the communities be reminded of their ultimate destiny and frustration. Gopal Krishna, an Indian academic, wrote may years ago:

> The inescapable truth seems to be that Hindu India cannot escape the consequences of its medieval defeat, however much it might try, and Indian Islam cannot overcome the consequences of the failure of its mission of conquest in India whatever it might do. The result has been on both sides, frustration, hatred, and apparent powerlessness to alter the situation.

But why call it frustration! Is it also not an opportunity, a hope? If such a huge mass of people, seemingly so unfriendly, have lived side by side for a thousand years without an Armenian massacre, without a Holocaust, or without a Rwanda, why can they not live happily for another thousand years? The nearest comparable tragedy was the massacre of Bengalis during the Bangladesh liberation war. But that was not an interreligious conflict, even though Pakistan tried to give it that colour.

It is all in our minds as to how we want to see ourselves. Let *epaar-bangla-opaar-bangla* be the role model. By extrapolating the model into our South Asian region, let us proudly remind ourselves that we are a unique people amongst whom one single individual, Rabindranath Tagore, composed the national anthems of three countries, Bangladesh, India, and Sri Lanka.

In an otherwise communally charged India we still proudly sing Pakistan's national poet Mohammad Iqbal's *Saare jahan se achchha Hindustan hamara* (best amongst all nations is my India). Can anyone say that Tagore's *amaar shonar bangla* does not also subsume the Bengalis of West Bengal?

Essay 6: Constructing a *Hindu Ummah*: The Globalization of Hindutva*

The way the 'Howdy, Modi' extravaganza was planned, executed, and marketed, one is bound to wonder, is a Hindu *ummah* under construction? At first glance, this characterization appears comical given that Islam, with which the idea of an *ummah* is associated, is Hindutva's *bête noire*. A Hindu *ummah* ought to be a contradiction in terms. Hinduism is doctrinally insular. In most cases its rituals and meditational practices are personal. Unlike Christianity or Islam, it is also non-congregational.

* 'Constructing a Hindu Ummah', *Dhaka Tribune*, 26 October 2019, https://www.dhakatribune.com/opinion/longform/2019/10/22/constructing-a-hindu-ummah, simultaneously carried as 'Constructing a Hindu Ummah', *Newsclick.in*, 18 October 2019, https://www.newsclick.in/constructing-hindu-ummah

Ummah is an Arabic word. It means 'people' or 'community'. Its political connotation, however, is loaded. It conceives of a community of 'believers', meaning Muslims, who are spread across nations. They are expected to coalesce around the goal of propagating Islam, as doctrinally sanctioned in Islamic theology. Being a proselytizing religion, Islam also has the notion of *Dawat-e-Islam* (invitation to Islam). It circuitously presupposes the superiority of Islam and, therefore, asks non-Muslims to join it.

Hinduism, on the other hand, doctrinally discourages conversion. The only proselytizing effort attempted within Hinduism was in the late nineteenth century by the Arya Samaj when it introduced the ritual of *shuddhi*, through which a converted Muslim or any non-Hindu could become a Hindu. But it was largely a non-starter. *Shuddhi* should also not be confused with the present *ghar wapsi* (return to the Hindu fold), which is nothing but political hooliganism by another name.

And yet, the possibility of a Hindu *ummah* is greater today than it ever was before: political Hinduism is active today in about 40 countries of the world. In Western democracies, say, the United States, its visibility is causing ripples in its domestic politics and also among the other religionists. This could hardly have happened overnight. How, then, can one conceptualize its rise?

Some questions, therefore, are inescapable: What is the origin of the Hindu *ummah*, how has it evolved, what forces drive it, and what will its international fall-out be? Does it prove Samuel Huntington right who talked about the 'clash of civilizations' in the post-Cold War world?

Before these questions are answered some conceptual clarity is in order. One can do so by juxtaposing the concepts of Islamic and Hindu *ummah*. Two important differences between them immediately become clear. One, unlike Islamic *ummah*, the Hindu *ummah* is not doctrinally sanctioned (as I noted above). And two, unlike the former, the Hindu *ummah* is remote controlled, from India.

It is alleged that Saudi Arabia too remote controls the Islamic *ummah*. Much as the Saudis would love for this to be true, it is not. At the macro level, Muslim countries barely show any unity, least of all under the leadership of Saudi Arabia. Leave alone the

Shias, who constitute about 15 per cent of the world's 1.8 billion Muslims, even Sunnis are not necessarily pro-Saudi. And most Sunni countries watch with suspicion the unwelcome Wahhabi influence in their societies.

The 57-member Organization of Islamic Cooperation (OIC) is barely taken seriously as an Islamic front, and even less so as a cohesive cluster in the classical *ummah* sense. If the latter has failed at the inter-governmental level, it has not fared any better at the societal level. The Islamic *ummah* seems to be successful only in a form of 'Islamic terrorism' which is cross-national and dreams of a return to the glory of the Caliphate. But even 'Islamic terrorism' has multiple power centres.

From the above discussion it is clear that Islamic *ummah* is there only in name. Yet we refer to it because we believe in some imaginary Islamic solidarity, a glue that brings it together. In the case of the Hindu *ummah*, Hindutva serves as this glue. Like the Islamic *ummah*, it too is not officially sponsored. But it is much more real than the Islamic *ummah* because it is semiofficially sponsored. The Rashtriya Swayamsevak Sangh (RSS) as its sponsor is now both the brain and brawn of India's ruling Bharatiya Janata Party (BJP), which continues to expand its influence across the country.

To make the formulation clearer, let the entire period of independent India be divided into two phases: when BJP was not in power and when it was in power. We can see that the seeds of a Hindu *ummah* were sown in the first phase itself. It was as early as 1947, the year India gained independence, that emigrant RSS members opened branches in Kenya and Myanmar. But these efforts were rudimentary and probably not overseen by RSS headquarters in Nagpur.

The first clear guidance in this regard came in 1953 when RSS supremo Madhav Sadashiv Golwalkar exhorted RSS *pracharaks* (workers) to launch a 'world mission to *propagate* the Hindu notion of the world as *a single family*' (emphasis added). In this call one can see the laying-in ceremony of the Hindu *ummah*.

Soon efforts were undertaken to enter Hindu communities in Nepal and Kenya, followed by similar activities in the UK. With the establishment in 1964 of the Vishwa Hindu Parishad (VHP), a militant Hindu affiliate of the RSS, the United States started appearing more prominently on the RSS radar. In 1970 VHP began its operation there.

With the systematic push for Hindutva in the early 1980s, through campaigns such as the *Ekatmata Yajna* (connotation: Hindus to think themselves as one soul), this overseas connection grew rapidly. In the beginning, it was difficult to distinguish between Indian-Americans, in general, and Hindu-Americans, in particular. But with the growing dominance of the BJP as a political force in India, this distinction has increasingly become clear.

This organized thrust for Hindutva that we notice in several parts of the world today is what makes a Hindu *ummah* a real possibility. At present, the RSS is active in at least forty countries through organizations like the Hindu Swayamsevak Sangh (HSS), the Overseas Friends of the BJP (OFBJP), the Hindu Education Foundation (HEF), the Vedic Foundation, the Hindu American Foundation, etc. With 15 per cent of the world population being Hindu (1,100,000,000 people), it is an important political development with inevitable consequences for international relations.

In this short essay it is not possible to do justice to the entire process of globalization of Hindutva but an American case study can throw some light on some of the critical issues involved. In any case, when one talks about the Hindu diaspora, one generally means Hindus settled in the West, and even then so primarily in the United States. Modi's two high-profile visits to America leave little doubt about this hypothesis.

America's Hindu connection is old. In the early days, it was not the Hindu immigrants but Hindu philosophy that attracted many eminent Americans. In the writings of the transcendental philosopher Ralph Waldo Emerson (1803-82) one can see the influence of the notion of *karma*. Helena Blavatsky's Theosophical Society (1875) had much to borrow from Hindu mystic philosophy. But it was Swami Vivekananda who hugely triggered American interest in Hinduism.

Vivekananda's electrifying speech at Chicago's World Parliament of Religions in 1893 impacted Americans so much that many joined his Vedanta Societies. In the subsequent years, the writings of Rabindranath Tagore, too, had a massive appeal because of his universalistic vision, which were themselves largely drawn from modern Hinduism.

The life and teachings of Mahatma Gandhi injected into American consciousness a profound vision about Hindu social ethics. By his spiritually inspired political thought, encapsulated in his vision of non-violence as a weapon against oppression, Gandhi profoundly influenced at least three eminent Americans: the civil rights leader Martin Luther King, Jr, the Christian pacifist and activist A.J. Muste, and the folk singer and activist Joan Baez (of 'we shall overcome' fame).

The current phase, however, is totally different. It is no longer the philosophy of Hinduism but Hindutva, or political Hinduism, which has assumed centre stage. This variety of Hinduism appeals little to Americans. Indeed, it is not meant to register their support. It aims at influencing American Hindus so as to make them serve as outstation cheerleaders of a particular political party in India that believes in Hindu nationalism.

It is common knowledge that America being a nation of immigrants will have all kinds of diaspora. Their respective mother countries do use them as lobbies to influence the American government in their favour. But the Hindu diaspora is a sectarian diaspora, not an Indian diaspora. As such, it contains a potential irritant for Indo-US relations, notwithstanding President Donald Trump's full-throated endorsement of Modi in the 'Howdy, Modi' event.

Representing a tiny number of Hindus in predominantly Christian America, it can expose the American Hindus to the distrust of the Christian majority. In response to the anti-Christian violence in India in the recent past, perpetrated by the same forces that dominate the Hindu diaspora in America, some American Christian organizations had called on the US State Department to take action. The fact that the latter almost routinely rebukes India for its shoddy record in terms of religious freedom must be factored in to understand this connection.

The other problem is more deep-seated and concerns the diminished influence of the Indian expatriate lobby in America. This lobby had played an important role during the signing of the

Indo-US civil nuclear deal in 2008. It may be recalled that when the importance of the Indian diaspora in America was first highlighted by Rajiv Gandhi by coining the word 'brain bank' in place of 'brain drain', his reference was to the 'Indian diaspora', and not the 'Hindu diaspora'. A recent study suggests that of the 966 Indian American organizations, 481 are religious organizations, and of these, 60 per cent are Hindu.

It cannot just be coincidence, then, that with the coming to power of Narendra Modi in 2014, Muslim Indian-Americans have largely been expelled from the community. The Indian Embassy in Washington no longer organizes an annual Eid reception. Both the massive pro-Modi events, first in Madison Square Garden in New York on 28 September 2014 and more recently in Houston (Texas) on 23 September 2019, were almost entirely dominated by rich Hindus. (Some Muslim Bohras attended the events as they support Modi in India, but they are an exception within the broader Indian Muslim community.)

An ironic sidelight to the event was that although the Indian-origin Muslim comedian Hasan Minhaj was denied entry to the event because of the digs he took at Modi on his Netflix show *Patriot Act*, he was featured in the event. Standing outside the stadium, Minhaj watched a livestream of the show and was amused to see 'his own face up on the jumbotron as one of the Indian-Americans being honoured for their contribution to the arts'.

Not all Hindus in America have turned Hindutva enthusiasts but those who have are more vocal and organized. Pieter Friedrich, a well-known American specialist on South Asian communities says:

> Those who oppose Modi often follow elections in India with great interest, and maybe even talk or write about them, but do little beyond. Those who support Modi host [or] organize rallies, training camps, and campaign events. While one side alleges that Modi staged a pogrom, thousands of volunteers from the other side return to India to physically canvass for his political party.

Let all Hindu-Americans, particularly the types that throng 'Howdy, Modi' events, be reminded that they have sworn to the US government on becoming American citizens that:

> I hereby declare, on oath, that I absolutely and entirely renounce and abjure all allegiance and fidelity to any foreign prince, potentate, state, or sovereignty, of whom or which I have heretofore been a subject or citizen; that I will support and defend the Constitution and laws of the United States of America.

They may also be reminded that America has a violent history of hostility against new immigrants; for example, against the Japanese-Americans during the Second World War. Only a decade prior to that the Americans had chanted against 'the menacing spread of Hindus'. It is elementary international politics that there is no permanent friend or foe; today's friend India can be tomorrow's enemy India.

Of all the people, Trump is probably least dependable in this regard. Today he may go to the ridiculous extent of calling Modi 'the father of India', but tomorrow that same Trump may say with equal aplomb 'Imran is the father of Pakistan', and hence, 'Modi and Imran are cousins'. He will then step in with his masterly real estate business skills to divide the real estate called Kashmir between the two cousins.

Anyone who has even an elementary understanding of how the US presidential election works would have noted that it was Trump more than Modi who played his cards better. By sharing the podium with Modi in front of enthralled Modi fans, Trump was trying to poach into the pro-Democratic Indian-American community to further his 2020 reelection prospects.* Texas has 38 votes in the electoral college, next only to California, which has 55. Trump cannot afford to lose Texas, which, though traditionally Republican, has of late shown a tendency of drifting towards the Democrats. In a close contest, the Hindu-American support will matter.

Let me conclude this essay with a lament. As soon as one becomes a religious fanatic he stops distinguishing between right and wrong because that faculty is no longer in their possession. It is true of all fanatics, Hindu, Muslim, Christian, or Buddhist. That is the risk in the expansion of the Hindu *ummah*, as was the case with the Islamic *ummah*, which degenerated into terrorism.

* Donald Trump has officially lost the 2020 presidential election to Democratic nominee, Joseph R. Biden.

It is chilling to note the expanded space religion is occupying these days in our lives across all continents. Even our social relationships are facing a crisis of confidence because of the phenomenon. Although most social media posts are garbage, some are quotable. Let me recall one: 'Want to convert a friend into an enemy? Discuss politics. If that fails, try religion.'

Postscript: This year, India is celebrating the 150th anniversary of Mahatma Gandhi with all enthusiasm. It would be instructive to know what the Mahatma had to say about the Indian diaspora. Though it was smaller then, limited almost entirely to Ceylon, Malay and the West Indies, where Indian indentured labourers had settled, his thoughts remain relevant today.

Addressing a congregation of Indian Tamils in Colombo on 25 November 1927, Gandhi said: 'Since you are earning your bread in this beautiful island, I would ask you to live as sugar lives in milk. Even as a cup of milk which is full up to the brim does not overflow when sugar is gently added to it, the sugar accommodating itself in the milk and enriching its taste, in the same way, I would like you to live in this island so as not to become interlopers and so as to enrich the life of the people in whose midst you may be living'.

Essay 7: Corona, Termites, and the Tablighis*

Three completely different things. One is a virus, the other is a pest, and the third is a religious congregation. How on earth could there be a connection between them? But tragically, there is. The

* 'More Dangerous than Any Virus', *Dhaka Tribune*, 22 April 2020, https://www.dhakatribune.com/opinion/op-ed/2020/04/22/more-dangerous-than-any-virus, simultaneously carried as 'A Case of People versus Cynical Politics', *Newsclick.in*, 18 April 2020, https://www.newsclick.in/case-people-versus-cynical-politics

connecting thread is hate, more dangerous than any virus we have known or are likely to know. Hate is, to update William Shakespeare, that 'green-eyed monster which doth moth the meat it feeds on'. The more we hate others, the more our hate-fuelled inferiority complex mocks us.

The whole world is now under the grip of a Coronavirus whose destructive potential is incalculable. We have seen two world wars, many earthquakes, floods and wildfires, a Tsunami, or even the Great Plague of London (1665-6) or the Spanish Flu (1918-20), but never have we seen such massive destabilization across all continents. By the time this column is out, the situation will probably be starker. There is little doubt that a vaccine will be found soon. But what will happen to the virus of hatred that is being nurtured on a daily basis in the name of spotting the original culprit? It is man's misfortune that he thinks that all his misery is because of someone else's fault. Just like for Trump's America it is the 'Wuhan Virus', for many Hindus it is because of the Muslims, through their agents like the Tablighi Jamaat.

Pandemics are not new. To put it wryly, they can be seen as the *harbingers* denouments of globalization. In the fourteenth century, bubonic plague spread across China, Central Asia, India, and the Middle East. In 1347, traders from Genoa and Venice passed it on to Mediterranean ports. Yellow fever and the hookworm reached America through the importation of black slaves from Africa. In the early nineteenth century, cholera migrated from India to Sri Lanka, Afghanistan and Nepal. It then reached the Arabian Peninsula, from where it spread to east Africa, Burma, China, Japan, Java, Poland, Russia, Thailand, and Turkey. The Austro-Hungarian Empire, Germany, Poland and Sweden were next, before it ultimately arrived in the British Isles, Canada, and the United States.

According to Jared Diamond, the author of *Guns, Germs and Steel* (1997), 'Smallpox, measles, influenza, typhus, bubonic plague, and other infectious diseases endemic in Europe played a decisive role in European conquests, by decimating many peoples on other continents. For example, a smallpox epidemic devastated the Aztecs after the failure of the first Spanish attack in 1520.' There is also the famous story of smallpox infected blankets gifted by British colonists to exterminate some specific Indian tribes in North America. During recent centuries, when the United States experienced massive immigration flows, fears were expressed that the immigrants were prone to import their native diseases.

It is against this background that our concern about the Corona virus must be seen. Until recently, Indians were made to believe that a major threat to their survival emanated only from the 'termites' that had infested every nook of India. The then BJP president and presently India's Home Minister, Amit Shah, referred to these 'termites', the unauthorized Bangladeshi settlers in India, in his election speeches to garner Hindu votes. During the three-week lockdown of India when millions of poor Indians hit the roads to desperately reach their native villages to avoid starvation, I eagerly tried to spot many of these 'termites' among the fleeing poor. But no TV or social media footage obliged me. That Amit Shah had played his anti-Muslim hate card was evident.

Tragically, the same hate card is once again on display at the mass level. In addition to its anti-Muslim strand, it now has an anti-North Easterner strand as well, just because many citizens from those parts look 'Chinese'. Ever since the news of the Tablighi Jamaat meet in Delhi (13-15 March) and its inevitable impact on the spread of the Corona virus has surfaced, a section of the Hindutva brigade has left no stone unturned to accuse Muslims at large for spreading the virus with the ostensible aim of killing Hindus. Vigilante groups are running amok in semi-urban areas asking for IDs from local vendors, just to target Muslims. Many old, out of context, videos are being uploaded on social media to spread all kinds of anti-Muslim venom.

What the Tablighi Jamaat did was idiotic, and the Indian state should have been watchful and prevented it from happening. But such idiocies are rampant across religions. If I start documenting them, this column will run out of space. And if you need to be reminded of how dangerous such fanaticism can turn out to be if it is not contained: In Patiala a Nihang (a member of a firebrand Sikh sect) chopped a police officer's arm off just because the officer and his team were enforcing a state-mandated lockdown.

Like India's Muslims, people from India's north-east are also being exposed to all kinds of abuse; not for their religious affiliations (many of them are Christians) but for their physical features. Such racial abuse has been reported in several parts of India. My former students from the region have been routinely mentioning to me these humiliations. In the present Corona context, I received an e-mail from one of them, Ms Lamneivah Sithou, a Thadou/Kuki from Manipur. With her permission, I am sharing it with my readers. See the anguish in her tone:

> Having lived in Delhi for more than a decade I have seen how we are subjected to racial discrimination as a matter of routine. Now that the Corona virus is supposed to have spread from China we are ridiculed on the streets and public places with such abusive comments as, 'you Corona Virus', 'Go Corona Go', and so on. These racial slurs hit at the core of our dignity as human beings. We are being reduced to insects. India's idea of 'Unity in Diversity' lies in tatters.

Then she makes a suggestion: 'Let the Indian parliament make a law against such racial attacks so that all its Indian citizens can live with equal dignity and self-respect'. Poor girl, she still entertains a lofty faith in our legislations.

One last point. It is disgusting to see how politicians around the world take their citizens for a ride in the name of religion. In India it is now endemic. What will happen to that country where secularism and liberalism become abusive terms? A secular person is abused as *sickular*, and a liberal as *libtard*, i.e. a liberal bastard. Even Prime Minister Modi thinks that his electoral victory indicated the end of secularism. Alas, how can one convince these people that secularism is an ideal, like honesty, truthfulness, etc.? One can criticize somebody as not sufficiently secular, but to discard secularism altogether as an idea amounts to throwing the baby out along with the bathwater.

Unfortunately the trend is not confined to India. Even the United States, which gave the world its first written constitution almost 250 years ago, and talked of separating the state from religion, is drifting away from its ideal. President Trump routinely plays to his Christian gallery. After having totally failed to tackle the Corona threat, he had the audacity to boast on 24 March, the day India began a three-week lockdown, that by Easter Sunday, that is 12 April, the Corona problem would be solved and 'you'll have packed churches all over our country'. Ironically, by that same Easter Sunday, America had recorded as many as 5,61,103 confirmed Corona cases and 22,106 deaths. Ideally, instead of 'packed churches' Trump should have promised 'packed offices and factories'. According to the economist Arun Kumar, in these three weeks, 16 million Americans had lost their jobs, which is more than what was lost in the entire financial crisis of 2007-9.

No one will dispute that religion is important in one's life. But one's religiosity has no business to intrude into another person's religiosity. Let me take my own example. I am a Hindu, but I am secular as well. Where is the contradiction? Do I not respect all other religionists as equal in every sense? Sonia Sikka, a West-based philosophy professor, makes sense to me when she argues that seldom do all members of a community blindly follow their religious tradition. In most cases, they are spiritual but not religious, because their inner voices serve them as 'critical insiders'. Those voices make them reflective and make them 'adopt the views and practices that cohere with their own experience and judgment'. And that judgment, I think, should not be anything but humanist.

Postscript: In any grim situation there is always a silver lining. When colonists encountered tropical diseases and realized that the germs did not distinguish between them, the colonial masters, and their servants, they spent enormous time and resources to understand these diseases and locate cures. The result was that in due course the world had the legendary Institute for Tropical Medicine in London and the Royal Tropical Institute in Amsterdam. Who knows, but it might be possible that at the end of the Corona menace we will have some unthinkable breakthroughs in our medical knowledge. And societally, too, we will know that there is a world of mutual trust and respect beyond the presently divisive religion-centric, race-centric, and power-centric polities. The best democracies of the West, which are held up as models today, had only until a few hundred years ago a gory history of religious conflicts. Human ingenuity is inexhaustible. As the poet Sahir Ludhianvi wrote, the gloomier the night, the brighter the sunshine. Let us be led by humanistic thinkers, not self-serving politicians.

Essay 8: UCC: Programmed to Remain Elusive*

A democracy presupposes equality of citizens before the law. As such, since there is one criminal code, there should ideally also be one civil code. Most Western democracies fit this model, although as their societies have become increasingly multicultural, they have been forced into making innovations that dilute the code's original rigidity.

The case of India is somewhat distinct. When it comes to family matters like marriage, divorce, inheritance, adoption, and maintenance, Indians are governed by their respective personal laws. But personal law does not signify private or individual law; rather, it means individual rights exercised by virtue of belonging to a particular community. For nearly a century now, many have demanded that India too ought to adopt a Uniform Civil Code (UCC), which will replace existing personal (i.e. community-based) laws and adjudicate all family matters under uniform rules.

A question many ask is why did the British, who ruled India for two centuries and who gave us the Indian Penal Code of 1861, not promulgate a similar civil code. Overwhelmed by India's mindboggling cultural diversity, they quickly discovered that the justice system they had inherited from the Mughals was quite efficient. This system relied upon religious laws, mainly Hindu and Muslim, to settle family matters. Accordingly, the British undertook a massive project to translate relevant Hindu and Muslim religious texts into English.

These translations provided the bases on which judges delivered justice. Over the years, judges came to depend more on their predecessors' interpretations of the translated texts, i.e. on case laws, than on the original translated texts themselves. In due course, compilations of these case laws came to be known as the Anglo-Hindu Law and the Anglo-Mohammedan Law. The British legal project thus was fundamentally conservative, invested in maintaining the existing social order so that their commercial interests

* 'Is a Uniform Civil Code Really Necessary? It'll Lead to More Lawsuits, More Courts, More Delays', *Outlook* (New Delhi), 9 September 2019, pp. 38-9. https://www.outlookindia.com/magazine/author/partha-ghosh/9312

were protected. Any potential desire to institute social reform was further discouraged in the wake of the revolt of 1857.

It was during India's nationalist movement, which had a distinctly progressive thrust, that the idea of a uniform civil code gained momentum as independent India's motto. The Constituent Assembly debated the issue threadbare, but the maximum it could achieve was to list a UCC among the Directive Principles of State Policy. Since nothing in those Directive Principles is justiciable, the matter has not moved an inch forward since. Those who refer to this commitment at every drop of the hat should remind themselves that the Directive Principles contain many other lofty ideals too, but seldom has even a tear been shed for their non-implementation.

India's leaders were faced with two possible routes forward after 1947: reform and codify existing personal laws, or, draft a model UCC to be debated and enacted? They chose the first route and the results are before us. It was in Nehru's first cabinet itself that the idea was broached. Given the fact that despite devastating Hindu-Muslim riots millions of Muslims had preferred to remain in Hindu-majority India, it was thought unwise to fiddle with their personal law and further threaten their sense of identity. Both Gandhi and Nehru supported this idea.

But in keeping with his commitment to the UCC, and because Hindus were the predominant majority, Nehru also pushed for the reform and codification of Hindu personal law. B.R. Ambedkar, as first law minister, prepared the necessary draft. But Nehru should have anticipated that a draft Hindu reform code prepared by a Dalit would be too much for caste Hindus to swallow. Not just the Hindu Mahasabha and RSS, but many eminent Hindu leaders within the Congress stridently opposed it. In the end, the draft was approved by Cabinet but never brought before parliament.

Realizing his political miscalculation, Nehru devised a two-stage strategy. In the first stage was passed the Special Marriage Act, 1954, which allowed any two adult citizens to register their marriage in court irrespective of, and free from, the requirements of their religions. The act had one shortcoming though, as I have learned from the esteemed legal scholar Tahir Mahmood. As many of its provisions were lifted from Hindu personal law, it disallowed inter-cousin marriage, a practice permitted among Muslims. In the second stage, Nehru relied upon his Brahmin law minister, H.V. Pataskar, to present Hindu law reforms not en masse but piecemeal. Pataskar made persuasive speeches to convince the legislators. Generally progressive, the Hindu Code (1955-6) did generate some collateral damage. For example, the gender-just systems of the Nairs in Kerala, Meiteis in Manipur, Meenas in Rajasthan, and the Jains got neutralized.

The political importance of the Hindu Code, however, lay elsewhere. That an elected parliament had interfered in matters of personal law signaled a radical step. When such a question had arisen in the Constituent Assembly a few years earlier, some Muslim members had argued that the parliament should have no authority to legislate over personal law. Ambedkar had at that time ruled in favour of the parliament's authority to do so. The passage of the Hindu Code marked the first instance of such legislative assertion.

There have been two other instances since. The second was when the Rajiv Gandhi government passed The Muslim Women (Protection of Rights on Divorce) Act, 1986. Although Gandhi is criticized by both secularist and Hindutva forces, if interpreted in democratic terms, it was a progressive move. The recent passage of The Muslim Women (Protection of Rights on Marriage) Act, 2019 signals the third instance. But a critical difference marks the first two from the last: Community concerns were summarily rubbished while passing the 2019 Act.

The lesson here is that the Indian parliament is powerful enough to usher in a uniform civil code. The Hindutva forces think that reforming Muslim personal law and a UCC are one and the same thing. They are not. Certain core facts, therefore, bear reiteration, again and again. One, personal law reforms do not lead to a UCC, they instead come in the way of one; two, UCC is a political matter for which consensus is needed, the legal nitty-gritties are peripheral; three, all religious and tribal communities, Hindus included, oppose the UCC; four, no political party is serious about the UCC and that includes the BJP; and five, there must be a draft UCC to start with. If the recent recommendation of the Law Commission is any indication such a draft is still light years away.

Under these circumstances, it is not parliament but the judiciary that is stealthily making progress; not towards a UCC, but towards, to use Werner Menski's phrase, the 'uniformization' of personal law. According to Menski, events in India seem to be following a two-pronged path. On the one hand, we see the harmonious management of age-old cultural diversities by effectively allowing a plurality of personal laws. On the other hand, we see attempts to address the pressures of real and potential gender and cross-community inequality 'through the intricate process of gradual harmonization of all Indian personal laws and [their] supervision by criminal and constitutional laws'.

Let the devil have the last point. Is a uniform civil code really necessary? More codification means more lawsuits, more courts, more expenses, and more delays. Already there are more than thirty million cases pending in Indian courts. In 1987, the Law Commission had recommended that there should be at least 50 judges for every 1,000,000 people. As recently as 2016, the law ministry revealed that there were just 18 judges per million. Upendra Baxi argues forcefully in favour of a non-state legal system where most poor people have traditionally gotten their justice. I think he makes sense.

Essay 9: Have the Farmers Stalled the Hindutva Juggernaut?*

It is time for Hindutva to watch out. The Narendra Modi government is facing a political challenge as never before. The challenge is daunting because it emanates from no political party but loosely organized farmers. Spearheaded by Punjabi farmers the agitation is gaining in strength every passing day with more farmers from all over India joining.

* 'Have Farmers Stalled the Hindutva Juggernaut', *Dhaka Tribune*, 21 December 2020, https://www.dhakatribune.com/opinion/op-ed/2020/12/21/op-ed-have-the-farmers-stalled-the-hindutva-juggernaut, simultaneously carried as 'Have Farmers Stalled the Hindutva Juggernaut', *Newsclick.in*, 15 December 2020, https://www.newsclick.in/Have-Farmers-Stalled-Hindutva-Juggernaut

Reminiscent of the 1988 Bharatiya Kisan Union-led farmers rally in Delhi, the present protests have assumed importance for their same apolitical nature. That has made BJP's job difficult. Until now, the BJP has successfully played its Hindutva card to dominate the political narrative and trounce its political opponents. The question, therefore, is will the farmers' agitation make the Hindutva juggernaut halt and allow a return to a level-playing field in Indian politics.

BJP's electoral gains over the years have been striking, including those in the recently held Greater Hyderabad municipal election. From a bare four in 2016, it won as many as 48 municipal divisions (out of a total 150) in elections earlier this month. Its vote percentage also rose massively to 34.56 points, which almost matched that of the regionally unbeatable Telengana Rashtra Samithi (TRS).

The Hyderabad showing was right on the heels of its victory in the Bihar elections held in October-November. There the BJP emerged as the dominant partner in the ruling National Democratic Alliance (NDA), relegating to the background its more powerful regional ally, Chief Minister Nitish Kumar's Janata Dal United (JDU). Had the BJP wanted, it could have claimed the post of chief minister, but keeping larger strategic interests in mind it let Nitish Kumar retain the position. The latter is no doubt aware that a small misstep and the BJP will replace him without much ado.

Whether in Bihar or in Hyderabad, the political card the BJP most vociferously displayed was that of Hindutva. There was extravagant use of such catchphrases as: 'beware of the divisive forces'; 'look out for the Pakistani lackeys'; 'condemn the pseudo-secularists'; 'drive out the Rohingya migrants'; 'remember who were behind the terrorist attack in Pulwama'; 'change the name from Hyderabad to Bhagyanagar (evoking the renaming of Allahabad and Mughal Sarai Junction as Prayagraj and Deen Dayal Upadhyay Junction, respectively)'; and finally, perhaps the most ludicrous of them all, 'there will be "surgical strikes" to drive out all illegal Bangladeshis'.

These tongue-in-cheek and demonstrably false contentions had little relevance for local politics but because they were dished out directly by the likes of Narendra Modi, Amit Shah, J.P. Nadda, and other top BJP leaders they were powerful enough to influence voters. Considering discretion the better part of valour, most other parties steered clear of the communal question by emphasizing seemingly more mundane matters. In Bihar, for example, the Tejaswi Yadav-led Rashtriya Janata Dal (RJD) danced to just one tune, the problem of unemployment. That it emerged as the single largest party and also won the popular vote by a significant margin serves warning to the BJP about the efficacy of Hindutva as an all-weather weapon. Still, Hindutva has not lost its shine.

In such circumstances, many Muslims in the Muslim-majority areas of Bihar increasingly gravitated towards the Hyderabad-based, Asaduddin Owaisi-led AIMIM (All India Majlis-e-Ittehad-ul-Muslimeen: All India Council for Unity of Muslims). And although Owaisi is no twenty-first century Mohammed Ali Jinnah out to divide the country, his success no doubt pleases the BJP, which would love to see an Owaisi-driven polarizing drive succeed, thereby further consolidating its Hindu constituency. After all, greater the Hindu-Muslim communal polarization, better the prospects for Hindutva to perpetuate its appeal.

Against this background of business-as-usual success, the BJP could scarcely have imagined that their Hindutva juggernaut would come to a grinding halt in the face of roadblocks mounted by the innocuous Sikh farmers of Punjab. It is the first time since Modi's elevation to power in 2014 that his government has not been able to browbeat protesters in the name of national security. The Sikh farmers have (so far) succeeded where the nation-wide cross-community protests by university students (including those form JNU) and anti-CAA protesters (led by common Muslims of Delhi) had failed.

Not that the BJP has not tried to make use of their well-tested deceptions to discredit the farmers. Most unabashedly, they branded the protesting Sikh farmers as secessionist Khalistanis who were being sponsored by forces from across the border, meaning Pakistan and China. Ever since the recent border row between India and China, 'foreign hands' has conveniently begun to connote not just Pakistanis, but the Chinese as well. (During Indira Gandhi's time, these so-called 'foreign hands' signaled American interference.)

Some BJP bigwigs even went to the extent of questioning the

credentials of the farmers. V.K. Singh, Minister of State for Road Transport and Highways, placed his foot squarely in his mouth when he declaimed that he could tell from their dress that that they were not farmers. How could a farmer, who is expected to be poor and in tattered clothes, look so well-fed and well-dressed? Obviously, this was what Minister Singh meant. One may recall that during the Jharkhand assembly election last year, Narendra Modi had similarly derided the Muslims who formed the bulk of the anti-CAA protesters in Delhi's Shaheen Bagh area. As if the Shaheen Bagh protesters had tried to conceal or were embarrassed by who they were.

Thanks to COVID-19 restrictions and certain recent Supreme Court rulings, street protests and open-air gatherings have been virtually delegitimized, granting unfettered reign to the BJP's anti-Muslim rhetoric. The BJP has also used this opportunity to pass one legislation after another, riding rough shod over legislative procedures. They have also let loose their social media troll army to browbeat all liberal, not necessarily anti-BJP, sentiments. Thus, even the depiction in *A Suitable Boy* of a kissing scene between a Hindu girl and a Muslim boy on the premises of a Hindu temple was enough to provoke demands that Netflix pull the show. A more subtle interpretation of the scene—that there is a Hindu temple in every nook and cranny of this country—was perhaps too much to expect from the rabble.

In any case, India's Muslims have been systematically marginalized thanks to the post-Nehruvian politics and do not constitute Hindutva's biggest enemy. The real enemies are the forces of democracy and liberal politics, both of which have been in steady retreat since 2014. But Muslims are important to the Hindutva project because their demonization keeps India's Hindu majority distracted, suppressing their inner societal and cultural contradictions.

From the beginning, the guardians of Hindutva know that so long as the marginal social classes within the Hindufold have a sense of political and legal oneness with the upper castes, they will remain satisfied, their actual societal suppression notwithstanding. The UP government may trumpet their recent anti-Love Jihad law, when of all marriages in the country only three to four per cent are inter-faith (likely even fewer in UP), but have they taken even a single step in the direction of encouraging inter-caste marriages among the Hindus? If and when Hindutva takes this up as its crusading motto, it will have takers even among the 'libtards' and 'sickulars'.

In light of the foregoing discussion, the farmers' agitation assumes importance because it shows that Indian politics should have concerns other than merely the Hindu-Muslim question, which the BJP has mastered to its advantage by posing it as the central question. Nobody knows what the ultimate outcome of the faceoff between the farmers and the state will be, but the visible climb down by the latter is a good omen for Indian democracy because in the process many other issues will also come to the surface. These include the indiscriminate arrests of activists and journalists in the name of national security and the overall deterioration of legislative and judicial processes.

Let me end this essay by asking the BJP one simple question. If everything is hunky-dory—India's growth story is in place, its indigenous anti-COVID vaccine is just a test away, all Muslim nations of the Gulf region are on best terms with India, the Americans are committed to sharing their sophisticated defence technologies, all conflicts with China are being coolly sorted out, farmers are all set to double their income in two years, the Kashmir problem is solved as it is now fully integrated into India, and, most importantly, India is now a corruption-free nation, for the first time since Independence—then why are India's Hindus (who comprise 80 per cent of the country) being made to feel so insecure about the country's politically and economically marginalized Muslims? Why must the community necessarily be demonized during every election, whether national, assembly or municipal?

In the forthcoming West Bengal assembly election we will see this naked communal dance as never before. The pro-CAA and anti-Muslim bugles are already audible. It is just a matter of days before the sound becomes deafening. Who cares about the inevitable fallout in neighbouring Bangladesh, where about 20 million Hindus reside? It seems that for the BJP government the seventeenth-century Treaty of Westphalia is their bible. It has taught them that cartographically Bangladesh is another country and hence India's domestic politics ends at India's Bangladesh border. I wish Prime Minister Sheikh Hasina Wazed had also read the same treaty text and had internalized its inherent ethos exactly the same way.

Postscript: In the 2019 Central Services Mains Examination conducted by India's Union Public Service Commission (UPSC), Question No. 10 of General Studies Paper 1 read as follows: 'What are the challenges to our cultural practices in the name of secularism?' In earlier days, when the word 'secular' had not been mocked as 'sickular', the question would probably have been phrased differently: 'What are the challenges to secularism in the name of our cultural practices?' More than the answers they may generate, it is the vast gulf between the questions themselves that reveals how much has changed in India's secular moorings.

CHAPTER 3

Kashmir Imbroglio

Essay 1: Kashmir Once Again: Is it Becoming another Hundred Years War?*

India and Pakistan are on the brink, once again. Ever since their first Kashmir war in 1947 they have seen so many wars, war-like situations, and cross-border fire exchanges that they have probably lost the count. As a child when I read about the Hundred Years War between England and France I used to surmise: How could a war continue for so long? But is not our Kashmir war becoming one such war? Even if good senses dawn on these nations to ward off the eventuality their TV and media warriors would continue to prepare the people for the war as if it amounts to watching movies? In the region Bangladeshis are the only people who really know what war really means.

The present India-Pakistan crisis had its origin on 14 February 2019 when the Pakistan-based Jaish-e-Mohammed deployed Adil Ahmad Dar, a 20-year old Kashmiri *fidayeen*, to explode his RDX-laden SUV on a CRPF convoy in Pulwama in Kashmir killing as many as 40. A terror strike of this scale is rare. A retaliation came on 26 February from the Indian Air Force which targeted a Jaish camp in Balakot in Khyber Pakhtunkhwa. The idea was to send the message that India reserved its right of 'hot pursuit' the way America did by attacking Osama-bin Laden's hideout in Abbottabad.

One does not know what happened to the Jaish base. Although

* 'Kashmir Once Again: Is it Becoming another Hundred Years War', *The Dhaka Tribune*, 8 March 2019. https://www.dhakatribune.com/opinion/op-ed/2019/03/08/kashmir-once-again

the BJP president Amit Shah claimed that 250 terrorists were killed and the Indian social media bragged that 300 to 600 were killed the Modi government was circumspect. The maximum it revealed was that the Israeli S-2000 bombs had hit four buildings inside Madrasa *Taleem-ul-Quran.* Pakistan said that the bombs fell on barren fields, a claim that seemed to have more takers in the international media. Let us accept all the versions for now as in such situations the biggest casualty invariably is truth.

On the following day, however, the situation became serious when Indian and Pakistani fighter jets got engaged in a dogfight in which one Indian Wing Commander, Abhinandan Varthaman, ended up as a hostage. Mercifully the crisis ended the day after as Pakistan released him as a 'gesture of peace'. Although it is difficult to know whether international good offices had worked or not still India's TV warriors kept claiming that Pakistan buckled under India's pressure. These omniscient commentators kept talking about the 'big picture'. In this jingoistic melee only one sane voice was audible. It came from none other than the former Army Chief of India, General Shankar Roychowdhury. In midst of the nailbiting wait for the release of the Indian captive he pleaded not to lose sight of the 'small picture' as well. He sensitized his viewers about the trauma that the Indian hostage and his family must have been undergoing and also how miserable Prime Minister Imran Khan must have been feeling for not being appreciated for after all it was he who had staked his macho reputation by announcing the unconditional release of the Indian POW for the sake of India-Pakistan peace (NDTV, 1 March, 8:00-9:00 p.m.).

The Kashmir question has been analysed so comprehensively over the decades that nothing new can be said in this short article. Professor Rasul Bakhsh Rais of the Lahore University of Management Studies (LUMS) calls it a 'stable instability'. But since both India and Pakistan are nuclear powers this 'instability', however 'stable', is potentially perilous. It is flawed logic that if nuclear America and Russia could survive the long-drawn Cold War why could not India and Pakistan. But remember America and Russia fought their wars through their proxies which served as the safety valves. India and Pakistan have no such luxury.

Let us understand that neither India nor Pakistan will give up their claims to the respective portions of Kashmir they occupy. However much India may say that the entire Jammu and Kashmir is an integral part of India it betrays conviction because there is hardly any corresponding effort to back up that claim. Rather since the slogan is repeated ad nauseam its seriousness gets compromised. On the contrary it reminds one of what the American humorist Ambrose Bierce lyricized in another context: 'Mark how my fame rings from zone to zone/A thousand critics shouting: "He's unknown!"'

So far as addressing the Kashmir problem in terms of its identity and autonomy demands are concerned only Atal Behari Vajpayee (1999-2004) and Manmohan Singh (2004-14) are recognized to have made some serious efforts. Those efforts surpassed even those of Pandit Jawaharlal Nehru though during his time the Kashmir Accord and the Kashmir Constitution happened. Nehru is more remembered for managing the problem through his puppets as chief ministers of the state. The present phase, of course, is the worst because the BJP/RSS Hindutva politics with its thrust on hyper nationalism is structurally incapable of appreciating any nuanced approach to the problem. Such notions as human rights, autonomy or cultural diversity are simply anathema to the Hindutva ideology.

Kashmir is the only Muslim-majority state in India and howsoever its Muslims may be culturally different from their counterparts in the rest of India there is a limit to this diversity particularly when the Hindutva militancy is in such a pervasive form. Its mass-based militant refrains in northern India like *ghar wapsi* (call to Muslims to return of their original Hindufold), *love jihad* (accusing Muslim men of enticing Hindu girls to marry them with the ostensible object of getting them converted to Islam), 'cow protectionism', anti-beef protestations, etc., have led to the lynching of many Muslims. Even when there is no violence these orchestrated slogans maul the dignity and self-esteem of Muslims at large as citizens of India. It is bad sociology to argue that Kashmiri Muslims are different and they are unconcerned about all these anti-Muslim invectives.

It is no surprise, therefore, that Kashmir is on the boil. In the last few years, just in civil unrest about 100 people have been killed in the Valley, 12,000 have been injured, and more than 1,000 completely or partially blinded by pellet wounds. The Srinagar parliamentary by-election of April 2017 had recorded as little as 7.14 per cent polling which was soon followed by a spontaneous student uprising. The Anantnag by-election had to be postponed again and again because the law and order situation was not conducive to hold it. The government had to frequently snap all 3G and 4G telecom services.

The most ridiculous thing happened when an army jeep tied up a Kashmiri boy on its bonnet to use him as a human shield to protect the soldiers from the young stone throwers. Calling it 'cruelty and cowardice' the *New York Times* editorialized (21 April 2017):

> Members of India's armed forces reached a new low in the long history of alleged human rights abuses in the Indian state of Jammu and Kashmir when they beat and then tied a 24-year-old shawl weaver named Farooq Ahmad Dar to the front of a jeep on 9 April, using him as a human shield against stone-throwing crowds. As the jeep drove through villages, Mr. Dar said, 'I saw people breaking into tears on seeing my state'. Mr. Dar, who says he never supported the separatists, complained: 'I voted [in the Sri Nagar by-election], and this is what I got in return. Do you think it will help India in Kashmir? No. It will give Kashmiris another reason to hate India.

However much the Hindutva ideologues may ask the Muslims to believe that they are not anti-Muslim, their message is written on the wall. Annual reports of India's Home Ministry and other independent studies make a pathetic reading of India's frequent riots in most of which Muslims are the victims. Not that Hindu nationalistic forces did not exist earlier but they were never on centre stage. It is also not true that the Indian state had not systematically poached into Kashmir's autonomy in the earlier years. But the dramatics that are now evident to nullify the autonomy clauses contained in Articles 35A and 370 of the Indian Constitution are unprecedented. That these dramatics are meant to enlist mass Hindu support makes common political sense.

It is interesting to watch how skilfully the Hindutva leadership has mastered the art of placating the Muslim nations in international forums yet simultaneously deriding the Muslim community at home. In the recently held Summit of the Organization of Islamic Cooperation (OIC) held in Abu Dhabi India's external affairs minister Sushma Swaraj not only spoke so eloquently about inter-religious bonhomie in India but also quoted from the Holy Quran to highlight its peace messages. But such things conspicuously lack in BJP-ruled India. Unlike other national parties BJP rarely fields Muslim candidates to fight for the parliament or state legislatures. At the local level anti-Muslim slogans often get vitriolic during the elections.

If India's Kashmir policy has failed what about Pakistan? For the sake of Kashmir it is most unlikely that it would wage a war against India. It is too risky given Pakistan's relative weakness on all parameters, more particularly its teetering economy. Given the fact that its Afghan border is vulnerable, particularly in the wake of an imminent US withdrawal, it would look for a safer and cheaper option. Here comes the efficacy of terrorism as a tool of its Kashmir policy.

Terrorists need no salary nor pension. If an appropriate mixture of radical Islamism and hyper-nationalism can be injected into their consciousness the rest will fall in place, a veritable *jihad* against India. Since no terrorist group has ever been able to dislodge an established state, not even al-Qaeda or Islamic State of Iraq and Syria, if they can be utilized for just their nuisance value to foment trouble in targeted areas it is a fair strategy. Pakistan's goal is to create such compelling circumstances under which the Indian state would have no option other than going for a negotiated deal on Kashmir.

Diplomatically who has gained from the India-Pakistan face-off over Kashmir is a moot question. The Indian government and most Indian commentators think that Pakistan has been internationally isolated. Even if it is true the question is whether that is a good strategy for India from a long term perspective. Given Pakistan's precarious economic circumstances the more it is isolated more its dependence on China, its 'all weather friend', will grow. It means more Chinese physical presence on Pakistan soil the way it has happened in Sri Lanka through the Hambantota port lease. It would not be surprising if it culminates in the stationing of Chinese troops on the Pakistani soil someday. If that happens that would be the ultimate failure of India's regional diplomacy.

There is no harm, therefore, to have a negotiated deal on Kashmir if it satisfies both the countries. I have been arguing for years that there is no escape for either state from recognizing the present Line of Control as the international border. The existing arrangement, as in the case of Korea and Palestine, has failed to promote peace. Kingsley Martin, the editor of the *London New Statesman and Nation,* was prophetic when he wrote as early as in 1953:

> [I]t is dangerous to allow a cease-fireline to harden into a frontier. The United Nations [plan] . . . in Kashmir, Palestine, and Korea has been patiently to isolate the dispute so that fighting ceased. In the case of Kashmir and Palestine it failed to have any effect beyond helping to settle the cease-fire line. Today it is clear that India and Pakistan cannot indefinitely endure the tension of indecision in Kashmir, while the relations between Israel and its neighbors remain dangerously bitter on a frontier that was never intended to do more than recognize a temporary *fail accompli.*

The solution to the problem in Kashmir is in statesmanship, not politics.

Essay 2: Kashmir Under Siege: Pent-up Helplessness can be Combustive*

'One man's beard is on fire, and another man warms his hands on it', so goes the Kashmiri proverb. No Kashmiri could have envisioned that a day would come when the proverb would haunt them with such ferocity. As they see the under restless uncertainty in the aftermath of the gutting of their 'special status' and wait in anticipation for yet worse things to befall them, much of the rest of India celebrates as if a territory has been conquered.

* 'Kashmir Under Siege: Pent-up Rage, Helplessness and Religious Politics Portend Terrible Consequences', *Dhaka Tribune*, 29 August 2019. https://www.dhakatribune.com/opinion/2019/08/29/kashmir-under-siege, simultaneously carried as 'In Kashmir's Silence, Read a Warning', *Newsclick.in* 7 August 2019, https://www.newsclick.in/Kashmir-Silence-Read-Warning-Religious-Politics

It is two weeks and counting that the local media is totally silenced. Even the otherwise informed, therefore, have no way of knowing what is happening in the Valley. Anuradha Bhasin, the editor of *Kashmir Times*, laments that in one critical sense at least the situation is even worse than what prevailed in the 1990s. Although journalists were targeted then too, they were targeted by both militants and the state machinery. Today, the democratic state has monopolized such repression.

The mood in Delhi's power circles is exactly the opposite. Six years ahead of its centenary, the Hindu nationalistic Rashtriya Swayamsevak Sangh (RSS), which views India as a nation of Hindus, for Hindus and by Hindus, has been presented with a much coveted gift: Muslim-majority Kashmir. They are thankful to their political arm, the Bharatiya Janata Party (BJP), for making it possible; an effort that started as early as 1951, when the BJP's forerunner, the Bharatiya Jana Sangh, was established.

The state of Jammu & Kashmir has all along been a test case for both India's secularists and its Hindu nationalists. If Jammu and Kashmir remained multi-religious with a majority Muslim population, it was a statement of success for India's secularists; but if it failed to remain as such, it was a victory for the Hindu nationalists. Buddhist-majority Ladakh was peripheral in this essentially Secular-Hindu contestation.

This critical element, the contest between secularism and a Hindu *rashtra*, is virtually missing in the present discourse over the future of Kashmir that was triggered by the fateful decision of 5 August 2019. On that day, Jammu & Kashmir, a constituent state of the Indian Union, disappeared and in its place emerged two Union Territories. One, the Union Territory of Jammu & Kashmir; and the other, the Union Territory of Ladakh.

Logically, given the BJP's known sympathy for the Hindu-majority Jammu region, Jammu and Kashmir should have been divided into three UTs, not two. It is possible that the RSS/BJP is testing the waters and once the surface turmoil subsides it may conduct a second surgery and further divide the UT of Jammu and Kashmir.

Leaving aside such speculations for the moment, let us instead consider the following: one, what has happened on the ground;

two, what is the state's history; and three, how can one address the handling of the Kashmir Valley, which has a history of protest and disaffection. To put it in poetic terms, what lies in store for the 'idea of India', or its so-called 'unity in diversity'?

Two constitutional provisions that governed the Indian state's relationship with the erstwhile Jammu and Kashmir state now stand de-operationalized. These are Article 370 and Article 35A. The first established the state's 'special status' vis-à-vis the Indian Union, though regular tampering with its provisions had reduced it to a hollow shell, retaining form but little of its original substance.

Article 35A was an addition to the Indian Constitution effected in 1954 through a presidential order that was never endorsed by parliament. As such, its legality was contentious and the matter was pending with the Supreme Court for adjudication. Given the actions of 5 August, any concern over its legality has clearly been overtaken by events. Or, might we still expect the Supreme Court to hear the case?

Of the two, Article 35A is the bigger bone of contention and Hindutva forces were particularly keen to get rid of it. The reason was that it gave the Jammu and Kashmir legislature virtually a blank cheque to decide who qualified as a 'permanent resident' of the state and was thus eligible for special privileges and rights when it came to public sector jobs, property ownership, state scholarships and other aid packages.

There is no dearth of such special privileges in many other states of the Indian Union but what mattered in the case of Jammu and Kashmir was that it was a Muslim-majority state and that the means of implementing the article were not constitutional. Ideally, its unconstitutionality alone should have been addressed, and not its contents. Politically, it is always important to assuage the fear of a minority community in a border region by allowing it to preserve its identity. It has been abundantly done in India's north-east (e.g. Nagaland). But obviously the Muslim factor weighed heavily in finding fault with Article 35A.

In the end, these are relatively simple questions that warrant relatively simple legal answers. Tackling them does little to help us deal with a larger, more complicated, question: what exactly is the

BJP trying to achieve through its Kashmir gamble? And that brings us to the even larger question: how will the BJP's Kashmir gambit affect India's broader commitment to secularism and federalism? In short, what will happen to its so-called 'unity in diversity'? Some, such as the French expert in South Asian affairs Christophe Jaffrelot, have already begun to posit that India is now set for a 'unity in unity' model.

Ever since the days of the Jana Sangh, Pandit Jawaharlal Nehru has been the *bête noire* of Hindutva forces precisely because he stood for secularism and federalism. Nehru has been dead now for more than 55 long years, yet his ghost continues to haunt the Hindutva right. Not a day passes that he is not ridiculed by these forces, either directly or through their social media outlets, as if he is the architect of all that ails India today. In the context of Kashmir, the accusations against him are boundless.

Many insist that Nehru was naïve to have incorporated the special status clauses for Jammu and Kashmir in India's constitution. Whatever little academic understanding I have of the situation prevailing in 1947-8 leads me to reject such a proposition. It is easy to read history backwards and blame Nehru for not accepting the entire state of Jammu and Kashmir as a full state of the Indian Union when the Maharaja of Kashmir had technically acceded to India.

But remember that the Maharaja had acceded to India under duress. Pakistan had attacked Kashmir. A popular movement led by Sheikh Abdullah was making the continuation of the kingdom as an independent entity (which the Maharaja himself desired) untenable. Hindu-Muslim riots had broken out in Jammu (triggered by Muslims and then massively retaliated by the Maharaja's men, who killed a large number of Muslims). In short, the situation was murky. The only redeeming feature was that Nehru and Abdullah were political buddies, which was a matter of enormous significance in the contemporary context. Article 370 was the sum total of this understanding, a compromise formula: the best out of a bad deal.

But as soon as Abdullah tried to be difficult by selectively using his communal as well as international cards, Nehru became as ruthless a statist as classical theories of statecraft would prescribe. He had no compunction in jailing Abdullah in 1953.

In politics, as in real life, symbolism matters. And therein lay the relevance of Article 370, which served the critical purpose of containing Kashmiri disaffection against the Indian state without appearing to be aggressive. Those aware of its prognosis over the past 70 years will know that it was mauled beyond recognition by successive governments. But Kashmiris could tolerate this watering down as long as its symbolism remained in place. By now de-politicizing the Article, the BJP has deprived itself of this symbolism. As the situation unfolds, both in the Valley and in Delhi, a heavy price may have to be paid.

The challenge now for the Modi government is how to proceed from here; particularly because it has burnt all political bridges. Among the first things the BJP did was to lock up any Kashmiri leader worth his or her salt. This included pro-India secular leaders like Farooq and Omar Abdullah as well as Mehbooba Mufti. How can politics be conducted in a political vacuum?

Prime Minister Narendra Modi has vowed to exorcise the ghosts of the 'political dynasties' of the Abdullahs and the Muftis from the state. Should not somebody remind the prime minister that until recently his own party broke bread with Mehbooba Mufti? Did not the BJP have a ruling alliance with Mufti's People's Democratic Party (PDP)?

The BJP appears to operate on the theory that as long as a dynastic politician is an ally (a junior ally at that), all is fine, for, ipso-facto she or he becomes a subscriber to the party's Hindutva ideology. The moment they oppose the BJP, they become a contagion that must be quarantined.

Given the fact that the BJP can draw upon virtually inexhaustible party funds to buy allegiance, it is more than likely that it will soon recruit second or third rung Kashmiri Muslim politicians to do its bidding in the Valley. The prevailing anti-India anger in the Valley may delay this outcome for some time yet but cannot, in all probability, prevent it.

Much may happen in the meantime. We know that the modern state has a tremendous capacity to suppress information and browbeat street unrest, but we also know that the modern state is equally vulnerable in the face of sustained popular unrest and allegations of human rights violations. One waits with bated breath for the time when the curfew will be lifted, and politics will return to the street.

It is an undeniable fact that the BJP has unleashed a frenzied religious politics that is bound to snowball. The ongoing Dalit agitations in Delhi and other parts of north India over the demolition of their deified icon Ravidas' temple in Delhi is just one indication among many that religion has now emerged as the sole mobilizing factor in Indian politics. Even the secular Aam Aadmi Party (AAP) now governing Delhi is fast changing its idiom to dent the BJP's Hindu base.

In the long run, this may be to the good, for unbridled religious politics will ultimately collapse under its own weight. But before that happens much damage to India's composite culture will have been done. The fear is that it would give rise to religion-fed terrorism, which the Muslim world knows much more intimately than does the non-Muslim rest.

In the absence of open-ended democratic politics, a sequestered Kashmir, which has so far seen Pakistan-sponsored and, to a lesser extent, home-grown terrorism, could become a veritable breeding ground for a much wider militancy. As the saying goes, an answer to bad politics is not no politics but more politics. Let us not get carried away by the current 'silence of the lambs' to console ourselves that 'all is well' (made famous by the Bollywood movie, *Three Idiots*).

It is useful to recall here the work of Paul Wilkinson, one of the doyens of terrorism research. Wilkinson has theorized that the ultimate goal of a terrorist group is to provoke the state to such an extent that it eventually indulges in competitive terrorism targeting the common man. Once that stage is reached, the terrorist group has a much larger catchment to draw its future recruits from. All those who are fascinated with the idea of a strong, no-nonsense state and dismissive of human rights activism are requested to reflect on this formulation.

I do not want to be a doomsday forecaster, but I also cannot forget what former Mumbai police chief Julio Ribeiro said in 2002. In the Shah Alam camp of Ahmedabad, where many Muslim victims of the Gujarat riots were sheltered, he observed a frightening silence among its youngest inmates. Ribeiro wrote prophetically in the *Times of India* of 24 April 2002: 'I do not know if the VHP [Vishwa Hindu Parishad] and the Bajrang Dal [a violent Hindutva brigade], who had been gloating over their "success" in Gujarat, visualised the danger to which they are exposing their innocent co-religionists somewhere, sometime in the future.' I pray his fears are not realized in Kashmir.

Since no discussion on Kashmir is possible without a reference to Pakistan let me touch upon that by making just one point. The abolition of Kashmir as a state in the Indian Union has neutralized India's moral superiority vis-à-vis Pakistan. The latter has always been ambivalent about its *raison d'être*, particularly after the creation of Bangladesh. But now its leadership will revamp its mass religious appeal: 'Didn't we say that Hindus and Muslims cannot live together as our Quaid-e-Azam had always feared?' It would legitimize the quasi-democratic, but actually militaristic, regime of Pakistan to the further detriment of the country's fragile democratic constituency, which has been fighting a most difficult battle for decades to change the face of Pakistan polity.

The problem of playing religious politics, which many parties do for votes, is that it is easy to light the fire, but it is much more difficult to extinguish it. Once the embers reach the masses, it spreads like wildfire, vitiating the day-to-day life of the common man. Sometime ago, a Hindu customer cancelled his Zomato food delivery order because the delivery man was a Muslim. Even more recently, the online hotel aggregator, OYO Rooms, denied a booking to a person because he was a Kashmiri Muslim. Though the OYO top brass took the particular staff to task for such obnoxious behavior, the damage had already been done.

The prospective client, a Jamia Millia Islamia student by the name of Malik Aabid, said: 'I appreciate this message [of apology from OYO] but I don't think me and my friend will be able to get over with the "humiliation" which we encountered on 17 August. It has alienated our sense of "other" [*sic*].' Multiply this sense of alienation, of being 'othered', by seven million and one may begin to get a sense of Kashmiri Muslim alienation following the obliteration of their state.

Postscript: During a recent visit to Cambodia, my son (himself half Kashmiri) encountered a local Kashmiri shopkeeper. Out of curiosity, he enquired which part of Kashmir, Indian or Pakistani, did the shopkeeper hail from. The response was evasive, but meaningful: *Kya pharak parta hai, hum to dono taraf se kuchle jaa rahe hain* (how does it matter, we are oppressed by both).

Essay 3: Kashmir and the Future of Indian Federalism*

One thing is virtually missing in the entire discourse on Narendra Modi's latest Kashmir blitzkrieg. Commentators are discussing its legal, historical and international aspects but not many are paying enough attention to its implications for India's federalism. Ever since Modi has assumed power there is a clear trend towards centralization of the Indian polity which furthers RSS's Hindutva strategy without appearing to be so.

What does the RSS want to see India as? It views India as a Hindu *rashtra* which should obliterate not only its diversity in terms of the different religious affiliations of its people but also the diversities within the Hindufold in terms of castes (by itself a laudable idea if conceived seriously). All those who believe that indigenous, read Hindu, blood is flowing in their veins are Hindu. That means Muslims and Christians who trace the religious origins extra-territorially are not Hindu unless they explicitly recognize that they are all local converts from Hinduism.

The theory goes totally contrary to what many historians and political scientists have argued. According to them India is a nation of regions, in constitutional parlance, a union of states. Their argument is based on India's historical experience of having different kingdoms or small princedoms despite the overarching empires of

* 'Kashmir and the Future of Indian Federalism', *Mainstream* (New Delhi), 57(35), 17 August 2019: 17-18. http://www.mainstreamweekly.net/article8942.html

the kinds that the Mauryas, Guptas or the Mughals built. Even the British depended upon the local satraps or zamindars to serve as their agents both for revenue collection or social peace keeping even if that meant oppression of the socially lower placed. They saw to it, particularly after the revolt of 1857, that they should not fiddle with the religious sensitivities of the people, either the Hindu or the Muslim.

The theory also talks about the linguistic diversity of India which virtually decided the Indian state system following the State Reorganization Commission's recommendations in mid-1950s. There are now 22 scheduled national languages and hundreds of recognized dialects. There are constant demands from many linguistic groups for inclusion in the list and the Indian state is theoretically not averse to the idea.

In contrast to the above, RSS emphasizes on Hindi, Hindu, and Hindustan though they often say different things at different times with nuanced meanings and messages. If one reads Modi's political strategy between the lines one will see how it is modeled after this three-H principle. First, knowing well that Indian national leaders will have to be conversant in Hindi which is spoken by about 44 per cent of Indians concentrated in the political heartland of India he has mastered the language to communicate with the masses. Undoubtedly he is the best mass communicator today, a challenge his rivals in other parties understand their hard way.

About his emphasis on Hindutva it is an open secret. He passes it on to the masses in two ways. One, through his totally unscientific emphasis on the greatness of Indian science even in the prehistoric times to the extent of arguing that plastic surgery existed then which can be testified by the fact that Lord Ganesh had an elephant's head. Even the best plastic surgeons of the world today cannot dare to undertake that kind of daring surgery. I refuse to believe Modi sincerely believes in what he says but since he also knows that such claims are honey to the ears of a large number of Hindus who want to bask in the glory of ancient Hinduism he misses no oppoerunity to push such myths.

Two, he uses a sociology of binary for his Hindutva politics. It is a time tested model of building one's greatness at the cost of a perceived challenger by highlighting its perceived weaknesses. It has worked at all times and climes. Historically, what else can be projected as a challenger to Hindu pride than the Muslims? The Partition of India has given this contestation a permanent certification. Modi has made it work at the grassroot levels by first creating an atmosphere for it and then by giving lip service so as to distance himself from the idea because it is ethically untenable. Only a master communicator can navigate this complex course, which he has successfully proved to be.

Now let me contextualize his Kashmir move to the third idea, that is, one Hindustan. His destruction of Article 370 is reflective of his disdain for federalism in spite of the Finance Commission's rulings in respect of distribution of the central revenue according to a particular criterion which is weighed in favour of states (at least cosmetically). Watch his policies carefully. His schemes, such as Ujjwala that distributes free gas cylinders to village households, direct transfer of financial benefits through Aadhaar-linked banking, food rations to BPL people similarly distributed, Pradhan Mantri Awaas Yojana, etc., are all meant to bypass the state leaderships in effective political terms.

These policies should be read alongside Modi's *Mann ki Baat* radio programme which is meant to serve the purpose of reducing the state leaderships to irrelevance. If such distributive mechanisms are to operate through the *panchayat* systems why a villager should at all look upon his state leader who is now a hostage to these central schemes? Just look at the antecedents of the introduction of the governor's (then presidential) rule in Kashmir in recent months. The complaint was that the Mehbooba Mufti government was not holding the panchayat elections and as such real assistance could not be reached to the masses.

To put it in perspective, compare Modi's *Mann ki Baat* with Pandit Jawaharlal Nehru's regular letters to the chief ministers so as to, first, make them aware about the state of the union, and second, to tell them that they were the veritable links between the Centre and the states. Modi's Kashmir policy is totally in contrast to this model and soon the heat will be felt across the Indian states, particularly those which are not ruled by BJP. That debate will soon be in the offing.

CHAPTER 4

Illegal Immigration and the North-East

Eassay 1: Sheikh Hasina Visit: Rising Hindutva could Damage the Future of India-Bangladesh Relationship*

Against the background of high hopes being generated at Sheikh Hasina Wazed's weekend visit to India, her first bilateral sojourn in seven years, some serious questions must be raised about the future of India-Bangladesh relationship. Just as elections do not necessarily indicate the health of a democracy, good bilateral relations seemingly reflected in memorandums of understanding do not by themselves ensure their durability. President Donald Trump, for instance, has cancelled several international agreements that his predecessor had signed. In South Asia, where domestic politics plays so much of a role in foreign policy, such possibilities are even more.

At present the contrast between the polities of India and Bangladesh is glaring. While Bangladesh is systematically shedding its Islamist credentials, India is treading into a Hindu nationalistic mode at the cost of its secular ethos. The question is not as to how India would behave in the changed circumstances. The question is how Bangladesh would.

Two decades ago, Samuel Huntington famously theorised about

* 'Sheikh Hasina Visit: Rising Hindutva could Damage the Future of India-Bangladesh Relationship', *Scroll.in*, 10 April 2017. <https://scroll.in/article/834027/rising-hindutva-could-damage-the-future-of-india-bangladesh-relationship>

what he termed as 'the clash of civilisations'. Though critically dissected then more as a concept, increasingly it might seem that he was on to something. Religion has made a comeback in politics and world's two greatest democracies, America and India, are probably leading the way, with Donald Trump and Narendra Modi heading them. It would be naïve to think that the Modi phenomenon is a nine days' wonder or that the impact of the rise of Hindu nationalism would be felt only in India.

South Asia is a civilizational space—nothing is local here, particularly the issue of Hindu-Muslim relationship. These communities command the largest presence in the region, with a billion plus Hindus and 450 million plus Muslims. Two things are pertinent to note in this context. One, both communities have a painful memory baggage, owing to Partition, in which some 22 million of them in almost equal numbers were killed, maimed and displaced, and, two, both are dispersed across the region in such a way that they have acquired majority and minority complexes simultaneously. Maintaining societal equilibrium in the entire region, therefore, is imperative.

This writer, in his long career in South Asian studies, came across innumerable—indeed, liberal—voices from the region reposing faith in India's pluralism and secularism. Since India accounts for almost three-fourths of the region's space, population, Gross Domestic Product, and armed strength, India is expected to put up a fight against retrograde forces. But lamentably the same India is now taking a cue from the rest.

ACTION AND REACTION

At present India-Bangladesh relations are on an even keel largely because Prime Minister Sheikh Hasina Wazed has been able to sideline the Islamists and stands strongly in the way of her country being used as a hideout for India's north-eastern insurgents. Though an agreement over the sharing of the Teesta water remains problematic, several bilateral irritants like land border and maritime boundary disputes have been solved.

Even on the connectivity and energy cooperation issues, significant progress has been registered. But one must not forget that, first, Bangladesh politics is ever explosive, and two, the spectre of China playing its card is ever present. It will be naïve to think that the pro-Islamist forces have been wiped out for good in Bangladesh, though many of their leaders have been hanged or jailed. Stray terrorist incidents do make news but probably that is the easier problem. The real problem is when the pro-Islamic and, therefore, anti-India forces would gang up to dislodge Hasina and along with her, her ideology of secularism. It is most likely that the current trend in Indian politics will embolden these forces to make it extremely difficult for Hasina to win her next election in 2019.

The more India's Hindutva brigade humiliates India's Muslims, today by making a fuss about *love jihad*, tomorrow by asking for *ghar wapsi*, the day after by beating and heckling meat traders on false charges of cow slaughter, the more Bangladesh's Hindu minority (9 per cent) will bear the brunt, if the events following the felling of the Babri Masjid in 1992 are any indication.

WEST BENGAL AND THE NORTH-EAST

Particularly worrisome is the probable rise of the Rashtriya Swayamsevak Sangh in West Bengal. If the Uttar Pradesh experiment is repeated there even in a small scale, resulting in Hindu-Muslim riots, thereby destroying the long tradition of communal harmony nurtured by all the governments since independence whether under Congress, Bangla Congress, Left Front or now the Trinamool Congress, this fire is bound to cross over into Bangladesh endangering the Bangladeshi Hindus who are ever conscious of their minority existence. Does the RSS understand this connection? Or, is it cynical enough, calculating that more the Hindus in Bangladesh are in jeopardy, the better its chances to expand its Indian constituency?

This brings us to the issue of the Bharatiya Janata Party's entry into the north-east. The recent Citizenship (Amendment) Bill, 2016, that makes it simple to confer Indian citizenship on Bangladeshi Hindus, in contravention of the Assam Accord of 1985, which clearly states that illegal migrants heading in from Bangladesh after 25 March 1971 would be deported, has already stirred up a hornet's nest in Assam besides further imperilling Bangladesh's Hindu minority, who are ever suspected by the majority there of their dubious loyalty to the nation. Destabilization of India's north-east is closely linked to the destabilization of India-Bangladesh relations.

The all-out efforts by the BJP-RSS to grab political power in Assam by stoking communal passions have worked well electorally. But it is potentially disruptive of peace in the state with a mind-boggling mix of ethnicities. At one level, it is *Adivasi* versus non-Adivasi, at another Hindu-Muslim, Assamese-Bengali, *Asamiya* Muslim-*Miya* (East Bengali) Muslim, just to mention a few. Depending on contemporary realities there are alliances and counter-alliances among them. But the most combustible one is the issue of migrations from East Bengal/East Pakistan before 1971 or Bangladesh after that. Since the migrants are both Muslim and Hindu, it gives a communal colour to the question, which BJP wants to cash on. If the Congress is accused of using the Muslim vote bank, the BJP is equally culpable of using the Hindu vote bank. Against the fear of Assamese speakers being outnumbered by Bengali speakers, the issue has created an explosive brew in which Bangladesh will have to be an interested party, whether it wants or not. Communal strife in Assam will put the state's Muslims at the receiving end. The cycle of action and reaction will have an effect in Bangladesh which would result in the country's Hindu minority facing the brunt. Politics in South Asia is not local and international relations are not confined to mere governments.

In the same context, one need not read too much into the BJP making systematic inroads into India's north-eastern region. Depending almost entirely on central financial assistance, no north-eastern state (barring Assam) can afford to earn the displeasure of the Centre. The tendency is to alternate between the Congress and the BJP as past experience has shown. During the Vajpayee days when the Gegong Apang government of Arunachal Pradesh had an alliance with the BJP, Apang had confessed that to this writer in no uncertain terms. To the query as to how he would react to (then) Deputy Prime Minister L.K. Advani's statement that by the end of 2003 all the Chakmas and Hajongs living in the state would be granted citizenship, Apang reacted sharply. He cautioned against any such step as it would be incendiary.

NEED FOR CAUTION

In the light of the above, therefore, Indian politicians need to realize that the flames of their narrow sectarianism will not remain confined within India's borders. There is no reason to be complacent that the good relations India has built with Bangladesh would be nurtured by mere diplomacy. In South Asia, it is statesmanship that weighs much more than diplomacy. Each government in India's neighbourhood is continuously engaged in a fire-fighting mode to ward off the challenges to its stability. And in each case, the forces that are pitted against it are the same obscurantist ones that we are seeing in India. If India's mass politics continues to be what it is at present, the pro-Islamist forces in Bangladesh could make a comeback coincidentally in the same year that Modi's BJP will go for its second run for power.

Essay 2: India's North-East on Fire: Bangladesh to Watch Out*

It is easy to split territories but not their people. Bangladesh and India have umbilical links which all the three seminal events in their history, the 1905 Partition of Bengal, the 1947 Partition of India, and the 1971 Liberation of Bangladesh, and now even the border fences and the enclave-exchanges, have failed to snap. As the theory goes, a nation which does not understand its geography is condemned by its history. India, Bangladesh and Pakistan seem to be learning it the hard way. So at least I will love to think.

It is common knowledge that religion plays an important role

* 'India's North-East on Fire: Should Bangladesh Watch Out?', *The Dhaka Tribune*, 3 February 2019. https://www.dhakatribune.com/opinion/op-ed/2019/02/03/india-s-north-east-on-fire

in the politics of the region. But class, ethnic and linguistic considerations too play their roles, sometimes with even greater assertion. The Modi government is doing the mistake of reducing its Assam policy to religion alone as is evidenced by its proposed Citizenship Amendment Bill 2016, which sounds more like an anti-Muslim manifesto. It proposes that all Buddhists, Christians, Hindus, Jains, Parsis and Sikhs who have migrated to India from neighbouring Afghanistan, Bangladesh and Pakistan before 31 December 2014 would be entitled to Indian citizenship. The only religious category that is excluded from the list is Muslim. Since the Muslim-majority Bangladesh is next door it is most likely that its flames will soon touch it. The bill is both bad politics and bad diplomacy.

It is faulty, both constitutionally and politically. Constitutionally it violates India's secular commitment. The way it is being projected, it gives the impression as if millions of non-Muslim minorities of Afghanistan, Bangladesh and Pakistan are seeking refuge in India. India's Intelligence Bureau (IB) says that there are only 31,313 such people. It is also not true that in these three countries only non-Muslims are persecuted. Millions of Afghan Muslims have taken shelter in Pakistan. In Bangladesh there are thousands of 'stranded Biharis' willing to be repatriated to Pakistan though they have been granted Bangladeshi citizenship. A non-Muslim Sri Lanka had forced thousands of Tamils, mostly Hindus, to take shelter in India during its ethnic strife. Also, it is unthinkable that the BJP does not know that scores of Indians routinely seek asylum in the West. In some countries many Hindu Indians have been caught running 'refugee smuggling' rackets.

Politically, the citizenship bill has been a disaster for BJP in its newly conquered north-eastern turf, particularly Assam. Intoxicated by its success in the 2014 polls, which the BJP misread as its Hindutva victory, it thought that this one-size-fits-all strategy will work in Assam as well. But in its over-enthusiasm, it mixed up the two strands of the Assam movement, one anti-Muslim and the other anti-Bengali, as one and the same. In the process it alienated the Assamese-speaking people almost entirely. The same forces which were in the forefront of the Assam movement are once again on the streets which include such respected academics as Hiren

Gohain. Once again one is hearing slogans demanding Assam's separation from the Indian Union.

The issue of illegal migrants or refugees from Bangladesh (Muslims, Hindus and others) affects not only Assam but also other north-eastern states in general. For Arunachal Pradesh the existence of Buddhist Chakma and Hajong refugees on its soil is a permanent eyesore though they have been granted Indian citizenship with voting rights. A few years ago, its then chief minister Gegong Apang had told this writer in categorical terms how these settlers were threats to his state's ethnic identity. Till date the same sentiments have not died down. All the governments of the north-eastern states have now sent notices to the Modi government to behave or face the music. One must not give too much importance to the fact that most of these regimes are pro-BJP. They have the record of changing their political alliances overnight.

A burning north-east is no good news for Bangladesh, particularly because of its emotive content. It is naïve to think that a religion-laden socio-political controversy in one part of South Asia can be quarantined within its locale for a long time. The region is a cultural whole and anything happening in one place has ripples across borders. If the communities happen to share the same ethnicity or religion such chances are much more. Some of the statements of BJP leaders are outright provocative: 'These crores [ten millions make a crore] of illegal Bangladeshis are like termites. They have devastated our nation by eating all our food and by grabbing the jobs of our poor. As soon as we win in the 2019 election we will see to it that each one of them is identified and pushed back to Bangladesh.' These words in Hindi thundered by BJP President Amit Shah in a Delhi rally on 23 September 2018 sounded much more vitriolic than what this sanitized English translation suggests. That the BJP has a record of displaying such hollow bravado is not new. In the aftermath of the Babri mosque demolition in December 1992 Delhi's BJP chief Madan Lal Khurana had played the same card to win the elections and become Delhi's chief minister. He became the CM but could not evict a single Bangladeshi even though he dramatically marched to the banks of Yamuna to do that. He realized that governance was an altogether different ball game than street politics.

Migration is a complex phenomenon which only oppressive dictatorships can tackle, for their means are inhuman. Democracies which cannot afford to disrespect human rights beyond a point have no escape from living with this problem whatever they may say or do. When such a powerful country like America with all its technological devices fixed at the Mexican border cannot handle the issue it is impossible for poorer nations like India to accomplish that miracle. Just like water seeking its own level no amount of political or physical obstacles can prevent the poor people from moving beyond the borders to look for greener pastures. India's north-east will have to live with the problem no matter what the politicians say. Still, what is possible, and must be done, is not to inject religion into the problem for then it would lead to inextinguishable societal conflagration.

As a ruling party BJP cannot afford to behave immaturely in an otherwise complex north-east, or for that matter anywhere. It must realize that Bangladesh politics, too, has a powerful Islamic fringe which thrives at the success of Hindu fundamentalism in India as was evidenced in the aftermath of the Babri mosque demolition. Whatever may be said in criticism of Sheikh Hasina's liberal and democratic credentials, she has at least kept the country's fundamentalist forces in leash. The Modi government will be ill advised to make her task more difficult.

Essay 3: NRC in Perspective: Which cannot be Cured, has to be Endured*

It is said that there are three kinds of lies in the world: lies, damn lies, and statistics. Over the years, the way the Government of

* 'Which Cannot be Cured, has to be Endured', *Dhaka Tribune*, 19 September 2019, https://www.dhakatribune.com/long-form/2019/09/19/which-cannot-be-cured-has-to-be-endured, simultaneously carried as 'NRC in Perspective: Which Cannot be Cured, has to be Endured', *Newsclick.in,* 19 September 2019, https://www.newsclick.in/NRC-perspective-which-cannot-cured-has-be-endured

India has dished out figures about illegal Bangladeshis in India one cannot help but conclude that it believes in the saying. After all, if the government actually knew the numbers, their statistics would not have swung between two and twelve million.

Amit Shah, the former BJP chief and now India's home minister, has made even more outlandish claims. During rallies leading up to the 2019 parliamentary election, he thundered: 'These crores [ten million make a crore] of illegal Bangladeshis are like termites. . . . As soon as we win in the election we will identify each one of them and push them back to Bangladesh.'

Mercifully, Shah did not take his promise to its logical, macabre, end. An infestation of termites is eradicated only by the use of pesticides. Once you label a people as such, the historical precedents take you directly to Hitler's gas chambers and his attempt to accomplish a 'final solution' to the 'Jewish problem'. Instead, Shah satisfied his audience by making the impossible promise that all illegal Bangladeshis will be pushed 'back to Bangladesh', the likelihood of which the Modi government has now categorically put to rest.

The cat is now out of the bag. After a five-year long exercise in Assam, involving about 50,000 personnel and incurring an expenditure of over 12,200,000,000 rupees, 1,905,657 individuals have been identified as 'non-citizens'. This figure is significantly lower than any figure the government has generally quoted. The number is surely to fall even further once appeals during the 120-day grace period are processed. As and when the entire process is completed, the number of illegal Bangladeshis will be embarrassingly small for all those who conjured up images of countless 'termites'.

And whatever the ultimate figure, we also know it will not be accurate. In the poor, illiteracy-ridden Third World there are inherent problems with such counts. Kamal Sadiq's study (*Paper Citizens*, 2009) on illegal immigrants in the developing world, with particular reference to illegal Afghans in Pakistan, provides empirical confirmation of this basic reality. When the poor do not even have a secure place to keep their meagre financial savings, it is bizarre to think that they will preserve pieces of paper whose contents they cannot read.

Among the mundane yet stubborn problems is how to deal with

names that spelt differently across cultural settings. I can refer to one such instance from personal experience. On 28 April 2014, a massive fire gutted a large number of shanties in Delhi's Vasant Kunj area. The victims were mostly Bengali-speaking Muslims from North Bengal. Presumably, some among them were illegal Bangladeshis who had acquired Indian ration and Aadhaar cards, becoming what Sadiq would describe as 'paper citizens'.

The Delhi administration decided to issue cheques for Rs. 5,000 as immediate relief to each affected family. But cheques require names and names require consistency of spelling. The administration issued the cheques in English, using spellings that match Urdu pronunciations: Umar for Omor, Jamila for Jomila, Shahidul for Sohidul, Jawaid/Javed for Jabed, and so on. Unable to demonstrate that the cheques were indeed for them, legitimate beneficiaries were denied relief.

As a Bengali, I immediately understood the problem and offered to help. I wrote directly to the then Lt Governor of Delhi, Najeeb Jung, to explain the issue and help negotiate the communication gap. I do not know whether my explanatory note helped, but the matter was soon resolved in favour of the affected. In the context of the NRC, we are beginning to see an increasing number of similar snags. Not merely Muslim names, even Hindu and tribal names have been mangled across linguistic lines.

These are, however, smaller issues. Assam's real problems are its multidimensional fault-lines. To mention just a few: linguistically, Assamese versus Bengali; communally, Hindu versus Muslim; intra-communally, Assamese-speaking Muslims versus Bengali-speaking Muslims (the so-called *miyah*), as well as caste Hindu versus lower caste Hindu; ethnically, tribals versus non-tribals on the one hand, and plains tribes versus hill tribes on the other; regionally, Upper Assam versus Lower Assam; and finally, in terms of affirmative action, Scheduled Tribes (STs) versus potential STs (six communities are currently demanding ST status).

At the supra-level, there is an overarching concern among the Assamese of cultural marginalization, which has been at the core of the Assam movement since the late 1970s. With the recent rise of the BJP at the centre and in the state, these cleavages have sharpened in two contradictory ways. The BJP's Hindutva push fits well with the movement's anti-Muslim dimension, but its proposed amendment to the citizenship act, which is sympathetic to Hindu immigrants writ large, irks the linguistic nationalism of the Assamese.

Recall that the BJP's bigger goal in east India is to corner the support of the Bengalis, who are the region's dominant linguistic group across Assam, Tripura and West Bengal. Added to the calculation the impending West Bengal assembly elections in 2021, the BJP may well decide to turn a Nelson's eye to the essential thrust of the Assam movement, that is, 'Assam for the Assamese'. Sacrificing a smaller pie for a bigger pie is commonsense politics, after all.

No wonder, therefore, that even liberal Assamese intellectuals like Hiren Gohain were up in arms against the Citizenship Amendment Bill 2016. The progressive streak in him made him oppose the bill on the grounds that it compromised India's constitutionally ordained secular commitment, but his sense of Assamese-identity-in-danger made him take the maximalist position that Assam might be forced to think in terms of seceding from the Indian Union.

There is no denying the fact that during the last hundred years massive migrations have taken place from East Bengal into Assam, upsetting the original demography of the region. The spark that set ablaze the prairie fire of Assamese insecurity was lit in 1931. In that year, the British superintendent of the Assam census, C.S. Mullan, made the following combustible remark:

> Probably the most important event in the province during the last twenty-five years . . . has been the invasion of a vast horde of land-hungry Bengali immigrants, mostly Muslims . . . [as a result of which] in another thirty years Sibsagar District will be the only part of Assam in which an Assamese will find himself at home.

As Gohain notes, it was a classic case of British imperialism 'running with the hare and hunting with the hounds'. After all, it was the Permanent Settlement of revenue collection in Bengal that had created the class conflict between Hindu zamindars and an impoverished Muslim farming community, which was in turn prodded to migrate to Assam in search of greener pastures. In the 1970s, when the All Assam Students Union (AASU) launched its stir against illegal Bangladeshi settlers, Mullan's statement was found most handy.

But it was not merely the census of 1931 that was important. The census of 1951 (there was no census in 1941 due to war) was also critical in three respects. In the first place, Bengali Muslims declared themselves as Assamese-speaking, which contributed to the cooling down of Hindu Assamese hostility against the Muslims. With the communalization of the Assam movement this has become increasingly irrelevant, however.

Shalim Hussain, a Bengali Muslim, laments in one of his recent writings that it is the constant refrain of his community that when they could not speak Assamese they were ridiculed for clinging on to their Bengali roots but now that they can fluently speak the language, they are accused of 'putting on a show'—a case of heads the Assamese win, and tails the *miyahs* lose.

Second, the separation of Sylhet, which contained 30 per cent of Assam's population, 90 per cent of whom spoke Bengali, following a referendum just before Partition made Assam an Assamese-majority state for the first time. As a result, the percentage of Assamese in the population increased from 30 in 1930 to 56 in 1951.

Third, a new distinction emerged post-1951 with respect to Muslim immigrants from East Bengal and their Hindu counterparts. While the latter were recognized as 'refugees', the former came to be seen as 'illegal immigrants' or 'foreigners'. It may be noted that The Immigrant (Expulsions from Assam) Act 1950 implicitly distinguished the Hindu refugee from the Muslim immigrant. Although this act was repealed in 1957, there was a 1965 secret administrative order of the Government of India that authorized the district magistrate to grant Indian citizenship to those Hindu refugees from East Pakistan who had settled in Assam for six months or more.

Parenthetically, one can find similarities between this 1951 development and what happened in Punjab. In the same census, many Hindu Punjabi refugees had declared Hindi as their language, which eventually led to a political rift between Punjabi Sikhs and Punjabi Hindus and contributed to the germination of the Khalistan movement in the 1970s and 1980s.

The cumulative effect of all these developments is that Assam is chronically disturbed. Now, with the overdose of religion injected into Assam's body-politic thanks to the BJP's Hindutva thrust, things are poised to unravel, with the repercussions inevitably extending into neighbouring Bangladesh as well. However much India may clarify that no illegal Bangladeshi in India will be pushed into Bangladesh (as if Bangladesh is going to accept any of them), the emotive content in the promise is humiliating enough to make Bangladeshi Islamists enlarge their constituency and dream of a return to power.

Politics is existential; but existentialism should have its limits. Demographic changes that happen for historical reasons cannot be reversed by quick-fix political engineering. They warrant statesman-like handling based on human rights and larger calls to multiculturalism, ideals that are embedded in the currently much maligned 'idea of India'.

Human history is replete with migratory movements and though it is politically fashionable these days to denounce immigrants, particularly if they are Muslims, as can also be seen in many parts of Europe, the end result is bound to be naught. Moreover, since the West is rich, it can ward off the 'problem', much as Australia and Denmark have done in their own ingenious ways. The Third World can ill afford to just throw away immigrants. Notably, contrary to the advertised greatness of the West, much larger numbers of immigrants have been absorbed within the Third World for cultural reasons.

One last point. The middle-class Indians who ridicule Bangladeshi immigrants must look to their own hankering for American green cards, if not American citizenship. Moreover, of the US population of about 330 million, about 10.7 million, 3.3 per cent, are illegal immigrants. With India's population at 1.3 billion, 3.3 per cent of that would translate to about 43 million. Are we Indians not becoming unnecessarily panicky in the face of this suspected Bangladeshi influx?

Let Indians also be reminded, as Neeraj Kaushal writes in her book *Blaming Immigrants* (2019): 'In proportion to world population, the number of global immigrants—people living outside their country of birth—is a modest 3 per cent. Not a deluge, not a surge, not a flood, not even a stream, but a trickle'. This is the reality for the last hundred years.

To see it from another perspective, even if India has 10 million illegal Bangladeshis it would mean less than one per cent of India's population. Indian Americans today constitute one per cent of America's population. After the Jews they are the richest ethnic group in the United States. Most middle-class Indians, BJP supporters in particular, are proud of them. But for the poor Bangladeshis only revulsion seems to be in store.

Postscript: Any border re-demarcation collaterally harms one community or the other. The transfer of Sylhet to Pakistan in 1947 subjected the Sylheti Bengalis to a double jeopardy. In search of security they first migrated to Shillong, then Assam's capital and a safe destination. But upon the creation of Meghalaya in 1972, Shillong became Meghalaya's capital and its politics was overtaken by Khasi chauvinism. This chauvinism subjected the immigrant Bengali community to utter humiliation, including instances of rape in broad daylight. The situation became so unbearable that Sylheti Bengalis were once again forced to migrate, this time out of Meghalaya, enduring a double displacement in one lifetime.

Essay 4: The Citizenship Amendment Bill: A Threat to the Idea of South Asia*

Let us not beat about the bush. The essence of the Citizenship Amendment Bill (CAB) can be collapsed into just one sentence: It is meant to reduce India's Muslims to second-class citizens; proof

* 'A Threat to the Idea of South Asia', *Dhaka Tribune*, 15 December 2019. https://www.dhakatribune.com/opinion/longform/2019/12/15/a-threat-to-the-idea-of-south-asia, simultaneously carried as 'A Serious Threat to Every Idea of South Asia', *Newsclick.in* 13 December 2019. https://www.newsclick.in/CAB-Serious-Threat-Every-Idea-South-Asia, reproduced in *Mainstream* (New Delhi), ANNUAL 2019, 58(1), 21 December 2019: 25-8.

of their Indianness endlessly demanded but never fully accepted. The subtext is to give Hindus the sadistic satisfaction of making Muslims know their 'real place' in Indian society. But for this explanation, it is difficult to find any other rationale behind the bill, particularly at this juncture, when pressing economic issues demand immediate attention. To take this purpose to its logical end, the BJP has also proposed a nation-wide compilation of a National Register of Citizens (NRC). In communally charged South Asia, with a recent past of religion-centric conflicts that have consumed millions of lives, the move portends dangerous possibilities for India's neighbourhood.

CAB prescribes that any Hindu, Buddhist, Christian, Jain, Sikh or Parsi who has been a victim of religious persecution in Islam-centric Afghanistan, Bangladesh and Pakistan and, as a result, has taken shelter as a refugee in India on or before 31 December 2014, will not be considered an illegal migrant. As the biggest Hindu-majority nation, India will offer them an easy path to naturalized Indian citizenship. The only community excluded from this benefit are the Muslims, even though they have suffered just as much religious persecution. The cases of Ahmediyyas and Shias in Pakistan, and of Hazara Shias in Afghanistan easily come to mind. In Bangladesh, the most advertised case is that of the author and activist Taslima Nasrin.

CAB is a politically clever formulation for it camouflages its pro-Hindu thrust by bracketing Hindus with Buddhists, Christians, Jains, Sikhs and Parsis. For demographic reasons, the vast majority of people who crossed the borders between India and undivided Pakistan after 1947, and later between India and Bangaldesh, were either Hindus or Muslims. Other communities were small in number. Among them, many indeed were Sikhs, but they were all gainfully rehabilitated in Delhi and its neighbouring states. In recent years, a small number of Sikhs of Afghanistan have arrived in India. They have either been granted refugee status by the UNHRC in collaboration with the Indian state or have melted into the local Sikh community. The Buddhist situation is different, and in this case the BJP government has cleverly dodged the issue of Chakma and Hajong Buddhists in Arunachal Pradesh. Although the latter were granted Indian citizenship several decades ago, massive local opposition means they remain semi-citizens who have been denied the right to vote. In any case, the states of Arunachal Pradesh, Mizoram and Nagaland, and now Manipur, plus the tribal areas of Assam, are currently excluded from the purview of CAB.

Instead of wasting so much cerebral energy and precious time, the BJP could have chosen a simpler formulation: Damn India's secularism, damn India's commitment to international human rights covenants; Muslim migrants from Afghanistan, Bangladesh and Pakistan are illegal settlers, whose fates will hang in balance perpetually; they should not even dream of becoming Indian citizens. Who cares to note that India has a haloed record of playing host to all kinds of oppressed communities from the region and beyond, whether they are from Afghanistan, Bhutan, Myanmar, Sri Lanka, Tibet or even Iran and other places? In the wake of the Bangladesh war in the early 1970s, India had famously sheltered about 10 million refugees from East Pakistan, at least 15 per cent of whom were Muslims. All this has happened in spite of the fact that India is not a signatory to the international refugee convention, to which it has expressed a principled opposition.

To put the CAB discourse in perspective, let us view it from four angles—political, economic, humanitarian, and regional. Politically, CAB gives further 'respectability' to communal politics in India, strengthening a trend that has been in the making for several years. We know that communalism exists in all South Asian polities, but we also recognize that it is undesirable in modern democracies. It is for this reason that every political party worth its salt publicly distances itself from communalism. Even the avowedly Hindu-chauvinistic BJP has been forced to shout from the rooftop that it believes in *sabka saath, sabka vikas, sabka vishwas* (together, let us all develop by earning everyone's trust). The last phrase *sabka vishwas* (everyone's trust) has been added recently to address Muslims' concerns in particular. But when it comes to playing day-to-politics, we have seen how hollow the slogan reads. My columns these past several months have dwelt extensively on this hollowness. Let me not repeat myself here.

In any case, the huge contradiction that exists in India today must not escape anybody's attention. On the one hand, there is a clear policy thrust to see the Union of India as one single political unit at the cost of states' rights; on the other, everything is moving in the direction of fragmenting India as a nation. One-nation-one-election, one-nation-one-tax, one-nation-one-ration card, and direct-benefit bank transfers from the central government to needy Indians over the heads of state governments (so as to establish direct communication between the Modi government and the people), tell one story. But this story is turned on its head when state domicile becomes the major criterion to reserve 60 to 80 per cent of government jobs for locals. Thus, the Indian state celebrates the abrogation of Article 370 that had granted Jammu & Kashmir special rights. In the same breath, and with great aplomb, that same Indian state also celebrates its commitment to protect the special rights of the north-eastern states. How could such diametrically opposite processes be simultaneously celebrated? Only lunatics or Muslim-baiters can appreciate this jugglery. After all, Jammu & Kashmir was India's only Muslim-majority state (now split into two Union Territories).

As a schoolboy in the 1950s, I was told that Inner Line Permits (ILP) to certain regions in India's north-east were a temporary necessity and would be done away with in due course, once these regions had been fully integrated into the Indian Union. Six decades later, not only do these permits continue, they are being reinforced. Beyond the three original states of Arunachal Pradesh, Mizoram and Nagaland, additional demands for ILP are now being recognized from Assam, Meghalaya, Manipur (already granted) and Tripura. Assam's deputy chief minister and BJP's most visible face in the region, Himanta Biswa Sarma, has categorically said that even those getting Indian citizenship under CAB would not be granted residency rights, nor would they be allowed to own land or run businesses in specified areas of Assam without the permission of the state government. The Asom Gana Parishad (AGP), BJP's ally in the state, is demanding safeguards on the pattern of ILP. No wonder then that large sections of north-easterners are protesting against CAB. Even a section of BJP's West Bengal unit feels that its recent electoral reverses are attributable to NRC/CAB blues.

In Manipur, Lancha Ningthouja, an Inner Line Permit activist, recently stated: 'There is a serious danger of the indigenous Manipuri population being wiped out along with their culture, history and languages. . . . *Why should we let outsiders take over our land entirely* (emphasis added)?' Note that 'outsiders' here refers not to a foreigner but to other Indians. Also note that Manipuris (read Meities in this context, and not the Kukis and Nagas) are Hindus and their worry is not the 'Bangladeshi' Muslim alone but also the Bihari and Bengali, who in most cases is an Indian Hindu. There is little doubt, therefore, that CAB is entirely an exercise in communal politics. If Assam's NRC drama could engage its people almost completely for three years, thereby paving the way for the BJP to consolidate its power in the state, it can reasonably be surmised that the CAB/NRC will engage the Indian masses for at least four years, to safeguard the BJP's victory in the 2024 elections. In the intervening period, the BJP's fifth column, the pliant media and the party's social media troll army, will ensure that the pot keeps boiling.

Moving onto economics, CAB is going to cause an unimaginable drain on the country's financial and human resources. Consider JNU professor Neerja Gopal Jayal's extrapolation of Assam's NRC experience. For a population of 33,000,000, the NRC cost INR 16,000,000,000 and involved a work force of 50,000 officials. Given India's 880,000,000 electorate, a nationwide NRC would then cost INR 4,260,000,000,000 (INR 4.26 trillion). Now add to this the huge cost in terms of money and time that millions of Indians will incur for registering themselves in the NRC. And to top it all, add the expenditures incurred to build and maintain the thousands of detention centres that will house the so-called stateless persons the NRC will identify. If the Assam NRC alone identified 1,900,000 'non-Indians', the national figure will likely be to the tune of 50,000,000. That means the Indian tax payer will have to bear the cost of millions of employable individuals, who have been forced out of India's labour force and into internment camps. For the average Indian it will be a double whammy: Heads he/she loses; tails the BJP wins.

From a human rights perspective, volumes have already been

written on Assam's NRC experience. Multiply that at least thirty-fold to have a preliminary sense of the misery that is in store for millions of poverty-stricken illiterate Indians. To understand this humble reality, one need not have read Marx or Mao. And yet, the Indian state continues to defend the NRC on the grounds that if one is unhappy with the outcome the doors of the courts are open. In India, even the well to do dread approaching the courts for both financial reasons and because they face inordinate delays. Yet, we expect that the destitute will seek legal remedy in the face of 33,000,000 pending cases. Just like chartered accounts are minting money these days thanks to the complexities involved in GST filings, it would soon be boom time for lawyers specializing in citizenship litigation. Yet another point, largely unacknowledged, is that the real sufferers will be poor Hindus. Having lived under the shadow of a muscle-flexing Hindu-majority India, poor Indian Muslims are ever conscious of the Damocles Sword that hangs over their heads. Unlike their Hindu counterparts, they are therefore more careful in maintaining their identity papers. I suspect this is the reason why many more Hindus found themselves struck off the NRC in Assam.

Last, and to my mind most important, the proposed CAB/NRC will do havoc with the notion of South Asian regionalism, especially if the exercise is taken to its logical end. Assuming that in due course India will end up with millions of impoverished Muslims languishing perpetually in detention camps, these millions will be fodder for fundamentalist politics. Groups in Pakistan will no doubt take advantage. But it is Bangladesh that may prove the bigger bogie. Given Bangladesh's restive 90 per cent Muslim community, how long can India think that Bangladesh should remain unconcerned? Illegal Bangladeshis are like 'termites' and each such 'termite' will be identified and thrown out of India, so claims Home Minister Amit Shah. But thrown where? Has not India committed at the highest level that Bangladesh need not worry, for the illegal Bangladeshis are India's internal matter? But who will tell India's leaders that communal politics is not India's monopoly alone? Bangladesh too has mastered the art. And lest we forget, 16 million out of its 200 million are Hindus.

One other reality my readers must be sensitized about. Nationality per se is no guarantee of one's complete identification with the nation, just like denial of nationality does not necessarily make one an enemy of the nation. Sri Lankan Tamils and Indian Tamils are both Hindus, yet in the context of Sri Lanka's national question, their respective positions are diametrically opposite. There was never any question about the citizenship status of Sri Lankan Tamils, yet it is they who wanted to secede from Sri Lanka. In contrast, Indian Tamils were always exposed to uncertainties about their Sri Lankan citizenship, yet they showed complete loyalty to the Sri Lankan nation, so much so that they even refused repatriation to India under the Shastri-Sirimavo Pact of 1964.

One last point. Much as it may be fashionable to do so today, everything in the world ought not to be viewed through the prism of religion. There are multiple ethnicities that get blended within an individual, something which social anthropologists call the 'elasticity of ethnicity'. But it is the tragedy of political classes the world over that they undermine these diversities in favour of one-religion-one-nation. India began the age of decolonization with the promise of reversing this trend. Alas, it too is no longer immune to the virus of reductive nationalism. As a result, South Asian nations that should be celebrating their diversity are successively becoming majoritarian. Who will tell them that behind the 70 years of post-Partition South Asia there stand seventy centuries of history? It is that much longer history, celebrated by Tagore in his poem *Bharat Teertho*, that makes the region what it is. Here is an excerpt:

> Keho nahi jane kaar ahobane kato manusher dhara/Durbar shrote elo kotha hote, samudre holo haara./Hethaye arjo, hetha anarjo, hethaye dravid cheen—/Shauk, hun dal pathan mogole ek dehe holo leen./Poschime aaji khuliachhe daar, setha hote sobe aaney upahaar,/Dibe aar nibe, milabe milibe, jabe naa phire—/Ei bharater mahamanaber sagarteerey.

Its free translation in English would read:

> No one knows to whose clarion call/Peoples responded and came/In streams/And joined the ocean!/Hither lived the Aryans, the non-Aryans,/The Dravidians, the Chinese, the Scythians,/The Huns, the Pathans, the

Mughals—/And merged into one body and soul,/Today, doors to the West are open/New ideas are flowing/Incessant giving and taking/Meeting and mingling are on/They will not return/From this supreme Ocean of Humanity/That is India [meaning today's India, Bangladesh, Pakistan and Myanmar].

Postscript: How many Bangladeshis know that the creation of Bangladesh deprived millions of Bengalis in the rest of South Asia and beyond of one of their most critical identity markers? As a *probashi Bangali* from Bhagalpur in Bihar, I recall that prior to 1971 whenever I had to go Kolkata I would call my visits 'journeys to bangladesh', that is, to the land of the Bengalis. Those who suspect my statement are advised to look up on YouTube the famous Kishore Kumar-Lata Mangeshkar song *main bangaali chhokra . . . main madraasi chhokri* from the 1958 Bollywood movie *Ragini.* Its Bengali protagonist goes on to claim, *humra Bangladesh mein har gori ke lambe baal* (in my Bangladesh every lass has long plaits). Many things, over thousands of years, have gone into the making of South Asia. It is a civilizational space worth cherishing. I wish the Modi-Shah duo understood this.

Essay 5: Silver Linings on India's Horizon*

Finally, Indians are in revolt. Enough is enough. Selling dreams of a 'new India' and simultaneously selling communal hatred cannot go on indefinitely. The people were probably waiting for a catalyst, which the Narendra Modi government unwittingly put on

* 'Silver Linings on India's Horizon', *Dhaka Tribune*, 30 January 2020, https://www.dhakatribune.com/opinion/longform/2020/01/29/silver-linings-on-india-s-horizon, simultaneously carried as 'CAA-NRC Protests Are Silver Linings on India's Horizon', *Newsclick.in,* 27 January 2020, https://www.newsclick.in/caa-nrc-protests-are-silver-linings-indias-horizon

their platter in the form of the Citizenship Amendment Act. For the first time in India's history, an act made citizenship contingent upon one's religion, targeting Muslims in particular. The government might have guessed that it would further strengthen its Hindu base. But the strategy seems to have boomeranged. It has electrified India's largely dormant secular constituency and put large parts of the country on fire. The agitators' demand cannot be simpler: 'please honour the constitution'.

India has walked down a similar path twice in its past. In 1974-5, student unrest against a fee hike in Gujarat culminated in a mass movement across north India that demanded *sampurna kranti* (total revolution). The slogan was coined by Jayaprakash Narayan, a Gandhian of the nationalist vintage and the driving force behind the movement. In 2011, yet another mass movement emerged around the nucleus of Anna Hazare's hunger strike against rampant corruption during Manmohan Singh's second term in office (2009-14). Both agitations resulted in changes of government. The first ended Indira Gandhi's rule (1971-7, that included her Emergency regime, 1975-7), while the second unleashed the Modi phenomenon.

Notably, both upsurges benefited the RSS/BJP. Thanks to their organizational base they were quick to appropriate them. The opposite is happening now. Leave alone being a part of the present upsurge, they are instead on its receiving end. At stake is India's secularism, which the BJP has been systematically attacking in the name of its Hindutva project. Large sections of students who were already up in arms against the Modi government have now been joined by a cross-section of Indians, most prominently Muslims, all of whom are outraged by the discriminatory aspects of the citizenship act and what has been generally happening to them of late. Howsoever the Modi government may try to obfuscate the issue, by making contradictory statements, the cat is out of the bag and the trick lies exposed.

Can 'Modi magic' still manage to douse the fire? Or have the battle lines between the forces of secularism and those of a Hindu *rashtra* been irrevocably drawn? The situation is ominous because the spectre of a virtual civil war is no longer a purely abstract possibility. The RSS has tasted blood during the Modi regime and it is unlikely to squander its gains easily. During Prime Minister Atal Behari Vajpayee's time it was marked by a constant, simmering tension between the government and the RSS. In the Modi era it is a honeymoon all the way.

Thanks to the expansion of its *shakhas* (branches) at the grassroots level across the country, the RSS has never been as strong as it is today. As Andersen and Damle point out in *RSS: A View to the Inside* (2019), since the early 1990s, the RSS has expanded its membership to about two million and become one of the world's largest NGOs. It organizes nearly 57,000 daily *shakhas*, 14,000 weekly *shakhas*, and 7,000 monthly *shakhas*. In 2016, these *shakha* meetings were held in 36,293 places spread all over the nation. To supplement this popular connection, there is a virtual reserve army of about 6 million alumni and affiliate volunteers. And the pace of growth continues to accelerate: From 51,332 daily *shakhas* in 2015, the number jumped to 57,000 in 2016.

Now add to this huge organizational base Modi's unprecedented personal popularity. Pandit Nehru and Indira Gandhi were also very popular, but Modi has far outpaced them. It is mindboggling to watch the mass hysteria reflected in such incessant chants as 'Mo-o-o-o-di, Mo-o-o-o-di, Mo-o-o-o-di' in all his rallies. No wonder, then, whether it is a state election in Jharkhand or a quasi-state election in Delhi, the only commodity BJP finds sellable, given its dismal governance record, is the Modi persona. That the overuse of the Modi trumpcard will eventually tell upon the health of the BJP in the long run (much as Congress' reliance on Indira did), is a subject for another time.

But it does beg one question: How long will the momentum of the present upsurge against Modi and the RSS/BJP be maintained? A leaderless movement does not generally last long. The fate of the Arab Spring serves as a stark reminder. But perhaps this comparison does not hold water. Unlike the Arab world, India has extended experience in democratic experimentation (starting with Mahatma Gandhi joining the nationalist movement in 1915).

India is also plural in multiple senses. As such, howsoever leaderless India's mass upsurges may appear, there is an in-built order to the spontaneous crowds that have now become routine.

Whether the upsurges will ultimately challenge the RSS/BJP juggernaut remains to be seen. In the meantime, three key developments, each positive, each a credit to the protesters, are impossible to ignore. One, the upsurges are spontaneous, with no party sponsorship. Two, they have brought the country's totally marginalized Muslims back into the political mainstream. And finally, students and the youth at large, whose grievances are essentially mundane, that is, lack of jobs and opportunities, have found broad-based support for their cause, evincing memories of the JP movement of 1974-5.

The most exciting element of these upsurges, however, is their demand for the restoration of the glory of India's secular and inclusive constitution. The sheer simplicity of this demand has even forced the RSS/BJP Siamese twins to play on the back foot. In a sight never witnessed before in India, men, women, and children have taken to reading aloud the Preamble to the Constitution of India:

> WE, THE PEOPLE OF INDIA, having solemnly resolved to constitute India into a SOVEREIGN SOCIALIST SECULAR DEMOCRATIC REPUBLIC and to secure to all its citizens JUSTICE, social, economic and political; LIBERTY of thought, expression, belief, faith and worship; EQUALITY of status and opportunity; and to promote among them all FRATERNITY assuring the dignity of the individual and the unity and integrity of the Nation; IN OUR CONSTITUENT ASSEMBLY this 26th day of November 1949, do HEREBY ADOPT, ENACT AND GIVE TO OURSELVES THIS CONSTITUTION.

On what grounds can the Modi government judge these protestors anti-national? That well tested, cynical trick was first deployed at a JNU student event in February 2016. By making dubious allegations that Kanhaiya Kumar, then the president of the JNU Students Union (JNUSU), had said 'let the country be dismembered into pieces', a new *sarkari* (i.e. government-sponsored) abuse was coined. Suddenly the country was overrun with the *tukde-tukde gang*, and anybody who disagreed could be charged under the draconian British-era Sedition Act. Kanhaiya Kumar's protestations that the videos of the event, screened by a pliant media unable to maintain basic journalistic standards, were doctored to malign him, fell on deaf ears; so much so, that the Delhi Police put him in jail. In an ironic turn, and no doubt much to the BJP's chagrin, imprisonment turned out to be a boon for Kanhaiya. He may have entered jail as a student leader, he stepped out an iconic, national figure, a spokesman for India's democratic values. His jail diary in Hindi, *From Bihar to Tihar* (name of the jail where he was imprisoned), is a runaway bestseller.

The BJP made Kanhaiya Kumar a hero. They are now repeating the mistake and making the current JNUSU president, Aishe Ghosh, a future heroine of Indian politics. It is surprising to see how much the party hates JNU, which is not only a leading university, but also one whose student community is congenitally vocal against the political establishment, be it the BJP, the Congress, or anyone else. Recall that during Indira Gandhi's Emergency, JNU students were particularly targeted and many languished in jail for months. But unlike during the Emergency, the BJP's animus against JNU appears to be driven by an intense disrespect for scientific temper and intellectual debate. As such, JNU is routinely criticized for its leftist politics. But this criticism ignores the fact that its students are politically progressive, inspired by an idealism that is essential to youth. After all, if one doesn't question norms and dream of a better world when one is young, it is far less likely one will do so when older. It is sad, therefore, to see them abused as the *tukde-tukde gang*, 'urban Naxal', and, most offensively, as 'anti-nationals'.

Let us face it: Indian youth and minorities today are restless. The Magsaysay Award winning TV anchor, Ravish Kumar, recently ran a long series on the state of higher education in India's Hindi heartland, which is, paradoxically, also India's political heartland. Whether the states are ruled by the BJP or the Congress, they suffer from total neglect in terms of teacher-student ratios, chronic absenteeism of teachers, virtually non-existing classrooms, libraries and toilets, and much else. Under these circumstances, it is evident that the political class has successfully brainwashed the middle classes, who otherwise would beg, borrow or steal to buy the best education for their wards. Instead of demanding better education, they toe the BJP line and complain about students misusing their 'taxpayers' money'. Where is their concern when the BJP spends INR 3,000 crore (£330 million, US $430 million) of their 'tax-payers' money' to build a statue of Sardar Patel, that too by sourcing most of the materials from the Chinese.

One last point. Of all liberal arts disciplines, history has earned the dubious distinction of being, on the one hand, dismissed as worthless and wholly dispensable, and yet on the other hand, the beneficiary of intense government meddling. In a recent speech in Kolkata, Prime Minister Modi authoritatively claimed that historians have only studied political power struggles; they have completely neglected the common man and his problems. I wish Modi's speech writer had done some elementary reading about the subaltern school of history. Professor Ranajit Guha pioneered the school about fifty years ago. By now, historians belonging to the school have produced volume after volume detailing precisely what Modi, falsely and ignorantly, laments does not exist. And they have influenced the way historians work the world over. But why am I not surprised? Modi has also tried to teach economics to Amartya Sen.

Postscript: At a conference held in Dehradun a year ago, I had a friendly chat with Prof. Murli Manohar Joshi, a long-time BJP MP and Vajpayee's HRD minister from 1999 to 2004. Joshi had delivered a talk in the morning focusing on the science-social science interface. The talk was brilliant, and after expressing my appreciation, I could not resist adding, tongue firmly in cheek: 'Sir, you should belong not just to the BJP, but to the entire country.' He immediately got my point. Why was it that politicians turn much saner and circumspect the moment they are out of circulation? Was Joshi not the same HRD minister who had actively promoted the RSS agenda to rewrite history from a Hindutva perspective? Sadly, that same project is now poaching into natural sciences as well, if one goes by the statements of India's present HRD minister, Ramesh Pokhriyal. One shudders to think about the day when India's Mars Mission rocket will lift off based not on astronomical calculations but on astrological conjunctions—waiting for the propitious *muhurta* (moment)!

Essay 6: CAA: Neither Statesmanship, Nor Statecraft*

Even the worst critics of Prime Minister Narendra Modi will concede that he is a great communicator. His forceful speech in parliament on 6 February 2019 in defence of the controversial Citizenship (Amendment) Act (CAA) was a brilliant act of political messaging. It reminded me of what historian Lord Acton had famously said: reforms far from averting a rebellion tend to precipitate it. Modi was Actonian at his best. In response to mushrooming anti-CAA protests across the nation, he not only displayed his energetic defiance, he also reconfirmed his commitment to the CAA.

It is not easy to write on contemporary politics for a historian like me. Politics is existential; history is transcendental. Therein lies my problem with the BJP's vision for the CAA/NRC/NPR. They justify it purely in contemporary terms, with little regard for the subcontinent's longer history and with a very limited vision for the future. To my understanding, the situation is much more complex: It requires acknowledging the challenges that a plural post-colonial society like India has to confront and, more importantly, it requires us to recognize that we as a society are the product of human migrations through all times and climes. Thus, when the BJP claims that it is fulfilling the unfinished task of the Partition, I am forced to look for other such claimants.

The original nation builders of India, in the forefront of whom were the Indian National Congress under the leadership of Mahatma Gandhi, had felt their task incomplete unless India became an inclusive and secular democracy. For the newborn Pakistan, its unfinished task was the incorporation of Kashmir into the Pakistani state. For Hindu nationalists, their unfinished task was to

* 'CAA: Neither Statesmanship, Nor Statecraft', *Dhaka Tribune*, 15 February 2020, https://www.dhakatribune.com/opinion/longform/2020/02/15/caa-neither-statesmanship-nor-statecraft, simultaneously carried as 'CAA-A Tired Game that Needs to be Retired', *Newsclick.in*, 13 February 2020, https://www.newsclick.in/CAA-A-Tired-Game-Needs-Retired

make India a Hindu *rashtra* and, if possible, delegitimize the Partition and reestablish *Akhand Bharat* (undivided India) again. These unfinished tasks are the longstanding demons that fuel today's CAA, which we cannot delink from the NRC despite the BJP's mendacious protestations.

Cross-national movements of people are in South Asia's DNA. Add to the mix poverty, illiteracy, and widespread corruption, and the massiveness of the task of citizenship certification becomes readily apparent. The cases of *Abu Hanif alias Millan Master* vs. *Police Commissioner of Delhi and Others* (2000) and *Abu Hanif alias Millan Master* vs. *Union of India and Others* (2001) provide interesting examples. Abu Hanif was an Indian Muslim, yet he was accused of being an alien since he lived among Bangladeshis. He faced immediate deportation to Bangladesh. The court, however, gave the verdict in his favour. The flipside of the same phenomenon also exists. It is easy to acquire citizenship by manipulating the system and becoming what Kamal Sadiq has called 'paper citizens'.

Let us take three recent experiences to see what different ramifications the institution of 'paper citizens' can assume in the Indian context: One, Hindu paper citizens in Jammu and Kashmir; two, Indian/Plantation Tamil paper non-citizens; and three, paper refugees.

One of the arguments put forward by the Indian government while diluting Article 370 in Jammu and Kashmir was that it would allow Hindu refugees from Pakistan who had settled in the state to become full citizens of India. According to the BJP, these refugees had long suffered from the handicap of not being state subjects. But as it turns out, most of these refugees had already managed to become Jammu and Kashmir subjects in the intervening period. In 2018, when a scheme was announced to provide one-time financial assistance of INR 5,50,000 to each of 5,764 such families, there was not a single taker. A one-time financial windfall was poor enticement if it might jeopardize their cleverly earned Jammu and Kashmir—i.e. Indian—citizenship.

The experience of Indian/Plantation Tamil expatriates from Sri Lanka offers us a second example, that which I call the story of paper non-citizens. As a consequence of the Shastri-Sirimavo Pact of 1964 and the Indira Gandhi-Sirimavo Pact of 1974, thousands of these Indian/Plantation Tamils were expatriated against their will and settled in Tamil Nadu, Kerala, Karnataka, and Andhra Pradesh (including present-day Telangana). Half a century later, they and their descendants continue to lead miserable lives. Most of them have no idea where their citizenship certificates are. And what papers they had were washed away in the 2019 floods. Now, multiply this story a hundred times over and we begin to get a sense of the plight of East Pakistani/Bangladeshi migrants in the states of Assam and West Bengal.

Our third experience is what I call the case of 'paper refugees'. These are people who have submitted their papers but been told that these papers are incomplete. Following the NRC exercise in Assam, we have now identified 19 lakh such people as non-Indians. Among them, 12 lakh are Hindu, six lakhs are Muslim, and one lakh are tribal (Christian?). If the CAA is taken to its logical end, only six lakh Muslims will remain as non-Indians. They would effectively be the so-called paper refugees, the Hindi word for whom would be the obnoxious *ghuspaithiyas*, who, like 'termites', would be blamed for poaching into India's resources. Given that West Bengal is three times as large as Assam, India will soon have 20 lakh paper refugees. Although 20 lakh is just 0.14 per cent of India's 137 crore population, the number is large enough to jolt West Bengal politics when the state goes to the polls in 2021.

In the midst of all the controversy that a nationwide NRC has kicked off, a recent *Indian Express* report offers a timely reminder of the challenges that lie in store. In 2003, the Atal Behari Vajpayee government conceived a pilot project to test the feasibility of issuing Multi-purpose National Identity Cards (MNICs). The pilot project covered about 31 lakh people in 13 districts spread across 12 states. After six years, the exercise was given up, having achieved only 45 per cent of the target. It was found impossible to gather information from rural people, especially those who were agricultural labourers, landless farmers, married females, or floating migrants in search of livelihood in towns and other villages.

My years of training in IR (International Relations) research have taught me two things. One, a state, any state for that matter, is a congenital liar; and two, statecraft is essentially amoral, in which taking the people for a ride is business as usual. In so far as the first is concerned, the BJP is already a past master. With respect to the second, however, especially when compared to the Congress, it has yet to master the art of statecraft. Let me give three examples.

One, the abrogation of Article 370 by the Modi government. By 2019, the article had already been fiddled with so much that it was hardly recognizable. Barring the abolition of the state through its bifurcation into two Union Territories, the BJP did nothing that Nehru and his successors hadn't already done, including imprisoning the tallest leader of the state, Sheikh Abdullah. To my pointed question to the Kashmir University professor Aijaz Ashraf Wani, the author of a 2019 scholarly study, *What Happened to Governance in Kashmir?*, 'which party has been worse for Jammu and Kashmir, BJP or Congress?', his categorical answer was: 'Congress'. But this was before the Modi government had abrogated Article 370. Wani may give a more nuanced answer now. Howsoever the Modi government might claim that normalcy has returned to the Valley, the situation remains grim and far from normal. To repeat: Statecraft is a complex business; it is not merely playing to one's galleries.

Two, the Indian state under the Congress was also pro-Hindu, its avowed secularism notwithstanding. For example, when in the 1950s and 1960s some controversies arose in Assam in respect of Hindu and Muslim immigrants from East Pakistan, a 1965 secret administrative order of the Government of India authorized the district magistrate to grant Indian citizenship to those Hindu refugees from East Pakistan who had settled in Assam for six months or more. It did not attract anybody's attention as a non-secular move. Similarly, it cannot be just a coincidence that prior to the exodus of Kashmiri Pandits from the Valley in 1990-1 most of the positions in Jammu and Kashmir's nationalized banks (such as SBI), AG office, post office, etc. (all controlled by the central government) should be manned almost entirely by them. I suspect that there must have been an unwritten instruction from the central government in this regard as well.

Three, the Modi government itself undid in its second term in office (May 2019-) that which it had so surreptitiously achieved in its first (2014-19). Through critical changes in the administrative 'rules' (not 'amendments') pertaining to *Passport (Entry into India) Rules, 1950* and the Foreigners Act, 1946, Hindus, Christians, Sikhs, Buddhists, Jains and Parsis were given preference vis-à-vis Muslims with respect to naturalization, or putting in detention centres. The imperatives behind the CAA, therefore, are not new. But as a duly passed Act (and not mere 'rules'), it has raked up an avoidable controversy because it had to be done through the parliament. It is probable that other calculations were in play, most notably the BJP's desire to make inroads in the 2021 West Bengal election, and in broad sense pamper its Hindu constituency. If so, it would not be statecraft but politics, once again aimed at playing to the galleries. Sheikh Hasina Wazed is right when she says that the act was 'unnecessary'.

Postscript: Raja Deen Dayal was probably India's first photographer. Between 1884 and 1905, he produced over 30,000 images of architecture, landscapes, and people. The sixth Nizam of Hyderabad appointed him his court photographer. His studio became the first Indian firm to receive a Royal Warrant from Queen Victoria. In his collection, recently on display in Delhi, there is a family photo of a Hindu nobleman of the Nizam's court by the name Pershad. This Pershad is shown with his several wives, both Hindu and Muslim. The photo also depicts a large number of children. Those born to Hindu mothers are wearing Hindu attire; those born to Muslim mothers are wearing Muslim attire. Setting aside our concerns over polygamy, is not the photo evocative of the possibilities of South Asian secularism, whose key defining feature remains its tolerance?

CHAPTER 5

Islamophobia

Essay 1: Islamophobia Must be Taken Seriously*

Everyone is praising Jacinda Ardern, the Prime Minister of New Zealand. Her unequivocal condemnation of the dastardly act of the Australian white supremacist Brenton Tarrant that killed 49 Muslims in Christchurch on 15 March 2019 has been unanimously lauded.

Calling it as 'one of New Zealand's darkest days' she told the world that,

> We were not a target because we are a safe harbour for those who hate. We were not chosen for this act of violence because we condone racism, because we are an enclave for extremism. We were chosen for the very fact that we are none of these things. Because we represent diversity, kindness, compassion, a home for those who share our values . . . [which] I can assure you, will not, and cannot, be shaken by this attack.

To comfort the psychologically battered Muslims she ordered a nationwide broadcast of the *azaan* the following Friday (22 March) led by Imam Gamal Fouda. She participated in the prayer with her head draped by black scarf. She referred to Prophet Muhammad's saying that 'the believers in their mutual kindness, compassion, and sympathy are just like one body. When any part of the body suffers, the whole body feels pain. New Zealand mourns with you; we are one.'

* 'Islamophobia must be Taken Seriously', *The Dhaka Tribune*, 3 April 2019. https://www.dhakatribune.com/opinion/2019/04/03/islamophobia-must-be-taken-seriously

But is Christchurch going to be the last such madness? Is Islamophobia not a veritable reality? Although everyone knows that terrorism is not the monopoly of the Muslims still why in large parts of the non-Muslim world they alone are seen as its vehicle? These questions beg answers. Who created the bogey and why? To what extent are Muslims themselves contributing to the process?

Religion-centric conflicts are not new. The Crusades (eleventh-thirteenth centuries) were long enough to sow the seeds of Christian-Muslim race for supremacy. In its recent phase the mutual doubt can be traced to the American hostage crisis of 1978 in which it was the Iranian clergy that had provided the anti-American leadership. Had it been secular probably the meaning of the resistance would have been different. This event, soon brewed with the American victory in the Cold War (1990), seemed to make the job easy for the US to explain that the danger to world order now on emanated from Islamism. Although the story was complex it was simplified for the world through such notions as *End of History* (Francis Fukuyama), OWL (Order, Welfare and Legitimacy theory of Edward Kolodziej), and *Clash of Civilizations* (Samuel Huntington).

The connection appealed to the non-Christian cum non-Islamic world which had its own reasons to subscribe to the idea. The Chinese found it handy to promote its Hanification project by othering the Uyghur Muslims in Xinjiang. For the Hindu nationalists in India who had a long history of anti-Muslim sentiment it was a shot in the arm. Even some Buddhist nations which had sizeable Muslim presence used it as a tool to justify their undemocratic highhanded-ness. Western intellectualism with its traditional base in the develop-ing world had little difficulty in spreading the fear. The 9/11 com-pleted the task.

What came first, anti-Islamism or Islamic terrorism, is one of those chicken and egg stories that can never be answered because every history has its history. In the present context let us at least know for certain that Christchurch was not a lone wolf affair. The day it happened, Fraser Anning, a senator from Queensland, said unequivocally:

What it highlights is the growing fear within our community, both in Australia and New Zealand, of the increasing Muslim presence. . . . Muslims may have been the victims today, [but] *usually they are the perpetrators. . . . The truth is that Islam is not like any other faith. It is the religious equivalent of fascism* (emphasis added).

Is it not surprising that no one ever meets a non-Christian white supremacist yet he is not a Christian terrorist. Likewise, it is never an Arab, Syrian or Nigerian terrorist, he is always Islamic terrorist. This raises the question as to why it is so, and from the answer one probably gets an explanation, partially though, to what this Islamophobia is, and why it is so pervasive across the non-Muslim world.

We just explained how the West has popularized it. Let us see now how the Muslim attitudes are a contributing factor too? Certain Islamic norms and practices, which are essentially insular, private and harmless, inadvertently encourage animosity for the Muslims at large. They insist on halal meat even in non-Muslim countries, their mosque sermons are often loaded with political messaging, they prefer Islamic vis-à-vis secular schooling in many Western societies, their schoolgirls insist on wearing the *hijab* (recall the controversy in France), they violently react to any kind of joke on their religion which is common with other religions, they, in most cases, insist that non-Muslims marrying Muslims must convert to Islam, and so on. These things do earn for them the notoriety of being fanatic.

In short, it is bad time for the world which is increasingly getting polarized on sectarian lines. Such UN initiatives like Alliance of Civilizations (2005) meant to find the roots of cultural polarization hold little promise for the simple reason that instead of being inspired by major nations like America or China which really matter it was sponsored by Spain and Turkey. No wonder that after 14 years hardly anybody talks about it though it has many signatories.

In the absence of any concrete action let us do what we always do the best, express some nice sentiments. After the 9/11 it was for the *Le Monde to say*: 'Today, we are all Americans'. Now it is for the world to say: 'We are all New Zealanders'.

Essay 2: Demonizing the Muslims: No One has Time to Go Beyond the Immediate*

Ever since the Al-Qaeda terrorist attacks on the World Trade Center and the Pentagon on 11 September 2001 (9/11) Muslims all over the world are 'under siege'. That's how the Pakistani-American sociologist Akbar Ahmed titled his book *Islam Under Siege* (2003). He could see how the tide of Islamophobia soon gripped the United States. Muslim charities were shut down, veiled women were humiliated, and commentators on the Fox TV paralleled the Quran with Hitler's *Mein Kampf.* The editor of the *National Review*, Richard Lowry, went to the ridiculous extent of asking for the 'final solution' by nuking Mecca.

Even eighteen years after 9/11 we do not see any abatement in the phobia. Rather it has spread beyond America, into Europe, Asia and other places. Muslim refugees from war-torn West Asia are the latest victims. In Europe the Muslim question is rife in its politics, TV programmes and social media. Even in our own region, in Hindu-majority India and Buddhist-majority Sri Lanka, Muslims are on the receiving end. The phenomenon has given pretexts to many governments to gloss over their failures and pass the buck to the Muslims.

Comically, Muslim countries, too, are taking advantage of the situation. In the name of 'Islam in danger', they are tightening their grips over their undemocratic regimes. Otherwise, they could have, particularly those who have so much clout in world politics because of their oil reserves, dented this baloney by putting pressure on the drifting nations. The Abu Dhabi Summit of the 57-memer Organization of the Islamic Cooperation (OIC) held in March this year is a case in point.

Far from telling India, even politely, about OIC's displeasure

* 'Demonizing Muslims: Why Islamophobia has Gripped Much of the World', *Dhaka Tribune*, 8 August 2019. https://www.dhakatribune.com/opinion/2019/08/08/demonizing-muslims, simultaneously carried as 'The growing phenomenon of demonizing Muslims', *Newsclick.in* 7 August 2019. https://www.newsclick.in/growing-phenomenon-demonising-muslims

with what had been happening in India in respect of Muslims' safety and honour, the organization invited India's External Affairs Minister Sushma Swaraj as the guest of honour and keynote speaker. That the Summit Declaration did not even thank her, itself weird, nor took any cognizance of her concern with regard to international terrorism is beside the point.

What is relevant to note is that the OIC was only interested to take India on board because it is economically vital. All those who think that international public opinion matters must be told that they are living in a fool's paradise. Didn't America maintain a flourishing trade with Hitler's Germany two years into the Second World War? By that time millions of Jews had already been killed. Our own beloved Subhas Bose was also merrily dealing with the Nazis. Devils can be enemies; devils can also be friends. National narcissism thy name is international politics.

Whatever be the dynamics of international relations the fact remains that social expressions about Muslims have turned rabidly hostile. Wherever they are in minority they are considered as religious bigots, who are ardently conservative. A litany of assumptions follows: that misogyny is in their blood, that their rigid food code only allows halal meat (pork especially forbidden), that they marry non-Muslims only on the condition that the spouse converts to Islam, that their veiled women are security hazards as terrorists can hide behind them, the list continues.

For historical reasons Muslims are the most dispersed community in the world, even more than the Christians who are much more in number (33 to 24 per cent). Compared to them Buddhists and Hindus are concentrated in a few pockets, even though Hindus comprise 15 per cent of the world population and Buddhists 9 per cent. As a result, the Muslim minority question is virtually a global issue which is not the case with other minorities.

In Western Europe, the Muslim presence is essentially post-colonial. England has a South Asian-African-Muslim diaspora, France has an African-Muslim (including Algerian) diaspora, and Holland an Indonesian-Muslim diaspora. Besides, all have Muslims from other regions as well. Germany, although not possessing comparable former colonies, has attracted Turks in large numbers from

1960s onwards. The present anti-Muslim ire, however, is targeted at recent immigrants, in particular, Syrian and Iraqi refugees.

European anxiety stems from the image that Islamist terrorists tend to create. These terrorists are quite unlike other terror brands. The Irish Republican Army (IRA) never displayed its Christian card. The Tamil Tigers, who were mostly Hindus, did not wear Hinduism upon their sleeves. The latter is particularly notable because they were fighting a Buddhist chauvinistic Sinhala state.

But these mental constructions, both insecurity-driven and culture-centric, do not pose any real danger to European life per se. Some countries where refugees are minuscule, such as Poland and Hungary, are also up in arms against them. Germany, which 'never had it so good' economically per Chancellor Angela Merkel's own admission, recorded as many as 3,500 anti-refugee incidents in 2016.

Are Muslims alone to be blamed for everything going wrong in Europe? Let us appreciate that refugees are not there for a picnic. Faced with dire circumstances back home, they had to run away. Can anyone deny that the refugee problem of Europe is intimately linked to America's security-centric machinations in West Asia? If European nations as members of NATO could not play an adequate role in the game, what business do they now have to confuse the consequence with the cause.

It is one thing to be worried about the refugees but quite another to play second fiddle to the Americans. The former foreign minister of Germany, Joseph Martin 'Joschka' Fischer, had once lamented that if at all the European Union wanted to play its rightful role in global politics it would have to behave like a 'power' and not rely only on 'experience'. So long that does not happen, America's wars will generate Muslim refugees who will for sheer geographical reasons turn up in Europe.

Let Europeans also be advised to peep into their own history before giving sermons to others not to 'invade' their continent as immigrants. I hope their school texts tell their children that between 1846 and 1930 fifty million of them had left the continent to settle in the Americas, Australia, New Zealand and South Africa. The natives in those lands certainly did not invite these Europeans nor did they volunteer to be subjugated by them, let alone exterminated.

The Islamophobia of South Asia is historically different from Europe, but varies little in terms of content. In India, it has much to do with Hindu nationalism, which has at least a hundred years of history. But only in its present form has it become virulent. Today, the mere suspicion that someone is carrying or eating beef can lead to their being lynched by a mob, which then has the audacity to video record the event and circulate it on social media with aplomb. Just for the heck of it Muslims are being forced to chant *Jai Shree Ram* (salutations to Lord Ram). If they refuse, which they have every right to, they are heckled and beaten, sometimes to death.

The matter has reached such ridiculous levels that even app-based services such as Uber (taxi) and Zomato (food delivery) are affected. There are reports of Hindus cancelling their trips or food orders upon discovering that the taxi driver or the Zomato delivery man has a Muslim name. The only silver lining is that the Zomato owner, a Hindu, has refused to budge, declaring that it goes against 'the idea of India'. He has not obliged his customers even though it has caused his company some losses on account of the undelivered food and also generated calls for boycott of Zomato on social media.

At the state level, the worst example of Islamophobia is the way the National Register of Citizens (NRC) is being compiled in Assam, with plans to extend the register nationwide. The assumption behind the exercise is that the Muslim immigrants from Bangladesh (Hindu and Buddhist immigrants are excluded as the government's statements indicate) are 'like termites [who] will completely lick off the country' and must be prevented from doing so.

One shudders to think what will happen when the NRC report will be out, latest by 31 August 2019. All reports so far have indicated massive flaws in the data. Reports also talk of widespread human rights violations. One thing is more or less clear: that the BJP anticipates particular trends in the findings. If the report does not show that the illegal Bangladeshis are overwhelmingly Muslim, and that they are overwhelmingly present in the border districts, then the party's political game will be lost. They will then have to reinvent their anti-Muslim tirade on some other grounds. They need to placate their Hindu constituency in Assam and the rest of the country, after all.

To have a perspective of the situation one must understand the area's history and geography. The region which comprises Assam, Bangladesh, West Bengal, and the several states of India's north-east was a united Bengal Province until 1874. There were incessant migratory flows from eastern Bengal to Assam from 1900 onwards. Among the contributory factors were, one, the greater density of population in eastern Bengal, and two, the rain-fed alluvial soil of the Brahmaputra and Barak valleys of Assam was ideal for wet paddy cultivation. Neither the political engineering of the Partition of 1947 nor the creation of Bangladesh in 1971 could obliterate these basic realities. In fact, both events triggered large scale migrations because of the violence that preceded and followed them.

To make the perspective even sharper, let us compare it with the US-Mexican situation. It is for historical and geographical reasons that erstwhile East Bengalis and formerly Mexican nationals are concentrated in the bordering regions. In America they are the hyphenated Mexican-Americans. India does not have the system of counting hyphenated ethnic categories. Still it is common historical sense that such people will be in large numbers in the border districts of Assam, Meghalaya, Tripura and West Bengal, just as Mexican-Americans are in large numbers in the bordering states of California, Texas, Arizona and New Mexico. We will also do well to remember that these states belonged to Mexico and were lost after the 1848 war with the United States. New Mexico, which had seceded from Mexico in 1836, is the exception.

The Islamophobia of Sri Lanka is comparatively new. It can be explained through a binary sociology. In the construction of Sinhala nationalism, besides a focus on Buddhism and the Sinhala language, it was also necessary to find an 'other'. That 'other' could be either the Sri Lanka Tamil community or the Muslim community, both of which are Tamil-speaking. As long as the Sri Lankan civil war was raging between the Sinhala-dominated Sri Lanka state and the Liberation Tigers of the Tamil Eelam (LTTE), Muslims sided with the state. This in turn drew the ire of the LTTE, which reduced many of them to refugees by evicting them from places where they were in good numbers.

But once the LTTE was defeated in May 2009, a new punching bag was required to sustain Sinhala nationalism. Because of Islamophobia around the world, including in India, the situation was conducive for anti-Muslim sentiment. One of the early pieces of evidences is the way Tsunami relief politics played out. Hambantota in the Southern Province, which was predominantly Sinhalese-Buddhist and also the constituency of Prime Minister/President Mahinda Rajapaksa, received much greater relief assistance than Ampara in the Eastern Province which had a Muslim majority. The latter suffered the LTTE wrath also.

After the recent attacks on churches by a local Muslim terrorist outfit anti-Muslim politics is in its most vocal form, bolstering the Buddhist militancy led by *Bodu Bala Sena* (Buddhist Power Force) that has been terrorising the Muslims for the past few years. Even an online campaign has been launched to scuttle the Sirisena government's move to set up the Sharia University, supposed to be Asia's biggest.

Rajapaksa's People's Front (*Podujana Peramuna*) is now all set to play its time-tested Sinhala-Buddhist card in the forthcoming presidential election. It is to be seen what kind of Muslim militancy it will result in. That there is a connection between majority high-handedness and minority extremism is well documented. If anyone thinks that Tamil insurgency had nothing to do with the Buddhist chauvinism of the 1950s as displayed through its 'Sinhala Only' language policy, one indeed has no sense of history.

Talking about sense of history I am amazed to see how little we learn from history which constantly warns us against arrogance, arrogance of the kind displayed by most majorities in most places. But they forget that the same majority is a minority somewhere else or at some point in history. After the Jews, Indians today are the most prosperous ethnicity in the United States. But less than a century ago (1929) they were reviled as 'illegal' immigrants. 'The menacing spread of Hindus' frightened the American state. Even the Nobel Laureate Rabindranath Tagore was subjected to such humiliation by the US immigration officials that he cut short his sojourn and returned home early.

Also intriguing is the notion that democracy is the solution to all societal problems. Strangely, however, the majority-minority cleavages seem to be sharper in democracies than in other systems. I recall an interesting conversation I had in Kathmandu in 2005 with a Muslim politician. Reflecting on the fall of the Hindu monarchy and the arrival of democracy in Nepal, he felt that since only votes mattered for the latter the Muslim minority had reasons to worry. Many years have passed since then but nothing has happened. Still, given the Hindu resurgence next door in India intercommunal peace in Nepal may not remain undisturbed for long.

It may as well be recalled that it was the Hindu Maharaja of Kashmir who had introduced a rule in 1927 according to which no outsider could buy land in the state. It was meant to protect the poor masses of the state, mostly Muslim, from the richer Punjabis next door who otherwise could have dispossessed them from their lands by offering big prices. But today's democratically elected Government of India is considering doing away with this age-old regulation so as to allow anybody to settle in the state.

Abraham Lincoln has given us the simplest definition of democracy: a government of the people, by the people, for the people. But seeing the majority-minority cleavages all over the world this definition needs some tweaking. Let it read now as: Democracy is a political contraption through which different communities, big or small, deal with one another so as to truly create a government of the people, by the people, for the people.

CHAPTER 6

Chinese Elephant in the Room

Essay 1: India-Nepal-China: Who Will Win this Three-legged Race?*

Even before the logic of globalization could sink in, it was overtaken by multilateralism, thus obfuscating both the processes. Soon the tendency was to return to the age-old wisdom of bilateralism though on the surface multilateralism ruled the roost. In the recent past three multilateral conferences have been in the news. First, it was the postponement of the Islamabad SAARC Summit, then it was the BRICS Summit at Benaulim (Goa), and then, alongside the latter, the BIMSTEC leaders' meetings with the BRICS leaders. But the curiosity was not about what the 7,300-word BRICS Declaration contained but as to how some of the bilateral relationships panned out in Benaulim. In any case the BRICS Declaration had little meaning having contained almost everything under the sun. What transpired in the bilateral 'summits', for example, in the one between the Prime Minister of Nepal, Pushpa Kamal Dahal 'Prachanda', and the President of China, Xi Jinping, became the query. This one-to-one conversation lasted for just twenty minutes after which the two were joined by the Prime Minister of India, Narendra Modi. Presumably, Prachanda and Xi had not simply discussed about the beauty of the Benaulim beach.

China-Nepal relations have political and strategic implications for India. The latter any day would be happier if Nepal pays more

* 'It's Complicated: The China factor in India-Nepal Relationship', *Scroll.in*, 23 October 2016<http://scroll.in/article/819705/its-complicated-the-china-factor-in-india-nepal-relationship>

attention to India than to China. Indeed that is always the case, but India wants more. For all India's small neighbours, Nepal included, their only diplomatic trump vis-à-vis India is their China card which they have learnt to flaunt whenever they feel the necessity of neutralizing India's 'over-lordship'. This tension is a permanent fixture in India's neighbourhood diplomacy. Although one has no clue as to what happened at the Prachanda-Xi meeting yet with hind sight one has reason to believe that it was a friendly exchange pointing towards policies aimed at all-round mutual advantage. Unlike in the past, China, of late, has shown more interest in Nepal's domestic politics. In May 2016 when Nepal's the then K.P. Sharma Oli government was on the verge of collapse on account of Maoist Prachanda's threat of withdrawal of support to the government it was the Chinese 'intervention' that saved the day for Oli. China reportedly counselled Prachanda to relent. According to some Nepal watchers this was the first time that China took a position on a purely domestic matter. Now the same Prachanda is at the helm of the Nepal government. China has reasons to feel assured. In contrast India has reasons for concern.

Prachanda's diplomacy could well be his country's traditional one: maintaining equal distance from both its big neighbours, India and China, or, to remain equally close to both of them. In that sense it is the Nepalese nationalism that speaks, and not whether it is a monarchy as it was in the past, or it is a republic, which it is at present. Or, whether the rulers are Maoists or not. In the 1970s it was the policy of the monarchy to declare 'Nepal as a zone of peace' meaning both India and China should keep off Nepal. Since those days China did not matter for Nepal's politics the message was clear: Nepal politics should be out of bounds for India. Now that China is actively engaged in Nepal's politics and diplomacy the tone of the Nepal leadership has changed. Prachanda has pleaded for how Nepal could serve as a 'dynamic bridge' between India and China. With the support from both these Asian giants Nepal could become a prosperous country, Nepalese newspaper *Himalayan Times* has reported Prachanda as saying: 'We wish to reap benefits of this geographical speciality by working as a dynamic bridge between the two countries'. Xi reportedly complimented Nepal for keeping an equidistant relationship with China and India while expressing his hope that in the future all the three countries would mutually gain. Indeed Modi had little option other than sharing this pious thought.

Nepal is a challenge for the Modi government not only for the China factor but also for how to deal with its ethnic question—the controversy between the Nepali and Madhesi (Indian origin Nepalese of the Terai region) identities. The challenge is at two levels, one, the Maoists are in power, and two, the Madhesis are a disgruntled lot whose disaffection can easily spill over into India as it happened in the recent past which resulted in the plugging of the open India-Nepal borders causing economic hardship to Nepal in general and to the Terai region in particular.

The nature of the Indian state which is essentially bourgeois can never be at ease with a Communist regime next door. It would have been so even if Congress had been in power. Under the present BJP rule it is even more expected. The RSS, which is the ideological mentor of the BJP, is avidly opposed to the Marxists/Maoists. They have not reconciled themselves to the demise of the only Hindu state in the world. During the anti-monarchy movement in the 1990s their sympathy was for King Gyanendra. There was nothing personal about it nor for the monarchy as an institution. It was in the hope that through him the Hindu state of Nepal would survive. In the meantime, on the one hand, Nepal has become a republic and left-oriented, to boot, while on the other, the BJP has captured power in India, after 2014 more firmly. The impact of these two developments are inevitable on the Terai politics. It is now a question of time when the ideology of Hindutva will find its footprints on the Terai soil (95 per cent of Nepal's 4.5 per cent Muslims are in the Terai). Mercifully the region has not so far seen any Hindu-Muslim conflict but more the Madhesis will feel marginalized in the politics of Nepal, and there will be politics of scale which is inevitable in a mass democracy, it will find expression in Hindutva-oriented politics, with or without visible support from the RSS/BJP. Under these circumstances the already complex relationship between India and Nepal is bound to be more complicated, the China factor further stirring the brew.

Essay 2: While India Slept*

It is elementary wisdom that in modern wars conventional military balance alone is not decisive. Had it been so, the Axis Powers would not have lost the Second World War, the Soviets the Cold War, or the Americans their Vietnam War. What ultimately matters is the intrinsic strength of a nation's polity and its resolve to take on any adversary with rock-solid determination, behind which lie an integrated society built upon a concrete and egalitarian economic base and correct international connections. As such, the final script of the India-China showdown has not yet been written. But if the trailers are to be believed, the omens for India are bad.

But first things first. What has really happened on the border? Has China actually intruded into areas that India considers its own, or at least into the so-called 'no-man's land'? If so, by how much? If China alone has violated the LAC (Line of Actual Control), what is this 'mutual disengagement' we keep hearing about? Why is India not clearly demanding 'Chinese withdrawal' from areas it has intruded into? Why did the Indian government send confusing signals in the beginning, from which it has yet to wriggle itself free? Have not the Chinese taken full advantage of this Indian 'faux pas' to bolster their domestic support base, which is in any case in their pocket, being the totalitarian state that they are.

In this hurly-burly, the one reality that stands out is that Indians were caught napping. To put it bluntly, they were lulled into complacency by the Chinese lullaby; Narendra Modi by Xi Jinping, much as Pandit Nehru by Mao Zedong and Zhou Enlai nearly sixty years ago. The core question is: Why is India always taken for a ride by China; why is it found defending or recovering land allegedly lost to the Chinese? Why this perpetual reaction, why no pro-action? The answer is simple: While India sleeps, China is active, even super active.

* 'While India Slept', *Dhaka Tribune*, 10 July 2020, https://www. dhakatribune.com/opinion/op-ed/2020/07/10/op-ed-while-india-slept, simultaneously carried as 'While India Slept', *Newsclick.in,* 10 July 2020, https://www. newsclick.in/India-Slept-China-LAC-Army

It is possible that the ongoing diplomatic parleys will make India convince China to restore the status-quo ante as of April 2020 (how each country would interpret that is a million dollar question), but will that alter the reality that China is head and shoulders above India in real terms? After all, barring comical claims of being the 'wisdom giver to the world' (*vishvaguru*), India has done little meaningful to narrow the ever-widening gap.

International relations is a cutthroat field. Power speaks through overall strength, not mere good intentions. Most of us in India, or probably anywhere else, are obsessed with comparing nations through the parameters of GDP or military balance. They are important indicators, but they often bypass in the calculations those that should figure centre stage: the masses.

Being a student of South Asian politics for decades, and having interacted with my counterparts across the region, I have convinced myself that howsoever much we may try to warn of growing Chinese influence in the region to our neighbours it cuts little ice. For them, both India and China are giants. When you sleep with elephants you sleep in perpetual fear, never sure to which way the mammoths will turn. For historical and ethnic reasons, these countries have more to worry from New Delhi than from Beijing. The latter is too far away and, in any case, India serves as a good buffer. Let India absorb the shock first. Pakistan's advantage is geo-strategic in any case.

More importantly, in constant search for resources and support to pursue their development agendas, the smaller South Asian nations love to make India and China compete over who can be a better friend to them. As a potential donor, China is much better positioned than India.

A decade ago, with the help of my economist friend Professor Taranath Bhat, I tried to make a comparative India-China chart to understand where we relatively stood in development terms. To make our chart look comprehensive we deviated from the beaten track of comparing GDP-PPP or military expenditures and arsenals. Instead, we looked for their respective commitments to their masses in terms of daily needs. Here are some interesting revelations based on data culled from World Bank and UNDP factsheets, the *China Customs Statistics 2011*, and the *Economic Survey of India* for the years 2010, 2011 and 2012.

The Chinese population stood at 1.35 billion, India's at 1.21 billion a decade ago. China's GDP in PPP terms was 9.87 trillion dollars vis-à-vis India's 3.91 trillion; annual per capita GDP in PPP terms was 7,599 versus 3,425; and the defence budget stood at 106.4 billion dollars versus 40.5 billion dollars, respectively. Now, consider these development indicators in terms of their reflection in people's welfare. In China, 29.8 per cent of the population survived on less than $2 a day; the corresponding share in India was 54 per cent. Adult literacy in China stood at 96 per cent, in India at 76 per cent; and the Human Development Index (HDI) ranked China at 101 and India at 134. China produced 16,200 doctorates in science and engineering every year, India barely 7,300; China had 520,000 vocational and training institutes, India just 12,260. China's child mortality rate (under 5 years per 1000) in 2010 was 18 compared to India's 63. China's per capita electricity consumption was 2631 kWh, while India's was 597 kWh. China's annual steel production of 683.3 million tonnes dwarfed India's figure of 72.2; in cement production, the ratio was 1,800 million tonnes to 220 million tonnes. In the ten years since we collected these figures, these trends have diverged, not converged.

In the context of the COVID-19 pandemic and the difficulties faced by the health services of both countries, it is instructive to remember that comparative expenditure on health was far higher in China. In 2010, the per capita expenditure on health in China was 265 dollars while in India it was barely 122. According to WHO statistics, the corresponding figures for 2017 were 441 dollars versus 69 dollars (yes, India reduced its spending on health!). If India wants to deal with China on an equal footing, each of these metrics matters.

One last point. The easiest thing in the world is to become a state-defined nationalist. The moment one becomes such a nationalist, his critical thinking goes into slumber and he basks in the glory of the greatness of his nation. His reverie is disturbed only when he realises that the world beyond his walls has not lain idle but has instead steadily encroached into his home. But by then it is already too late. His house has been burgled in and his pride punctured.

To my mind, the most frustrating field of social science research is IR (International Relations). The reasons are numerous, but for our purposes here two prominent ones will suffice: one, the inherent compulsion for IR scholars to toe the official line; and two, its fundamental weakness to be normative, howsoever remotely. This is exactly what has happened to India's China policy. Our state-sponsored nationalism has lulled us to such an extent that we have lowered our guards to an unimaginable level.

There is absolutely no harm if Narendra Modi warmly hugs Xi Jinping or decides to swing merrily with him on the Sabarmati lawns. But India's external affairs minister, S. Jaishankar, should certainly have known better than him to take any of these activities at face value. Indeed, his childhood education ought to have proved sufficient. The son of India's doyen of international strategic studies, K. Subrahmanyam, Jaishankar must surely have learned early and learned well that in international politics what matters is an adversary's power, not his intentions. Furthermore, one would assume that in a democracy a foreign minister has the ear of his prime minister.

Postscript: In 1938, a year before the beginning of the Second World War in Europe, Winston Churchill wrote *While England Slept.* His point was simple. England had not prepared itself sufficiently to deal with Nazi Germany's economic and military build-up. The book was an indictment of Neville Chamberlain's so-called 'policy of appeasement'. Among its readers was a young John F. Kennedy, future American president. In 1940, Kennedy graduated from Harvard College, having written a thesis titled 'Appeasement at Munich', which was largely inspired by Churchill's book.

That same year, he sought to publish it as a book, and chose a title that would pay homage to the book that inspired him: *Why England Slept.* Publication was likely facilitated because of the good offices of his rich and influential father, Joseph P. Kennedy, then the American ambassador in London. The older Kennedy even approached the famous British political scientist Harold Laski to write a foreword for the book. But Laski declined, dismissing the book as the product of 'an immature mind'. Laski was convinced that it would not have found a publisher had it not been written 'by the son of a very rich man'.

The younger Kennedy had the last laugh, however. *Why England Slept* sold 80,000 copies in America and England and earned him 40,000 dollars in royalties. He donated part of the money for the reconstruction of the war-ravaged British city of Plymouth. With the remainder he bought himself a Buick convertible.

Essay 3: The China Syndrome and the Spectre of Cold War 2.0*

An uncanny peace prevails on India's China border. The Indian government first falsely assured everyone that no Indian territory had been lost to China. More recently, it has conceded that the border situation is tense, and that India is prepared to retaliate militarily if the situation so demands. Against the background of all kinds of contradictory statements over the months, this clarity is welcome. But since the state—any state—is a congenital liar, one does not know what is actually in store and to what extent people are being taken for a ride.

The date of 15 September marked the second instance since the abrogation of Article 370 in Kashmir (August 2019) that the Indian government has categorically referred to the illegal Chinese occupation of 1,33,180 sq. km of Indian territory, including Aksai Chin, portions of POK, and vast stretches of Arunachal Pradesh. Several meanings can be adduced from the statement.

* 'The China Syndrome and the Spectre of Cold War 2.0', *Dhaka Tribune*, 20 September 2020, https://www.dhakatribune.com/opinion/op-ed/2020/09/20/op-ed-the-china-syndrome-and-the-spectre-of-cold-war-2-0, simultaneously carried as 'China Syndrome and Spectre of Cold War 2.0', *Newsclick.in*, 19 September 2020, https://www.newsclick.in/India-China-Border-Spectre-of-Cold-War-2.0

One, India is preparing for an all-out war with China to regain its lost territories. It may be honey to the ears of our self-styled nationalists, but given the power differential between the two nations, it would likely be a case of 'fools rush in where angels fear to tread'. This is, therefore, ruled out, though India's message is loud and clear:

> [T]he situation this year is very different both in terms of scale of troops involved and the number of friction points, we do remain committed to the peaceful resolution of the current situation. At the same time, the House [Lower House of Parliament] can be assured that we remain prepared to deal with any contingencies.

Two, the statement is meant to play to the galleries. Anyone who has analysed Narendra Modi's blitzkrieg style diplomacy carefully must have noticed that it is heavily loaded in favour of catering to the domestic audience. Even his meetings with NRIs in developed countries were primarily meant to communicate with their families and friends back home in India. At present, Modi is the uncrowned king of India. All that his devotees want to hear from him is that everything is hunky-dory and when the crunch comes, he would teach China a veritable lesson. After all, who does not like a feel-good atmosphere? Modi knows how to mollycoddle this 'all is well' mentality.

Three, more than India, it serves China's interests. Diplomatic parleys with the Chinese to defuse the situation and reclaim almost thousand square kilometres of Indian territory have been ongoing for several weeks now. Nowhere has one come across any Chinese commitment, either in the joint statement, or in the two separate statements released to mark the conclusion of the India-China meeting of foreign ministers, between S. Jaishankar and Wang Yi, on 10 September 2020. Nor was there any reference nor any demand from the Indian side that China must restore the status-quo ante as it prevailed in April 2020.

Fourth, by referring to the loss of more than a hundred thousand square kilometres of Indian territory in the sixties, and not the thousand square kilometres in the last few months, the Modi government has reverted to a well-worn strategy: blame Pandit Jawaharlal

Nehru. Politically, this rhetoric served BJP well in its ascension to power, and there is no reason to think that it cannot continue to pay dividends. Who cares to ponder that this huge territorial loss was also staring Modi in the face when he was indulging with so much aplomb in his personalized diplomacy with Xi Jinping? Evidently, this territorial loss did not come in the way of the Wuhan Spirit or the Mamallapuram Summit.

Fifth, and most importantly, now that the much-hyped bonhomie between India and China has so terribly soured, what should India's larger diplomatic game plan be? Ever since President Donald Trump's rise to power, Modi has wholeheartedly stood by the former's side, conscious of the fact that not only do the Indian Americans matter in American politics, but that they also constitute a huge source of support for the BJP through their financial and cultural connections to India. As the COVID pandemic has devastated his presidency, Trump has increasingly resorted to playing the anti-China card to retain his electoral base. Is Modi preparing to play ball with Trump?

Against this background, it is not surprising that Trump would try to rope India into the snare of 'Cold War 2.0', the prospect of which he has aggressively encouraged. Simply put, the idea connotes that just like the world was divided between American and Soviet camps during the original Cold War, the second iteration will be a war of nerves between those who side with America and those who side with China. The slogan is certainly not without attractions, particularly at the present juncture of India's discomfiture with the Chinese. But should India take the bait? Whether the idea survives the US presidential election or not is another matter, but it will certainly not be easy for a subordinate power like India to adjust to the ever-changing requirements of a superpower like America. Caveat emptor!

India must, therefore, swallow this Cold War 2.0 recipe with a pinch of salt. We would do well to remember that from the end of the Cold War until 9/11, when Islamic terror became the focal point of US global strategy, it was Japan that occupied the role of America's prime adversary. Debates in American academia during those years centered on the impending economic tussle between

America, Japan and Western Europe. There was increasingly strident talk of a 'car war', with fears that American marques would be overrun by Japanese ones. Tough trade negotiations eventually forced Japan to budge and accept a quota for exports to America, leading Noam Chomsky to jibe that ultimately it was not trade, but aid that salvaged the America economy! China was nowhere in the reckoning then.

Like the US-Japan car war, what we see between America and China today is a technology war. Who will beat whom in the realm of Artificial Intelligence (AI) is the question. In this twenty-first century great game, India will matter marginally. Some in India may still hope that when the chips are down, the US will come to India's aid. But that is not how superpowers behave. They see to their interests first (and last). Notice that in the many instances that President Trump has offered to mediate between India and Pakistan on Kashmir or between India and China in their border row, not once has he taken a clear pro-India position.

One last point. In the ultimate analysis, a nation will have to fend for itself. Foreign tie-ups help but they are no substitutes for national strength. After all, foreign policy does not float in a vacuum. And what matters most for national security are internal stability and strength. At present, India suffers from many fault lines. Indian society was never as polarized as it is now. The Indian economy was never worse off than it is in now. Indians were never as poorly informed as they are now. Even such a major event like the Chinese intrusion into our territory was obfuscated for three months by contradictory statements emanating from the highest levels. Let it be said without mincing any words: honest questioning of the government is the best form of nationalism. By that token, there is an alarming dearth of nationalism in India today.

Postscript: International politics is one of the most discussed subjects in middle class living rooms, yet it is also one of the least understood. Sometimes, even serving diplomats have no idea what their political masters are up to. Henry Kissinger's secret trip from Islamabad to China in 1971, which was meant to pave the way for the Nixon-Mao Summit the following year, was not known even to senior officials of the American embassy in Islamabad. The lone exception was the US ambassador, Joseph Farland.

For everyone else in the embassy, as well as in the international press, Kissinger was recuperating in the Nathia Gali hill resort in Abbottabad, a three-hour drive from Islamabad. He had supposedly been advised by the doctor to rest his 'Delhi Belly', a parting gift from his just-concluded India trip. Another real-life story from the Cold War days comically underscores the point. At the height of US-Soviet tensions in the early 1950s, it was written on the wall of the men's room at UNHQ: 'This is the only place where you know what you are doing'.

Essay 4: The India-China Quagmire: How Not to Negotiate from a Position of Weakness*

CENTRALITY OF POWER

The theory is rather simple: colonial wars created borders, post-colonial nations scramble over them. In South Asia these so-called borders routinely complicate regional security. Between India and China the bones of contention are the disputed boundaries in the Ladakh region and the McMahon Line (1914) in Arunachal Pradesh that separates it from Tibet. Between Afghanistan and Pakistan it is the Durand Line (1893/1901), which is arguably a crisis in the waiting. One need not search for morality in those imperial exercises for all that mattered to the British was their strategic interest. Power, as understood in international politics, constituted the warps and woofs of the system those days, as they are even now.

The ongoing border conflict between India and China will be put to rest someday depending upon who bargains for what based upon their intrinsic power. Although the definition of power has undergone changes over the years the bottom line is still the re-

* 'The India-China Quagmire: How Not to Negotiate from a Position of Weakness', *Policy Watch* (New Delhi), 9(11), November 2020, pp. 10-15, https://www.rgics.org/wp-content/uploads/The-India-China-Quagmire-How-Not-to-Negotiate-from-a-Position-of-Weakness.pdf

spective military strengths. The other backup variables are: economic base, societal cohesion, structure of the national ambition as buttressed by ground preparations, etc. India does not stand measurably vis-à-vis China on any of these counts. One fundamental advantage for India, however, is its democracy provided it is duly put to use.

CURRENT BORDER BLUES

An uncanny peace now prevails on the India's China border. The Indian government first falsely assured the nation that no Indian territory had been lost to China. Later, on 15 September 2020, through its Defence Minister Rajnath Singh, it categorically informed the Lok Sabha that China had over the years either occupied, or illegally claimed, approximately 133,180 sq. km. of India's land, including Aksai Chin, portions of Pakistan Occupied Kashmir (POK), and vast stretches of Arunachal Pradesh. The statement *inter alia* said:

> [T]he situation this year is very different both in terms of scale of troops involved and the number of friction points, we do remain committed to the peaceful resolution of the current situation. At the same time, the House can be assured that *we remain prepared to deal with any contingencies* (emphasis added).

Notably, there was no reference to the recent territorial advances made by the Chinese.

What meanings can be adduced from the statement? Here are some probable explanations. One, India is preparing for an all-out war with China to regain its recently lost territories, and more importantly, its bruised prestige in the world, more particularly in the region. The Delhi-based *Outlook* magazine (21 September 2020) even carried a cover story with the title: Is war inevitable? It might have excited India's self-styled nationalists, but given the power differential between the two nations, such a scenario is very risky to visualize. Prime Minister Narendra Modi rightly avoided all kinds of jingoism. He even steered clear of mentioning China by name. The war is, therefore, unlikely, though India's message is clear: this far and no farther.

Two, the statement is meant to play to the gallery. Anyone who has studied Prime Minster Narendra Modi's blitzkrieg style diplomacy[1] should know that it is heavily oriented towards bolstering his domestic support base. It started from day one in 2014. In his inaugural ceremony he invited all the eight SAARC heads so as mark a new beginning for the organization. But today SAARC is in tatters. Later, his meetings with NRIs in developed countries were primarily meant to communicate with their families and friends back home in India. At present, Prime Minster Modi is the uncrowned king of India. All that his supporters want to hear from him is that everything is okay on the India-China front and when the crunch comes he would adequately teach China a lesson.

Three, more than India, it serves China's interests. Diplomatic and military parleys with the Chinese to diffuse the situation and reclaim more than a thousand square kilometers of lost Indian land have been going on for several weeks now. But one has not come across any Chinese commitment to restore the status-quo ante. Neither the joint statement nor the two separate statements released after the meeting of 10 September 2020 between S. Jaishankar and Wang Yi, the foreign ministers of the two countries, mentioned anything to that effect.

In a web-based colloquium organized by the National Committee on US-China Relations held on 9 October 2020 under the title: 'Tensions in the Himalayas', the Chinese participant, Professor Shen Dingli, categorically underlined the disputed nature of the India-China border and suggested that the best way to prevent the situation from further deterioration was to declare a 'demilitarized zone' and wait optimistically for a better situation to emerge sometime in the future, which could be years away. His proposed solution was to first define a reasonable area of dispute, then to turn the area into a temporary area of peace as per the Line of Actual Control (LAC) ideally defined by both countries. This would be a temporary solution thereby turning the area of dispute into an area of stability, disengagement, and demilitarization. This way, China and India would learn to respect each other and find a more long-term solution.[2] Shen indeed was not speaking on behalf of the Chinese government but Chinese academics know their government's mind better than their Indian counterparts.

Fourth, and most importantly, now that the much-hyped bonhomie between India and China has soured, what should India's larger policy vis-à-vis China be. It has two major aspects: one, how to match China economically which determines the intrinsic strength of a nation, and two, how to create a world opinion against China as an expansionist power. The latter may not make China return the territory it has already grabbed but it can at least prevent it from any such filching in the future.

INDIA-CHINA ASYMMETRY

In spite of all the tall talk about India emerging as the *vishvaguru* (wisdom giver of the world) and that the shining global profile of India is making the country one of the top seeds in the international race for supremacy, the reality is quite different. From my personal experiences in Europe and America after this *vishvaguru* business became quite popular in India I can say with a sense of responsibility that this claim is grossly misplaced, primarily created in India by its own electronic media with hardly any taker abroad barring a section of the NRIs. There was a time in the 1990s and early 2000s when India studies were becoming popular in many of these countries but by the end of the first decade of this century India studies started getting replaced by China studies. It was not for any love for China but simply because the latter mattered more to them in economic and strategic terms. If 'know your enemy' is the gospel of all Area Studies programmes it meant simply that. In contrast India lost its glamour, was increasingly seen as a poor nation seething with all kinds of social tensions.

This author was startled to see how his lecture on 'India in South Asia' at the University of Ljubljana (Slovenia) in March 2015, by when BJP was well entrenched in power with its election manifesto having proudly proclaimed the country as *vishvaguru*, was completely hijacked by a volley of questions on gangrapes in India. Although the Nirbhaya gang-rape tragedy was almost three years old by then, it continued to catch the imagination of the students. These are hard realities Indians trumpeting about Indian glory sitting in India's middle class drawing rooms must realize. Almost during the same time it became a big news in India how the German Chancellor, Angela Merkel, had inaugurated the Indian pavilion at the Hanover international trade fair in the presence of Prime Minster Narendra Modi. But in the German media the event hardly figured as an important news.

In contrast, Deng Xiaoping, the builder of modern China, is famously associated with the statement, 'hide your capacities and bide your time'. One is not sure whether he really said so, or in what context, but the slogan has certainly been translated into reality. An India-China comparison done about a decade ago underlined the gap between the two nations. For example, China's GDP in PPP terms was 9.87 trillion dollars vis-à-vis India's 3.91 trillion; annual per capita GDP in PPP terms was 7,599 dollars versus 3,425; and the defence budget stood at 106.4 billion dollars to 40.5 billion dollars. China's annual steel production of 683.3 million tonnes dwarfed India's figure of 72.2; in cement production, the ratio was 1800 million tonnes to 220 million tonnes.[3]

In terms of welfare, 29.8 per cent of the population survived on less than $2 a day in China, the corresponding share for India was 54 per cent. Adult literacy in China stood at 96 per cent, in India at 76 per cent; and the Human Development Index (HDI) ranked China at 101 while India at 134. China produced 16,200 doctorates in science and engineering every year, India barely 7,300; China had 520,000 vocational and training institutes, India just 12,260. China's child mortality rate (under 5 years per 1000) in 2010 was 18 compared to India's 63. China's per capita electricity consumption was 2631 kWh, while India's was 597 kWh.[4]

The gap has persisted. In defence while the per capita spending in China is $182 it is less than a third of that in India. In 2019 India spent about $71 billion on defence while China as much as $261 billion. During the last ten years Chinese defence spending has more than doubled while that of India only by half. It may be argued that the Indian armed forces are more battle-hardened than the PLA but on balance the advantage is clearly with the Chinese.[5] Also, the Chinese venture capital is well entrenched in India with more than $8 billion invested in most successful Indian startups. China supplies many goods and services that India needs.[6] Just to take a recent COVID-related example, sometime early this year it was thought that one of the possible drugs for the pandemic was hydroxychloroquine (HCQ) of which India was the biggest producer accounting for almost 70 per cent of the global supply. But one of the essential ingredients of the medicine came from China. It is possible that this dependence may gradually decline but it will not happen overnight.

India is looking for a larger economic and strategic role in the Indo-Pacific region. But there also it would require fine tuning keeping in mind, on the one hand, India's strategic participation in the Quad (America-Australia-India-Japan), and then on the other, its exit from the Regional Comprehensive Economic Partnership (RCEP). One must remember that China is aggressively pursuing its economic interest in the region, leave alone strategic. In recent years ASEAN has overtaken the United States and soon it may even overtake the European Union as well as China's largest trading partner.[7] How to adjust India's Act East Policy with this frame is a huge challenge.

PLAYING BALL WITH AMERICA

Ever since President Donald Trump's rise to power, Prime Minster Modi has wholeheartedly stood by him considering the fact that not only the Indian-Americans matter in American politics but also because they constitute a huge source of support for BJP. As the COVID-19 pandemic has devastated the Trump presidency which may lead to his defeat in the forthcoming presidential election it is in India's larger interest to watch out its steps before treading into the over-hyped anti-China net spread by the Trump administration. The ultra-right pro-Trump think tank, Committee on the Present Danger: China (CPDC), which is massively manned by former military and intelligence officers, is on an overdrive to declare China as enemy *numero uno.*[8]

The US idea is to create a conducive climate for an impending Cold War 2.0. But India must carefully respond. One may recall that from the end of the Cold War until 9/11 when Islamic terror became the focal point of US global strategy, it was Japan that occupied the image of America's prime adversary. Debates in American academia centered on the impending economic wrangle between America, Japan and Western Europe, most significantly Japan.[9] China was nowhere in the picture. Like the US-Japan rivalry then, what we see today is an impending technology war between America and China. Who will beat whom in the realm of Artificial Intelligence (AI) is the question? In this twenty-first century 'great game' India is unlikely to matter. In the India-China context some may hope that when the chips will be down for India the US will come to India's rescue. But that is not how superpowers work. They take care of their interests first. One may have noted that on several occasions President Trump tended to offer mediation between India and Pakistan, or between India and China, but rarely did he take any pro-India position. At best he was diplomatically nuanced.

CONCLUSION

In the ultimate analysis, a nation will have to fend for itself. Foreign tie-ups do help but only to a limited extent. What matters most is the national strength structured on security preparations, internal stability, and economic strength. Lately, India has been suffering from many fault lines. Barring the Partition days, Indian society has never been as polarized as it is now. The Indian economy has never been worse off than what it is in now which the COVID-19 pandemic has further battered. Indians have never been as poorly informed by the state as they are now. Even such a major event like the unlawful Chinese occupation of our territory was obfuscated for months by inconsistent official statements.

Let me end this essay with a self-effacing perspective. Sometime in 1985 the London University historian Kirti Narayan Chaudhuri speaking at the Heidelberg University made a point which may be recalled here. He said that history had its course, its own philosophy, not necessarily fathomed by the decision makers of the day. By early twentieth century many thinking Brits had apprehended that the end of their Empire was in the making but they could not arrest the process. In his memoirs *Present at the Creation* (1969) the US Secretary of State, Dean Acheson, confessed that everything within America's power was done to prevent the 'fall' of China to the Communists in 1949, but America could not succeed.

How, therefore, will the India-China conflict finally end no one knows. In keeping with our academic reticence we can simply pray that these two Asian giants would not decide to fight to the finish the inevitable consequence of which is mutual destruction. To avoid that disaster let India swallow the humiliation this time but start preparing forthwith to avoid its repeat. Timely retreat is an essential element of war strategy.

NOTES

1. Partha S. Ghosh, *BJP and the Evolution of Hindu Nationalism: Savarkar to Vajpayee to Modi*, New Delhi: Manohar, 2017, pp. 437-46.
2. https://www.ncuscr.org/events/himalayas-tension
3. For the complete table, see Partha S. Ghosh, 'An Enigma that is South Asia: India versus the Region', *Asia-Pacific Review* (Tokyo), 20 (1), May 2013: 100-20.
4. Ibid.
5. Nalin Mehta, 'To Take on Chinese "Wolf Warriors", India Must Fix Military Asymmetry,' *Sunday Times of India*, New Delhi, 28 June 2020.
6. Uday Balakrishman, 'A Strategic Dealing with China', *The Hindu*, New Delhi, 2 October 2020.
7. Zorawar Daulet Singh, 'On the Economy, Don't Disengage with China', *Hindustan Times*, 28 July 2020.
8. Atul Bhardwaj and Inderjeet Parmar, 'Trump's Desperation and the Manufactured China Threat', *Economic and Political Weekly* (Mumbai), 55(31), 1 August 2020: 10-12.
9. See, Lester Thurow, *Head to Head: The Coming Economic Battle among Japan, Europe and America*, New York: William Morrow and Company, Inc., 1992.

CHAPTER 7

SAARC: Hoping Against Hope

Essay 1: SAARC: Fom ICU to Morgue?*

India is gloating at its success in sabotaging the 19th SAARC Summit scheduled to be held in Islamabad on 15-16 November 2016 by deciding to boycott it. What is even more gratifying for New Delhi is that other constituents of the grouping have followed suit, first Afghanistan, Bangladesh and Bhutan, and subsequently Maldives, Nepal and Sri Lanka. From a diplomatic standpoint it is no mean achievement given the fact that one is used to hear of India's neighbours 'ganging up' against India, but it is now Pakistan versus the rest. One is yet to know what kind of diplomatic pressure India exerted on the latter to make them toe its line but it is common sense that it was inherent in the situation. First, SAARC without India amounts to Hamlet without the Prince of Denmark. Accounting for three quarters of the region in terms of almost everything important like area (after Afghanistan's entry into SAARC in 2007 this is slightly less), population, GDP, and military expenditure, India and SAARC are virtually interchangeable. Without India the organization is defunct. Second, those who went by India's decision may be small but they also know geopolitics. Barring Afghanistan, their borders touch India's borders, not Pakistan's.

But there is a larger question. Imagine that the summit takes place as scheduled. Then, barring the homilies exchanged among the leaders and some routine resolutions passed, the entire atten-

* 'SAARC seems to have been taken to the morgue from the ICU. Here's why it needs to be revived', *Scroll.in*, 7 October 2016 <http://scroll.in/article/818357/saarc-seems-to-have-been-taken-to-the-morgue-from-the-icu-heres-why-it-needs-to-be-revived>

tion would be on how India and Pakistan thrash out their bilateral differences on the sidelines of the conference over the question of Kashmir and more generally over Pakistan-inspired terrorism. Herein lies the bane of SAARC. It is so much overshadowed by the India-Pakistan encounter that it has become nothing but a failed experiment. No wonder that intra-regional trade is as little as 4.6 per cent of the region's total international trade. Here is some comparison: it is 40 per cent in NAFTA, 26 per cent in ASEAN, and 67 per cent in EU. Further, the region accounts for about 25 per cent of the world's population but contributes barely 2.5 per cent to the global trade, that too primarily because of India.

Let us not, therefore, shed our crocodile tears at the tragedy of the summit's non-show. The two principal members of SAARC, India and Pakistan, have other ambitions. It is generally the view in India that for the failure of SAARC Pakistan is responsible. The fact is that India is equally responsible. India has found the substitute of SAARC in sub-regional and sub-regional plus cooperation looking eastward, and Pakistan has found the same by looking extra regionally westward and also towards China in a big way if the China-Pakistan Economic Corridor (CPEC) is any indication. The corridor runs through the Pakistan Occupied Kashmir right up to the Gwador Port in Balochistan. Hardly has the Summit controversy gone out of focus, the majority of SAARC members, barring Pakistan, are busy talking about the prospects of the Bay of Bengal Initiative for Multi-Sectoral Technical and Economic Cooperation (BIMSTEC) consisting of Bangladesh, India, Myanmar, Sri Lanka, Thailand, Bhutan and Nepal.

India and Pakistan, and in a lesser sense everyone else, may now wail at all diplomatic forums over the 'death' of SAARC and blaming one another of killing it. But all these thirty years of the grouping's existence the maximum they all have done is not to snap its respiratory support cord. Otherwise how can one explain that the SAARC summit meeting which is supposed to be an annual affair is still debating its 19th summit which ideally should have been its 31st? Many of the summits could not be held simply because some bilateral tension came in the way. Yet, strangely, the

SAARC constitution prohibits any discussion on bilateral matters. They spend their time and money on less important issues and that too by sheer passage of resolutions, not by their faithful implementation. Does SAARC matter in global reckoning? Minimally, to be charitable to the grouping. The latest edition of the *Encyclopaedia Britannica* in its 2011 Year Book did not even mention SAARC while listing the regional groupings from across the globe. But it did not fail to list the ASEAN, another Asian grouping.

Mark Twain once said: 'A person with a new idea is a crank until the idea succeeds'. The same is true of SAARC. It is a great idea but it has to succeed. And before that happens the cobweb that has been woven in our interstate relations will have to be cleared, which is easier said than done. Two factors matter the most, one, India's unprecedented rise yet not enough to impress its neighbours that much, and two, the shadow of China which provides a constant source of anxiety to India but which is a positive factor for the rest of the region. This dichotomy comes in the way of South Asian regional consciousness. Closely connected to this is the question of India's greatness image. People do not overlook that India is the world's largest importer of weapons while China is one of the largest exporters. In bilateral economic terms China is India's biggest trading partner. Against this background when India expects that India's neighbours must give more importance to India instead of China the diatribe sounds hollow.

The future of the South Asian region, SAARC is just one instrument, is in its peoples which the respective leaderships fear the most as reflected in the increasingly stricter visa regimes. There is no doubt that if India and Pakistan loosen these regimes there will be a huge improvement in bilateral relationship. But unfortunately the present situation is just not conducive for that. But the sooner the 19th summit is held the better. It should not be anybody's case that the present stand-off between India and Pakistan lingered indefinitely for it is pregnant with dangerous possibilities. There is no other organization than SAARC that is particularly suited to facilitate this process its general failure notwithstanding.

Essay 2: Playing the COVID Card to Sustain the SAARC Nonsense*

On 14 March 2020, typical to his style of indulging in personal diplomacy by springing surprises, Prime Minister Narendra Modi summoned a video conference. It was meant to look like a 'virtual' web-based SAARC 'summit'. In no time his diplomatic blitzkrieg enthused a set of cheer leaders in India and other places in the region to organize a few webinars to promote the idea as if the stalled SAARC process had been resumed. They may have added some variety to their lockout-induced boredom, but the actual game remained where it was. To my understanding the exercise was nothing but that of one-upmanship between India and Pakistan in which the participation of other member-countries was just a legitimizing formality.

Everything has multiple uses. Even a pandemic like COVID-19 is no exception. President Donald Trump has been proving that every day through his diplomatic offensive against China. By naming it as the original sinner in spreading the Coronavirus he has accused the Chinese of using the disease to win their war of supremacy against the Americans. Within our region, India was trying to resuscitate a dying SAARC through the expedience of COVID-19 diplomacy. Pakistan was the target, and it retaliated in kind. Who cares whether SAARC as a vehicle of peace and progress works or not?

Even at its healthiest, SAARC was a lame horse. That horse is now further debilitated by this pandemic. Under the circumstances, if some South Asian cooperation, however cosmetic, can make the horse trot again, surely that is not a bad thing. But to expect it to gallop will be asking for the moon. Some commentators tend to term this effort as the beginning of a SAARC 2.0, as if SAARC 1.0

* 'Playing the Covid-19 Card to Sustain the SAARC Nonsense', *Dhaka Tribune*, 20 May 2020, https://www.dhakatribune.com/opinion/op-ed/2020/05/20/playing-the-covid-19-card-to-sustain-the-saarc-nonsense, simultaneously carried as 'Playing the COVID-19 Card to Sustain the SAARC Nonsense', *Newsclick.in*, 20 May 2020, https://www.newsclick.in/SAARC-Indian-Pakistan-Narendra-Modi-Imran-Khan-COVID-19

was a success. Let us take stock of what exactly happened at the SAARC video meet. But before that some background may be helpful.

In my reckoning, SAARC is a failed project. An alternative view is possible provided one reconciles oneself to a change in the very definition of SAARC; that is, SAARC minus Pakistan. In so far as India is concerned, it would have loved a truncated SAARC sans Pakistan. But the problem is that it is not sure how the other members would react to such a reconfiguration, barring probably Bhutan whose foreign policy is, for all practical purposes, dictated by India. The alternate view must also have a high tolerance for the theatrics that SAARC routinely indulges in. This is something that every member state seems quite happy about. Theatricality, after all, is in South Asia's DNA.

For the purposes of diplomacy, other SAARC members would prefer to walk a tight rope rather than simply agree with what India wants. They were willing, for instance, to boycott the Pakistan-chaired 19th SAARC Summit in November 2016 to mollify India's anger after the Pakistani terror attack in Uri, but not much else beyond that. They certainly do not endorse Pakistan's actions, but they are also mindful that Pakistan is also their only leverage against Indian hegemony in the region.

Nepal has an additional technical reason too, particularly in the current context. After having chaired the 18th SAARC Summit in Kathmandu in November 2014, it has effectively become a chair-in-perpetuity unless a 19th summit is indeed held. That number itself is telling of SAARC's failure. Remember that SAARC was set up in 1985 and, procedurally, it was expected to hold a summit annually. Under normal circumstances, therefore, 2020 ought to have marked the Association's 35th summit, and yet, we find ourselves still stuck on number 19.

At the moment SAARC is caught in a technical mess. One is not sure how to characterize the 19th summit that was supposedly 'held' in Islamabad. Barring Nepal, the then SAARC chair, none of the remaining six members participated in deference to India's fury. On the one hand, Pakistani Prime Minister Nawaz Sharif 'addressed' the 19th SAARC Summit, which means that the summit was held; and yet on the other hand, he 'postponed' the summit, which means he himself understood that the summit was not to be officially recognized. Moreover, he declared that new dates would be announced soon. We are still waiting.

In technical sense, therefore, Nepal is the longest surviving chair of SAARC, having assumed that role in November 2014. One can understand its discomfiture when it says that 'a conducive environment be created soon to ensure the participation of all member states in the 19th SAARC Summit in line with the spirit of the SAARC charter'. In short, SAARC cannot move an inch until Pakistan reconvenes the 19th summit and all member-states participate in it, most notably India. Pakistan will have to bell the cat but in order to do so a conducive diplomatic climate has to be created to ensure India's participation. The condition India has set for Pakistan is an impossible one. Not only must it shun all its terrorist activities in India, but it is India alone that will certify that it has done so. See the catch?

It is against this background that one may analyse India's SAARC diplomacy in the era of COVID-19. What happened at the video meet was just a half step taken by India to gauge the regional mood. Most importantly, would Pakistan play ball? Pakistan did play ball but with a twist. Unlike other SAARC nations, which were represented at the highest level, Prime Minister Imran Khan sent his special assistant on health to represent Pakistan.

Clearly, Pakistan did not want India to steal the show and claim credit for restarting the SAARC process through a back door, especially when procedurally that task was Pakistan's in its capacity as the chair. Any objective observer of regionalism should find this India-Pakistan game of ping pong disgusting. But that is what the reality of SAARC is. In any case, the first round of COVID-SAARC diplomatic tango between India and Pakistan ended this way. In the second round, it was Pakistan's turn to take the other half step. As agreed in the 14 March video conference, a virtual meeting of the senior health officials was held on 24 April 2020 in which all the eight SAARC member-states, including India, participated.

In the overall context of the 35-year-old SAARC story, what does one make of these two exercises? If one hopes that they would contribute to end the deadlock by softening India's stand and allowing Pakistan to reconvene the 19th SAARC Summit with India in attendance, it would be too simplistic a reading of the India-Pakistan reality.

There are two questions we need to ask in evaluating the purpose and outcomes of the two meetings. One, did they effectively address the COVID fallout on regional economies, which already were showing signs of serious devastation. Two, did they contribute to break the India-Pakistan deadlock, which is at the core of SAARC's current crisis? So far as the first goal is concerned, each nation is already doing its best to arrest the economic damage to its economy. There is little that SAARC can offer. With regard to the second, the answer is: No.

To understand what a serious intervention should entail, consider what the European Union (EU) has been doing. On 8 April 2020, midway between the two SAARC COVID-related video meets, the EU came out with a comprehensive work plan on how to deal with the economic challenge posed by the pandemic. Among the many suggestions put forward by the EU was an invitation to the Eurozone to present within two weeks proposals on the economic response to the COVID-19 pandemic, and to a call to take stock of actions taken thus far so as to outline a comprehensive and coordinated economic response. It proposed to bolster the health care sector and civil protection mechanisms through fiscal measures to the tune of 3 per cent of EU's GDP.

The EU also decided to allocate 37 billion euros for a Coronavirus Response Investment Initiative to allow the hardest hit member-states to get access to financial support of up to 800 million Euros in the current year. It also launched a 750 billion Euro Pandemic Emergency Purchase Programme (PEPP) to expand the range of eligible assets under the corporate sector purchase programme (CSPP) so as to ensure that all sectors of the economy could benefit from supportive financing conditions that enabled them to absorb the Corona shock. There were many other details too in the EU plan.

In comparison, even before the SAARC proposal towards building a COVID-19 Emergency Fund could take-off, it faltered on procedural issues, a victim of diplomatic wrangling between India and Pakistan. Besides the fact that the fund was a modest one of about $19 million, to which India contributed the lion's share of $10 million, controversy arose with regard to its handling agent. To sideline Pakistan, theoretically the current chair of SAARC, it was decided that the fund would be operationalized neither by any individual member nor by the SAARC Secretariat. Instead, each contributing state would be responsible for approval and disbursement of the required funds in response to requests received from others.

On the face of it, this was a harmless arrangement. Pakistan, however, smelt a rat. It refused to contribute anything to the fund unless it was agreed upon that the operating agency would be the SAARC secretariat. Only thus, Pakistan contended, would it qualify as a SAARC initiate and pave the way to restart the stalled summit process. It is likely that Pakistan will register the support of other member-states on the matter. Pakistan's foreign minister, Shah Mahmood Qureshi, has held phone conversations with his counterparts from Bangladesh, Maldives, Nepal, and Sri Lanka. Tellingly, he did not consult his Afghan and Indian counterparts. Bhutan was ignored outright, for reasons explained above.

Qureshi's conversation with his Bangladeshi counterpart, A.K. Abdul Momen, are especially revealing here. Following the conversation, Pakistan's position on the fund was outlined in a Pakistan Foreign Office readout, which said: 'Discussing the need to share resources, it was underlined that SAARC Covid-19 emergency fund should be placed under the Secretary General of SAARC and the modalities for its utilization should be finalized through consultations at the earliest'. The current Secretary General of SAARC is the veteran Sri Lankan diplomat Esala Ruwan Weerakoon, who recently succeeded Pakistan's Amjad Hussain Sial.

The conclusion is simple. From day one, SAARC is an amphitheatre where Indian and Pakistani gladiators display their muscles and other member-states occupy the bleachers, cheering one, then the other. Their vested interest is in perpetuating the game, not in victory for either gladiator. It is a tragic truth that we South Asians love to privilege form over substance. Take the example of India's latest return to a worn-out cliché, 'self-reliance'. From the days of Tagore's *Ghare Baire* (1916, The Home and the World), through Nehruvian India's emphasis on a mixed economy, we have heard about this ideal and its many avatars. After having exhausted its stock of pompous (form over substance) schemes like 'Skill India', 'Make in India', and so on, the Modi government has returned once again to that well-worn shibboleth of self-reliance, relying cynically on the economic crisis wrought by COVID-19. If the idea presupposes the end of India's honeymoon with globalization, one would be intrigued to see how it in any way promotes regional cooperation. After all, even in the best of times, South Asian economies are competitive, not complementary.

Essay 3: SAARC: How to Negotiate the Strategic Trap?*

INTRODUCTION

The South Asian Association for Regional Cooperation (SAARC), a regional grouping comprising Afghanistan, Bangladesh, Bhutan, India, Maldives, Nepal, Pakistan and Sri Lanka, is now 35 years old. As per the SAARC constitution the organization should already have held its 34th Summit and been preparing for the 35th. Curiously, however, it has not yet been able to formalize its 19th Islamabad Summit of November 2016. On the question the organization is caught in a technical bind. In the 19th 'summit', barring Nepal, the then SAARC Chair, all the remaining six members had abstained in deference to India's fury against Pakistan's massive terrorist attack in Jammu and Kashmir's Uri town in September 2016, not even two months prior to the summit. Against this

* 'SAARC: How to Negotiate the Strategic Trap', *Policy Watch* (New Delhi), 9(5), May 2020: 21-6, https://www.rgics.org/wp-content/uploads/Policy-Watch_Indias-Place-in-the-world.pdf

background what sense one makes of the supposedly 'held' Islamabad summit? On the one hand, Pakistani Prime Minister Nawaz Sharif had 'addressed' the summit, which means that the summit was held; and yet on the other hand, he had 'postponed' the summit, which means he himself meant to announce that the summit was not to be officially recognized. He had declared that the new dates would be announced soon which has not been done so far. In short, SAARC is a lame duck now.

THEORY OF REGIONALISM

There must be something fundamentally wrong with the organization because for it is not for the first time that an annual meeting could not be held on time. The phenomenon has become the norm rather than an exception. Going by regional theory SAARC is a conceptual oddity. Its contradictions were evident even in 1985 when India and Pakistan, its two leading members, had celebrated its birth rather unenthusiastically. They would probably have been happier had the baby not been born at all. However, since other smaller nations in the region were keen about it, neither of them wanted to give the impression that it was the villain of the piece. They did join the grouping yet continued to remain vigilant about each other's moves so as not to be caught on the wrong foot. Over the years these suspicions have become sharper, and, contrary to the expectations of smaller nations, the SAARC forum has provided them with yet another opportunity to wash their dirty linen. To complicate matters, China, the elephant in the room, has exacerbated the contradictions which smaller member-nations, Pakistan in particular, have taken full advantage of to neutralize India's natural preeminence in the region.

Two basic handicaps plague the SAARC, one, strategic incongruity, and two, power asymmetry. No major regional organization in the world suffers so much from these limitations. During the Cold War, nuances notwithstanding, India was seen as pro-Soviet while Pakistan, pro-American. In the post-Cold War period, while India managed to improve its equations with the United States the China factor got further entrenched, Pakistan playing its China card more stridently to the detriment of India's power projection in the region and beyond. India indeed has made up its relations with China over the years, which now has become India's biggest trading partner, but the ghost of India's 1962 defeat in its China war haunts the Indians till this day. Unsettled border issues routinely prick India's sensitivities to the glee of most of India's neighbours, Pakistan in particular. The fact that both India and Pakistan are now nuclear powers have added to the anxiety.

So far as regional asymmetry is concerned, prior to Afghanistan's entry into SAARC in 2007, in terms of size, population, GDP, military strength, and share of the region in global trade, India accounted for almost three-fourths of the region. Afghanistan's inclusion somewhat changed the territorial reality but not in respect of other parameters. If this is compared with other regional organizations like the European Union (EU), African Union, Agadir (free trade agreement among Egypt, Jordan, Morocco and Tunisia), or Association of Southeast Asian Nations (ASEAN) it would be seen that India towers over its neighbours as in no other grouping. The only exception was NAFTA (now defunct) in terms of certain critical parameters. But, unlike SAARC, America was indisputably the predominant constituent of NAFTA. In the first place it was a superpower and second, there was no China-type factor influencing the organization. In no way could Canada or Mexico play ball with Washington. In all practical sense there was strategic congruity. Canada and Mexico could ill afford the luxury of pricking the US strategic sensitivity. Although Mexico's membership in NAFTA did annoy its neighbours like Bolivia, Uruguay and Venezuela, the economic advantages of its American partnership far outweighed those pinpricks.

BAGGAGE OF HISTORY

From the day India and Pakistan came into being in 1947 over the ruins of the British Indian Empire the two nations have been at their daggers drawn. Generally it is argued that this conflict emanates from the two fundamentally contesting theories of their nation-building strategies, namely, a two-nation theory versus a composite India theory, that is, a one-nation theory. While true to a large extent, in my understanding the conflict is even more foundational. It is rooted in their respective conceptions of identity after their independence. While India's identity was a rooted one, that of Pakistan has been in the constant search of one. Let it be underlined that both the words/phrases, Pakistan and South Asia, are just 70 odd years old, while the notion of India is eternal, it is there from the cradle days of global history. The Greek warrior Alexander came to India as early as in 326 BCE. The beginning of Christianity in India was marked as early as in 52 CE when St. Thomas had arrived in Kerala. India's western coasts had trade relations with the Arabs even in ancient and medieval times. During the Renaissance, Christopher Columbus and Vasco da Gama searched for sea routes to India. In colonial India Indology was a huge draw in Western academic circles. India was always the reference point to name new areas. Ergo, we had the Indian Ocean, West Indies, East Indies, and Indo-China. The company that pioneered the British Empire in South and Southeast Asia was called the East India Company. Even the name Indonesia was derived from Indos Nesos, 'Indian Island'. The Dutch company that traded in Indonesia was called the Dutch East India Company.

This in-built advantage of India cannot be matched by Pakistan however it may try by obliterating all references to its Indian (read Buddhist/Hindu) past as is evident from its history books that gloss over the country's ancient pre-Muslim India barring the civilizations of Harappa and Mohenjo Daro, the physical ruins of which earn substantial tourist revenue for the state. There is rampant distortion of history in the country just to show the greatness of Muslims in general and the sub-continental Muslim rulers in particular. SAARC, therefore, presupposes the overshadowing of Pakistan and the identification of the region primarily with that of India, which logically cannot go well with Pakistan's quest for identity. The resolution of this question is easy to romanticize but difficult to sell politically. Still there is no harm for hoping against hope to see how SAARC can contribute to regional peace and co-operation, or prepare at least a conducive mood for the same. Here is a brief history to put the subject in perspective.

THE GENESIS

The idea of South Asian regional cooperation was first mooted in the 1970s. During 1977-80, President Ziaur Rahman of Bangladesh suggested, let the seven states of South Asia (Afghanistan was politically unstable and in 1979 it fell under Soviet occupation) work out a cooperative arrangement to ameliorate the stark economic problems of the region. Although the proposal did not evoke much enthusiasm to start with, it caught the imagination of the regional elites once there were changes in the regional leaderships. It was the time when the political leadership of South Asia was changing hands into a new generation. In India Indira Gandhi's Congress party had been replaced by the Janata Party led by Morarji Desai, in Pakistan Zulfiqar Ali Bhutto was replaced by Zia-ul Haq, and in Sri Lanka Sirimavo Bandaranaike was replaced by Junius Jayewardene. In Bangladesh Ziaur Rahman had consolidated his position and there was no immediate threat to him from the pro-Mujib secularist forces. All these leaders had a pro-US image and, unlike their predecessors, tended to build regional relations upon new premises. In India there were talks of a 'genuine non-alignment' meaning de-staining its pro-Soviet image.

Ironically, however, the first effective step towards building SAARC was taken at a time when the political landscape of South Asia had almost returned to its earlier state. Indira Gandhi had staged a dramatic comeback in India, which coincided with the Soviet intervention in Afghanistan and the return of the US-Pakistan 'special relationship'. Indira Gandhi's virtual endorsement of the Soviet forward move in Afghanistan sharpened the strategic cleavage between India and Pakistan. Still, while all this was happening, in May 1980, Ziaur Rahman sent formal letters to the six South Asian leaders urging serious thought on their behalf for the creation of SAARC. The appeal received lukewarm endorsement. Without directly referring to the political questions and without touching upon sensitive regional issues, the leaders thought it worthwhile to explore areas of mutual economic cooperation just to begin with. It was the time when North-South dialogue had practically run its course and the global recession was increasingly crippling the world economy. Hardest hit was the oil-importing developing world to which South Asia belonged. By the mid-1970s the real growth rates had touched a low of almost two per cent. The 'second oil shock' of 1979-80 worsened the situation. In 1980, the balance of trade record of all South Asian countries was pathetic. Against this background, South-South Cooperation in general, and regional cooperation in particular, occupied high priority on the South's developmental agenda. The creation of SAARC was seemingly a matter of time.

Several meetings soon took place at the secretarial level to identify areas of cooperation. The highlight of these meetings was the evolution of a consensus that no 'bilateral or contentious' issues would be discussed. Interestingly, the first point was on India's insistence and the second, on both India's and Pakistan's, the other countries having no particular reason to worry about them. On the contrary, they would have preferred the inclusion of bilateral issues which could have given them confidence to deal with India, the colossus, which was contemptuously characterized as the 'Big Brother'. In a way, therefore, it was a diplomatic gain for India. In August 1983, the ongoing process was given a political push. At the First Foreign Ministers' Conference in New Delhi, the South Asian Regional Cooperation (SARC) Declaration was adopted. Following this the organizational structure of SAARC was finalized.

THE ORGANIZATION

In December 1985 at the first summit meeting in Dhaka SAARC was formally launched. The assembled leaders decided in favour of a council of ministers and a secretariat, certifying their enduring commitment to the organization. In February 1987, the SAARC secretariat came into being with a secretary general and four directors. Later, the SAARC council of ministers was formed consisting of the foreign ministers of respective member states. The organizational structure of SAARC was a four-tier arrangement. At the lowest level were the technical committees of experts and officials formulating programmes of action and organizing seminars and workshops. Next was the standing committee of foreign secretaries to review and coordinate the recommendations of the technical committees, which was to meet at least once a year. Above this was the foreign ministers' conference, also to be held at least once every year to grant political approval to the recommendations of the standing committees. At the apex was the summit meeting to be held annually (more frequently if required) to give political significance to the programmes. In 2007 Afghanistan was added to the group a process which was in the making since 2005.

THE RECORD

So far, eighteen summits have taken place, namely, Dhaka (1985), Bangalore (1986), Kathmandu (1987), Islamabad (1988), Male (1990), Colombo (1991), Dhaka (1993), New Delhi (1995), Male (1997), Colombo (1998), Kathmandu (2002), Islamabad (2004), Dhaka (2005), New Delhi (2007), Colombo (2008), Thimphu (2010), Male (2011), and Kathmandu (2014). About the 19th summit there is a technical confusion that we have discussed in the beginning of this essay. Notwithstanding this uneven summitry record SAARC has a fairly impressive list of meetings, seminars, studies and reports that it has sponsored. The calendar of activities released by the SAARC secretariat from time to time enumerates a large number of activities pertaining to such diverse developmental fields as agriculture, animal husbandry, horticulture, health and sanitation, forestry, population, meteorology, postal services, drug trafficking and abuse, integrated rural development, transfer of technology, sports, transport, telecommunication, women's development, trade and commerce, and others.

SAARC's activities are not confined to developmental issues only. Even such an issue as terrorism, which has been hanging fire in Indo-Pak relations for several years and has serious political overtones, has constantly received attention. Despite deep-rooted divisions among the SAARC countries over this question, they have adopted a convention against terrorism. Its highlight was the identification of offences, which 'shall be regarded as terrorist and for the purpose of extradition shall not be regarded as a political offence or as an offence inspired by political motives'. The convention provides the necessary follow-up through the signing of bilateral extradition treaties, which however have not yet been signed. In the 15th SAARC Summit held in Colombo (2008) the SAARC Convention on Mutual Legal Assistance in Criminal Matters was one of the most significant and tangible step. The convention, which was signed by the Foreign Ministers of the eight SAARC states sought to provide the legal basis that aimed to harmonize different domestic legal systems of countries which would facilitate mutual legal assistance in criminal matters, namely investigations, prosecution and resultant proceedings. The convention thus obviated the need to negotiate separate bilateral agreements with individual countries in the region, which has not been carried forward though.

SAARC's biggest success is in the field of energy cooperation and connectivity but the problem here is that they are all being operationalized at the sub-regional level involving Bangladesh, Bhutan, India and Nepal (BBIN connectivity project, for example) thereby re-conceptualizing SAARC sans Pakistan. The choice is one's own, whether to treat it as the organization's success, or its ultimate failure. Obviously the latter, objectively speaking. Also, one of the major thrusts of SAARC when it was launched was to promote free trade in the region. But after all these years of hectic brainstorming by the region's economists and other stake holders the result is virtually nil. Intra-regional trade still accounts for merely 5 per cent of the region's global trade. The hard reality is that even in the best of times, South Asian economies are competitive, not complementary. The economic integration of the region remains a pipe dream.

SAARC AND COVID-19

There was a flicker of hope recently to revive the paralysed SAARC when on 14 March 2020, against the background of the scourge of the COVID pandemic, India took the initiative to call a web-based SAARC 'summit' to address the problem. Though India and Pakistan continued to play ball on their expected lines still at least they all agreed to contribute to a common emergency fund. The respective contributions to the fund in US dollars were as follows: India, 10 million; Sri Lanka, 5 million; Pakistan, 3 million; Bangladesh, 1.5 million; Afghanistan and Nepal, 1 million each; Maldives, 200,000; and Bhutan, 100,000: total US$ 21.8 million. Two negative points, however, haunt. One, there is still no agreement over following one single procedure in terms of disbursing the funds, and two, compared to, for examplc, the European Union, the SAARC fund is too small to be meaningful. A similar EU fund goes into hundreds of billions of dollars and, administratively, it is far better organized.

SOME CONCLUDING THOUGHTS

One does not need to be either a diplomat or a politician to expect a few basic things from the SAARC. Agreed that to ask it to discuss bilateral or contentious issues would still be a tall order. But one can start with a couple of innocent confidence building moves. At academic and Track II levels the region has had enough discussions on confidence building measures (CBMs) which mostly have concentrated on avoiding accidental nuclear wars or escalating border skirmishes. Let the agenda be taken to the people's level now. South Asia is a civilizational space where all kinds of sects and ideologies have coexisted, not always peacefully, but not that unmanageably either. One is not asking for the reordering of the present state system which would amount to asking for the moon. All that one is asking is to take two small steps, one, more tourist flows, particularly between India and Pakistan, and two, more intra-regional academic exchanges. The region's obsession with security has made the region one of the most insecure in the world.

It is high time that SAARC is rescued from its impending collapse. Let the Indian leadership be statesmanlike by making the situation conducive for Pakistan to summon the stalled 19th summit without insisting upon it to officially renounce terrorism (such promises were made in the past as well). Let India accept the reality that it is not impossible to deal with a terrorism-promoting Pakistan. India has done so in the past. Pakistan's presence in the SAARC will not make it renounce terrorism as its policy tool but it would, at least potentially, temper its adventurism. A regular SAARC summit together with a relaxed visa regime that boosts tourism and academic exchanges would go a long way to melt the cloud, hopefully. Let this new regime be tried for just five years. Heavens will not fall if it does not work. Let us concede that most big accomplishments start with small dreams.

CHAPTER 8

Negotiating an Uncertain World

Essay 1: 'It's a Mad, Mad, Mad, Mad World'*

Why choose the title of a 1963 American comedy to headline this month's column? At first glance, the plot of '*It's a Mad, Mad, Mad, Mad World*' has nothing to do with what I am going to discuss. And yet, in one essential sense, it drives home my point. Just like the movie hovered around the madcap pursuit of $350,000 in stolen cash by a diverse and colourful group of eleven strangers, the 193 nations of the world today are chasing security and material success without really achieving either. International and regional systems are in a quandary and hypernationalism across continents is wreaking havoc on institutions that were created to build an orderly world after the Second World War.

On international security, the more the world claims it has eradicated the menace of international Islamic terror, the bigger that challenge becomes. This past October the US security forces killed the dreaded ISIS chief Abu Bakr al-Baghdadi. American President Donald Trump assured everyone that the world would now be 'a much safer place'. But we had received much the same American assurance just eight years ago, when the United States had elimi-

* 'It's a Mad, Mad, Mad, Mad World', *Dhaka Tribune*, 24 November 2019, https://www.dhakatribune.com/opinion/longform/2019/11/24/it-s-a-mad-mad-mad-mad-world, simultaneously carried as 'It's a Mad, Mad, Mad, Mad World', *Newsclick.in*, 23 November 2019, https://www.newsclick.in/It%E2%80%99s-Mad-Mad-Mad-Mad-World, reproduced in *Mainstream* (New Delhi), 57(51), 7 December 2019: 22-5.

nated Osama bin Laden and dismantled Al-Qaeda. The ISIS, however, emerged from the ashes of Al-Qaeda almost immediately. Perhaps it is time to replace that old saying, 'the king is dead, long live the king': 'terrorism is dead, long live terrorism'.

The world has learnt to treat the symptoms of terrorism but is unable to address the disease itself. The days of running with the hares and hunting with the hounds are probably not gone. One does not need to delve into the intricacies of how US military-industrial interests have dictated American policy in West Asia to recognize that the invasion of Iraq was grossly unethical. On totally unfounded (if not engineered) assumptions that Saddam Hussein had amassed stockpiles of Weapons of Mass Destruction (WMD), Iraq, and in the process the entire region, was devastated beyond recognition. It is all fine that bin-Laden and al-Baghdadi have been eliminated but has the world system done anything to penalize the original sinners?

At some point in the 1950s the regional security champions considered it prudent to decentralize the job of international security in order to make it more efficacious. Western Europe pioneered the idea by establishing the European Common Market (ECM) in 1957. In due course, the ECM grew into the European Union (EU), the Euro Zone, and the Schengen Treaty. Soon, the EU contagion spread to other continents. But under its own weight, the experiment is facing virtual collapse today. Take the case of India. After getting disillusioned with SAARC, it started romancing ASEAN with such policy pronouncements as 'Look East', 'Act East' and 'Act Indo-Pacific'. But when the crunch came to sign the 16-member Regional Comprehensive Economic Partnership (RCEP) it backtracked on the grounds that it did not have enough competitiveness in specific trade items to take on challenges emanating from China, Australia, or New Zealand. Was this reality unknown all these years that one would have to reach the signing stage to back out?

This is true not only of India but almost all nations. Some time ago I did a rough calculation to see how many countries were members of how many groups. When I totaled the memberships, it was roughly 400, but the total number of nations in the world was only 192, implying that many countries were members of multiple organizations. Here is a list of some such organizations: Agadir, African Union, Arab League, ASEAN, ASEAN Regional Forum, BASIC, BIMSTEC, BRICS, CACM, CC, GCC, CEFTA, CIS, ECOWAS, EU, EurAsEC, EFTA, G-8, G-20, IBSA, NAFTA (now defunct), RCEP, SAARC, SCO, and UNASUR. Inter-national trading arrangements are a grand hotchpotch now. And although the World Trade Organization (WTO) determines the broad contours of global trade, there are well over 400 Regional Trade Agreements (RTA) that complicate its operations.

National leaders crisscross the globe, busily attending meetings for one or another of these organizations. They use the resultant publicity in print and electronic media back home to sidetrack people's attention from their day-to-day domestic problems. Prime Minister Modi's frequent foreign visits also provide ample fodder to cartoonists and stand-up comics. One such stand-up quip goes: 'Our multinational prime minister visited India yesterday on a seven-day official trip'.

The underlying story behind this mushrooming of regional organizations is that there is an acute desperation on the part of most nations to do something quickly to arrest the growing popular disenchantment with an existing growth model that is weighted heavily in favour of an increasingly small section of people. According to recent studies, the richest one percent of Indians own 58.4 per cent of the country's wealth, while the richest 10 per cent own as much 80.7 per cent. Given the noise level of democratic politics, politicians across the board rely on two ways to contain these frustrations. One, by putting the blame on international factors; and two, by diverting people's attention using divisive and majoritarian issues such as religion and culture. Appealing to base human instincts to divide and rule is a well-tested political strategy. Even the developed Christian countries have not been able to fully escape the religion trap. But since their democracies typically have deeper historical roots, this problem has yet to become unmanageable.

The Islamic world, however, has become a prime victim, as is evident from the unprecedented growth of Islamic fundamentalism in a large number of Muslim countries. That it would eventually degenerate into terrorism is historical wisdom and already the case in many places. As a result, the misdeeds of tiny groups of Islamist terrorists are making Muslims at large suffer from a sense of siege. Today, Muslims as a community are despised across the globe; yet few care to note that the victims of Islamist terror are mostly Muslims. Strangely, however, the most callous about this phenomenon are the so-called leaders of the Muslim world, particularly those who can matter the most as they are sitting on huge reserves of oil and gas, something which the international economy is critically dependent upon. Leave alone doing anything effective to stem the rot, they are indirectly promoting the phenomenon by fanning fundamentalism at the mass level. Many of them are socially and politically oppressive and provide no space for democratic freedoms. Any free sentiment is muzzled in the bud. The brutal killing of the Saudi journalist Jamal Khashoggi by the Saudi secret police is an open secret.

The latest entrant to the game of religious politics is Hindu-majority India, which has started displaying symptoms of Hindu militancy heretofore unheard of. Ever since Hindutva (political Hinduism) has been ascendant in Indian politics, and particularly after the BJP came to power in 2014, Hinduism has lost its philosophical and spiritual moorings and become perverse and jingoistic. Since any jingoism has to have an enemy for binary reasons, Muslims have become its *bête noire.* In the beginning, Christians were also targets, but for tactical reasons the focus is now entirely on Muslims. Anti-Christian visibility is fraught with risk: America is Christian and its three-million plus prosperous Indian American community has a huge stake in maintaining good Indo-US relations.

The Hindutva madness is reflected both in the BJP's politics and in its cultural statements. Muslims constitute about 15 per cent of India's population, but they are increasingly becoming political non-entities. In 1980, when the BJP was launched (earlier it was Bharatiya Jana Sangh), there were 49 Muslim Members of Parliament (MP). The two BJP MPs in that parliament were both Hindu. Today, when the party has an absolute majority in parliament with 303 seats out of 545, Muslim MPs number only 27; not one belongs to the BJP. In the state of Uttar Pradesh (UP), historically the hub of Muslim politics, the political face of Muslims is now pathetic. Yogi [meaning: a Hindu saint who has renounced all mundane allurements] Adityanath (whose real name is Ajay Singh Bisht), known for his fire-eating anti-Muslim statements during the election campaign, is now UP's chief minister. Prior to the election, criminal charges were framed against him for making those statements as they had violated not only the election code but also certain provisions of the Indian constitution. Upon becoming chief minister, Bisht summarily closed all those cases. The underlying political message is clear: Hindutva fanaticism trumps the law.

In the cultural realm, particularly in the way in which the cow is being venerated or in the way Hindu mythology is being glorified beyond proportion, Hinduism, now increasingly indistinguishable from Hindutva, resembles a tribal, animistic religion. The cow is a traditionally revered animal among Hindus but of late this reverence has degenerated into a frenzy. In the process, the Indian cow (yes, not foreign cow) is having a gala time. She can according to her sweet will jaywalk on city streets, become a traffic hazard on national highways, and rampage through standing crops. If a cow gets killed in a traffic accident the driver has more to be worried about than if he had run over a pedestrian. In the latter case, he would be taken to court; in the former, he may receive fatal mob justice on the street itself.

And so, in the digitally modern and 5-trillion-dollar-economy-aspiring India, cow dung and cow urine have become the country's new supercomputer chips. According to many BJP leaders and party supporters, an Indian cow's excreta will cure cancer, hypertension, and diabetes. A touch of her body will control blood pressure. The latest in this litany of nonsense is that her milk contains gold, which is why it is yellowish in colour. One of the BJP loudmouths went overboard on TV to even claim that cow dung is as valuable as diamonds. I now wait for the day when Indian banks will start offering loans against mortgaged cow milk or cow excreta! A hilarious footnote to this cow story is its anti-climax in Kashmir. By abrogating Article 370, the Indian state has legitimized beef eating in this Muslim-majority state. Under the Jammu & Kashmir Reorganisation Act, which has bifurcated the state into two Union Territories, the Indian government has repealed 153 state laws. Among those repealed laws is the 157-year old Ranbir-Penal-Code-dictated beef ban.

Hindutva fanaticism is playing havoc with India's scientific temper, one of Pandit Nehru's most cherished values. Today, it is trumpeted ad nauseam that primitive Hindus had plastic surgery, Internet, test tube babies, missiles, aircrafts, aerodromes, pen-drives, remote sensing, and much else! It seems that had there been Nobel prizes in ancient times 90 per cent of them would have gone to the Hindus. No less important a person than India's education minister, Ramesh Pokhriyal, has announced that it is astrology, and not science, which should be given more importance in school and university curricula. A few years ago, Chicago Professor Wendy Doniger's book *The Hindus: An Alternative History* was attacked by the Hindu right in America, who insisted that it defamed the followers of the faith. Her Indian publisher was forced to withdraw the book from circulation in India.

The Hindutva hoopla has now reached another realm, putting a religious stamp on two languages. Thus, Sanskrit is now the monopoly of Hindus, and Urdu is a Muslim language. Recently, when a Muslim scholar was appointed an assistant professor of Sanskrit in Banaras Hindu University (BHU), his colleagues (and many students) protested vehemently, as if knowledge of Sanskrit is the birthright of Hindus (read Brahmins, in most cases) alone. But the hypocrisy of the Brahmin community is such that when the Mughals were in power, they helped Dara Shikoh translate the 52 Upanishads. During British rule, when some Europeans developed an interest in Indology, the Sanskrit-knowing Brahmins did not mind teaching them. They conveniently redefined *mlechchha* (untouchable, which included Christians in the contemporary sense) in violation of the injunction of the *Skanda Purana* that had ordained that if a Brahmin taught Sanskrit to a *mlechchha* the teacher would be excommunicated. After all, their pupils belonged to the ruling class.

The mirror image of Sanskrit is Urdu, about which the Hindu right's central narrative is straightforward and wrong: It is an alien language identifiable only with Muslims who are outsiders. Any student of the history of Urdu language knows that it has evolved from Hindi. This thesis was authoritatively argued by Pakistani scholar Tariq Rahman in his 2011 book *From Hindi to Urdu: A Social and Political History*. Besides, Urdu is designated as one of the 22 Indian languages in the Eighth Schedule of the Indian Constitution. Yet, Panjab University, in a wisdom all its own, recently designated it a foreign language. It is possible that it was done inadvertently but given the anti-Muslim/anti-Urdu hysteria that has gripped north India, such accidents have greater propensity of occurrence. (Parenthetically, let both Hindi enthusiasts and Urdu baiters note that the greatest Mughal emperor, Akbar, spoke Bhojpuri.)

Postscript: Against the background of the beef ban lunacy in India, which has caused several cases of lynching over alleged eating, possessing, or trading in beef, it is amusing to note that one of the best breeds of beef-producing cow in America is called 'Brahman'. The Brahman's origin is traced to the mid-nineteenth century, when four Indian breeds, namely, Gujarat, Gir, Ongole (now in Pakistan), and Krishna Valley, were crossbred with certain American varieties. In 1924, the American Brahman Breeders Association (ABBA) was registered to promote the interests of this beef packing industry. ABBA is now headquartered in Houston, where Prime Minister Narendra Modi, a great anti-beef crusader, had his grand 'Howdy, Modi' extravaganza this past September.

Essay 2: When a Superpower Loses*

Big powers do not lose wars, they lose interest in wars. That is how they explain their defeats. By the early 1970s, when it was more or less clear that the Americans would not win their war in Vietnam, they popularized the notion of 'Vietnamizing' the war. The idea was to tell the world that it was time for the Vietnamese people to

* 'When a Superpower Loses', *Dhaka Tribune*, 15 March 2020, https://www.dhakatribune.com/opinion/op-ed/2020/03/15/when-a-superpower-loses, simultaneously carried as 'When a Superpower Loses', *Newsclick.in,* 11 March 2020, https://www.newsclick.in/When-Superpower-Loses

manage their own affairs. It was as if the Vietnamese had invited the Americans to solve their problems in the first place. But since it was 'America the Superpower', the idea had its takers in the global media and among academics. Mercifully, there was no social media then, otherwise it would have gone viral overnight.

No such phrase is in circulation now with respect to America's withdrawal from the Afghan War, though in some sense it means much the same, provided we agree with the Americans that the Taliban are the only spokesmen for all Afghans. The bilateral deal was struck on 29 February 2020, following 18 months of interactions between the US Special Representative, Zalmay Khalilzad, and the Taliban. It is clear that between the two sides, it was the Americans who were keener to strike a deal, not the Taliban.

Ideally, there should have been at least three parties to the deal, if not more: the US, the Afghan government, and the Taliban. But over the months, the Afghan government's involvement was systematically marginalized. After all, the Afghan government troops were not posing any challenge to the American troops; the challenge was only from the Taliban. As a result, in real terms the government mattered little. But what particularly irked the latter was that it was virtually taken for a ride; so much so, that the Americans seemed to commit on behalf of the government that 5,000 Taliban prisoners in government custody would be released. One will have to wait and watch how the intra-Afghan dialogue, scheduled to commence from 10 March 2020 (seemingly put on hold due to intra-government strains), proceeds. In all likelihood, basking in the glory of their 'victory', the Taliban will dominate the negotiations from a position of strength and increasingly ignore the government.

In short, America has left Afghanistan at the mercy of the Taliban, marking the complete collapse of its commitment to eradicate international, read Islamist, terrorism from the face of the earth. In the aftermath of 9/11, almost the entire world was behind George Bush in his anti-terrorist 'crusade'. But America squandered that opportunity. Its die-hard supremacist approach to global politics blinded it to such an extent that it reverted back to its age-old game of bullying anyone and everyone who even remotely questioned its hegemony. Libya, Iraq and Afghanistan were reduced to utter chaos without achieving even the semblance of what America, and the liberal world at large, had longed for.

The present Taliban deal seals that failure with ominous possibilities for a broader West-Central-South Asian region that is already rife with all kinds of sectarian tensions. And yet, most analysts have shifted attention elsewhere, explaining the deal in terms of America's domestic politics, in particular President Donald Trump's bid to play-to-the-galleries, keeping in view the November 2020 presidential polls. But if a superpower plays petty electoral games at the cost of international order, there are reasons to question its very claim to holding to that status. It is true that during the previous election, candidate Trump had promised his prospective voters that if elected to power he would end the Afghan war. Some might say he is, therefore, duty-bound now to redeem his pledge. But does that befit a responsible great power?

A comparison here with the American retreat from Vietnam in the seventies may be instructive. In Vietnam, too, America retreated leaving the field open to the Vietnamese Communists. But the circumstances and the potential consequences of the decision were not as ominous. In international security terms, America left Vietnam to a potentially stable and progressive regime that was not expected to jeopardize the regional order. In fact, on the contrary, the Vietnamese had the wherewithal to stabilize the situation in the region (admittedly, an impending conflict of interest with China would lead to war in 1979). In contrast, an Afghanistan under the Taliban has all the attributes to destabilize an already explosive region.

Unlike the Vietnamese Communists, the Taliban are fanatically Islamist and will take every possible step to repress Afghan women and nip in the bud anything even remotely liberal in nature. In that sense, Pakistan has to be especially worried because its politics have been vertically divided between progressives and traditionalists from its very inception. The ten years under General Zia-ul Haq (1978-88) witnessed the worst form of conservative ascendancy and many retrograde Islamic laws passed during the decade remain in place. Today, Pakistan is one of the most unstable nations in the world, accused of being a key breeding ground of international Islamic terrorism. That it is also one of worst victims of such terrorism tells its own story.

Given this reality, Pakistan may love to appropriate the Taliban's victory as its own, but at some future date it may well have to face another Bangladesh-type secessionist demand. Any thinking Pakistani, familiar with the controversy surrounding the legality of the Durand Line and its division of Pashtun dominated areas, ought to wonder: When will Pashtun nationalism ask for its pound of flesh?

There are three factors, in particular, that Pakistanis may like to ponder. One, the spectre of an impending civil war in Afghanistan involving multiple warring factions. These include intra-Taliban factions with or without the involvement of al-Qaeda and the IS (notwithstanding any commitment the Taliban might have made to the Americans), as well as intra-government conflicts between the pro-Ashraf Ghani and pro-Abdullah Abdullah factions. Two, the youth bulge. About three-fourths of Afghans are below the age of 35 and in our internet age these youth promise to be a dangerously unpredictable lot. Finally, the fate of Khyber Pakhtunkhwa (formerly North-West Frontier Province). Combine the first and second factors and they could well challenge Pakistan's federal polity. A future irredentist demand for a greater Afghanistan that will include Khyber Pakhtunkhwa may not be as fantastical as it seems.

In any case, the re-emergence of a militantly Islamist Taliban is bound to exacerbate regional tensions because India is also in the midst of an unprecedented wave of Hindutva aggressiveness. As the siege mentality of its 14 per cent Muslim community (about 200 million in absolute terms) increases, so does the risk of broader India-Pakistan-Bangladesh tensions. To add to the complexity are the two Buddhist supremacist states of Sri Lanka and Myanmar. The common factor between Hindutva India on the one hand, and these two Buddhist nations, on the other, is that they all view their Muslim minority populations with distrust. It is only a brave augur who will predict stability in South Asia. It is against this background that the American exit from Afghanistan has to be read.

One last point. The fact remains that the Taliban were America's creation in the first place. The conventional wisdom is that once one creates a Frankenstein, one is bound to be eventually devoured by it. But since the creator in this case is a superpower, it can escape this inevitability by pushing someone else forward to take the call. The natural choice is the Afghan government because it happens to be the weakest of the three.

Postscript: Stan Lee's popular comic *Spider-Man* popularized the Peter Parker principle: 'With great power comes great responsibility.' But great powers are also profoundly reckless. Here is how America behaved during the Bangladesh liberation war. Secretary of State Henry Kissinger had characterized Yahya Khan in private as 'that butcher' who unleashed a reign of terror in East Pakistan. But what did Kissinger do?

When the US Consul in Dhaka, Archer Blood, repeatedly informed him about the pogrom being unleashed by the Pakistani junta and reminded him about America's 'international moral obligations to condemn [the] genocide', Kissinger, unmoved, remarked: 'That Consul in Dacca does not have the strongest nerves'. President Richard Nixon concurred.

To no one's surprise, Blood was promptly recalled to the State Department and assigned an insignificant desk. He retired years later; his career effectively throttled because of the telegrams he sent from Dhaka. In contrast, the 'legendary diplomat' Henry Kissinger won the 1973 Nobel Peace Prize for his success in inking the US-Vietnam ceasefire (which collapsed soon). By then, Bangladesh had already won its freedom, surviving a massive genocide in which hundreds of thousands of Bengalis perished.

Essay 3: 'Who Will Guard the Guards?'*

The brutal killing of George Floyd, an African-American, by the Minneapolis (Minnesota) Police Department has made me to return to the question that my former colleague, the Late Nirmal

* 'Who Will Guard the Guards', *Dhaka Tribune*, 23 June 2020, https://www.dhakatribune.com/opinion/op-ed/2020/06/23/op-ed-who-will-guard-the-guards, simultaneously carried as 'Who Will Guard the Guards', *Newsclick.in,* 21 June 2020, https://www.newsclick.in/Who-Will-Guard-the-Guards.

Mukarji, had asked some thirty years ago in an article in *Seminar* (October 1990): 'Who will guard the guards?'. Mukarji was India's last ICS officer and retired as India's cabinet secretary in 1980. During our conversations in the early 1980s, when we both were fellows at Delhi's Centre for Policy Research, I remember his deep concern about the deteriorating standards of Indian policing and the systematic subordination of the service to the political class. Being almost thirty years younger to him, his words had dinned into my ears like the truth of the Vedas. I wonder how he would have viewed things today had he still been alive.

Thirty years is a long time in politics. And yet, little in the debate has changed, whether it is India or the United States. In 1997, former CBI Director Joginder Singh lamented that, 'It would be a travesty of justice to expect policemen to be angels in such an atmosphere and to hold them responsible for all that is happening in the country. Police are violent because the society permits it and even wants the police to suppress violence with equal violence.'

Now consider Donald Trump's words. In the context of the America-wide protests against the George Floyd incident he unequivocally recommended the following in a 1 June 2020 video conference with governors and law enforcement officials: 'You have to dominate. If you don't dominate, you're wasting your time. They're going to run over you, you're going to look like a bunch of jerks.' He then reportedly scolded the governors and threatened to intervene in their states without, of course, considering if he had the authority to do so. But his message was clear: 'We're strongly looking for arrests, we do have to get much tougher.'

Since there is so much talk lately in India about Indian-American bonhomie, particularly at the highest levels, it would be instructive see whether the two nations are actually comparable. Are the comparisons confined merely to their respective leaders' mutual hugs, or do they stem from competitive failures in ensuring societal harmony because of majoritarian politics; in Trump's case white supremacism, in Modi's case Hindu machismo? A more comprehensive comparison between the two nations may help remove many obfuscations that blur our vision.

For starters, much as we may love to bask in the reflected glory of our past, neither are we *vishvaguru* (wisdom giver to the world) nor are we a superpower. The more we trumpet our ancient 'wonders', the more we expose ourselves to ridicule. If we do figure in international headlines, it is usually for all the wrong reasons. The George Floyd episode has given the world yet another opportunity to point to our own failings alongside America's and, in the process, those of other democratic societies similarly afflicted. If inter-racial bitterness is a bane for America so too are inter-caste and inter-religious conflicts for India.

Barring these murky commonalities, India and America are very different. India's per capita income is $2,200, America's is $65,000. Population density in India is 412 per sq. km, in America it is 34. GDP-wise, the numbers are $2.9 trillion versus $21.5 trillion. On defence spending, $71 billion vis-à-vis $732 billion. Beyond these material parameters, India has just 73 years of democratic experience against 233 for America. And perhaps most tellingly, it is Indians who flock to America for jobs and naturalization, not the other way round. Those of us who ridicule poor Bangladeshi migrants in India and label them 'termites' ought to take note of this.

There are historical contradictions as well. In 1776, when Americans declared independence from Britain, the latter were just starting their 190-year-long domination of Indians. The battle of Plassey had been fought only nineteen years earlier. By 1787, when the Americans were drafting the first written constitution in the world, the East India Company had already fought two colonial wars against Mysore. It would fight and win another two by the end of the century. In the following hundred years, first the East India Company and then the United Kingdom would establish effective control over all of South Asia. In the corresponding period, America resolved its federal problem in favour of an indissoluble federation.

Across a longer historical arc the American experience is of course less of a match. India has a history that spans multiple millennia, while American history is barely five hundred years old. No wonder, then, that the Indian federal experiment, unlike America's, is mindboggling in its diversity. It has emerged out of both centrifugal and centripetal tendencies of the past two thousand years. The political scientists Susanne and Lloyd Rudolph had famously characterized India as a 'nation of regions'. The America experience, in contrast, is largely centripetal thanks to its changing frontiers fuelled by westward expansion, a phenomenon that has no parallel in the world.

India's linguistic diversity is also maddening compared to the still primarily monolingual reality of the United States. English is the language of America, although it has never officially been declared as such. In recent years there have been demands to declare Spanish as a second language in some states, but that is all. Before the United States was launched there was also talk of declaring German as the official language of Pennsylvania. But it found limited traction. In fact, the proposal only asked for German translations of all government documents to accommodate Pennsylvania's large community of German-speakers.

For all their differences, India and the US share one important feature that ought to compel comparisons and mutual learning. That common feature is their weakness to build inclusive societies. Both are afflicted by the disease of majoritarianism and the symptoms are becoming more and more virulent. In America, it is expressed through white supremacism; in India, through Hindutva chauvinism. In America, African-Americans are at the receiving end; in India, the Scheduled Castes (Dalits) and Scheduled Tribes as well as the religious minorities, most notably, Muslims.

To be sure, the problem does not lie in their respective constitutions, which have adequate safeguards against discrimination, nor in the provisions that have been made for affirmative action or positive discrimination. Instead, the problem lies in the manner in which racist-religious politics plays out in both countries. The current global conservative ascendancy feeds the process. The only redeeming feature is that the liberal (an abusive term among sections in India now) publics in both the societies continue to battle for change, pushing in particular for structural reforms of the law and order machinery.

In America, public pressure now appears so strong that serious questions are being asked about police funding. The present practice of arming the police with army-surplus weapons is under the scanner for it has made the American police the most heavily armed police force in the world. In the larger context, the taming of the gun lobby is also on the agenda. Much, of course, will depend upon how these demands are articulated in the forthcoming presidential debates and upon who ultimately wins, and with what promises.

In India, demands for police reform have a long history. They have been institutionalized through successive police commission reports, none of which are short of remedial suggestions. But political indifference, if not outright opposition, has always come in the way. It was as early as 1981 that a Police Commission Report highlighted the gravity of the problem of communalism in the Indian police force. Tasked with inquiring into the communal riots in Bhiwandi, Jalgaon and Mahad in Maharashtra in 1969, the Report passed severe strictures against the special investigation squads that had been set up to investigate crimes committed in the course of these riots. It observed that these squads had 'acted in a partial and biased manner against one community [Muslims]'.

Years later, a 1999 study conducted by senior police officer Vibhuti Narain Rai showed that Indian Muslims had little trust in police interventions in riot situations; they preferred the army instead. The same is evidently true in India today. In some sense, the danger is endemic, for alongside the communalization of the police force there are also clear indications of its politicization. Many suspect and fear that a similar process is unfolding in the Indian armed forces as well. God forbid such processes attain completion. For India will then have reached a point of no return. Pakistan's experience offers grim warning. The only hope against such a runaway consolidation of power are our still vibrant, albeit beleaguered, public sphere, and the handful of standup comedians, who bravely and unstintingly speak comic truth to ruthless power.

Postscript: George Floyd had his forerunner thirty years ago in Rodney King, another African-American. The news of his brutalization at the hands of the Los Angeles Police Department led to massive race riots in Cincinnati, Cleveland, Detroit, and Newark. Contemporary India has faced similar Hindu-Muslim riots. The

Provincial Armed Constabulary (PAC) of UP and the Bihar Military Police (BMP) have been accused of siding with Hindu rioters. Curfews in many cases turned out to be 'comparative curfews', meaning further harassment for Muslims. In the 1989 Bhagalpur riots, it was found that the Hindu police not only did not quell the riots, but they actually participated in them. Allegedly, they did not even spare the families of their Muslim colleagues.

Still worse, as has been noted by historian Gyanendra Pandey in the case of Bihar, police records were meticulously destroyed to permanently foil any future inquiry. Given the current communal reality of Indian politics, no one should be surprised if police investigations into the communal riots that rocked Delhi in the last week of February 2020 are shoddily conducted. And let us also not forget that the raging fires and the loss of over fifty lives did not even register on Donald Trump, then in the midst of his official visit to India. But then Trump, like his host, is no apologist for inter-racial harmony, in his own country or elsewhere.

Essay 4: The American Election: Federal Experiences of Two Democracies*

America's presidential election is around the corner. Though a routine political event, its significance is much wider. Whatever we may say about the fading shine of America as a superpower, its worth as an underwriter of global order remains undeniable. Unsurprisingly, therefore, who will become the next US President is speculated upon all over the world with a share-market level of curiosity.

* 'A Tale of Two Democracies', *Dhaka Tribune*, 27 October 2020, https://www.dhakatribune.com/opinion/op-ed/2020/10/27/op-ed-the-american-election-federal-experiences-of-two-democracies, simultaneously carried as 'The American Election: Federal Experiences of Two Democracies', *Newsclick.in*, 26 October 2020, https://www.newsclick.in/the-us-election-federal-experince-of-two-democracies

The election is slated for 3 November. The process, however, has already begun with what is called 'early voting'. The system has been designed to accommodate those voters who may, for one justifiable reason or another, find it difficult to vote on the day of election. Many Western democracies, as well as Thailand, follow this practice. Although not designed with COVID-19 in mind, early voting has been welcomed by many who worry about the added risk of exposure because of crowding on 3 November. According to the *Washington Post,* until 19 October about 36 million Americans had availed themselves of the early voting option, which accounted for 76 per cent of the total early votes registered in the 2016 election.

America is essentially a two-party system and the result will effectively be known on 3 November itself. But because the process is technically indirect, the official outcome will not be arrived at until votes in the Electoral College are tallied on 14 December. And it is only on 6 January 2021 that the result will be formally announced and on 20 January that the new presidency will be inaugurated.

The American system is structured in such a way that the candidate who gets the higher number of popular votes may not necessarily win the election. In the 2016 election, Hillary Clinton polled 2,868,686 votes more than Donald Trump. Still, the latter won because he got 304 electoral votes compared to Clinton's 227. All those in India who think that the American-style presidential system is the cure for India's problem-afflicted parliamentary system should do their homework better.

It is intriguing why the Americans have retained this faulty system from as early as 1789, when their first president, George Washington, was elected. The answer is to be found in the nation's unflinching faith in federalism. America has gifted to the world not only its first written constitution, but also federalism as a model of government.

In the late eighteenth century, when the thirteen British colonies (represented today by the number of stripes in the American national flag) decided to fight their colonial master, they did so without a clear notion about how to politically organize themselves if they succeeded in driving the British out. Being ethnically diverse for having seen different waves of immigration from Europe, these colonies were often suspicious of one another, their common cause against Britain notwithstanding.

In 1783, they defeated the British and four years later drafted their constitution. To accommodate their mutual suspicions, however, they had to work out two complex compromises. The larger colonies wanted the president to be elected through popular votes so that they could control political power. This was known as the Virginia Plan. The smaller colonies, ever suspicious of their bigger counterparts, demanded that each colony be considered equal so that everyone's interests were protected. This was known as the New Jersey Plan.

The impasse was resolved through the creation of a bicameral legislature, that is, the US Congress. The lower house, the House of Representatives (popularly called Congress), would satisfy the principles of the Virginia Plan, while the upper house, the Senate, would meet the ideals of the New Jersey Plan. It is this history that explains why the US Senate is the most powerful 'second chamber' in the world.

The Electoral College (EC), which was improvised to elect the president, would comprise the total membership of the House of Representatives plus the total membership of the Senate. Later, the District of Columbia, that is, Washington DC, the capital, was permitted to send three members to the House of Representatives, albeit with restricted voting rights. At present, the EC has 538 members: 435 (House Representatives) plus 100 (Senators) plus 3 (Representatives). At first glance this division may appear to favour the House, but we should note that 12 of 50 American states are so thinly populated that they each send just one or two Representatives to the House but elect as many as 24 Senators.

There was one other important form of legislative engineering during this period. The question arose as to what ought to be done about the millions of slaves in American society. The southern states, where most of the slaves were located, wanted the number of their seats in the House to be decided by counting these slaves as well. But the northern states wanted them to be excluded for the purposes of census so that they could outmanoeuvre the slave owing states, primarily to protect their economic interests. Neither side asked for the slaves to be treated as equal American citizens.

This controversy was resolved through a three-fifths compromise. Irrespective of the number of slaves in any particular state, for the purposes of the census, every five slaves would be counted as three citizens. This calculus would then be used to determine the size of representation in the House of Representatives. It was as a result of such machinations that the state was enshrined as a fundamental unit of political power.

And it is for this reason that although most of the national-level polls predict a much larger vote share for Democratic challenger Joe Biden, the result of the election itself is far from a foregone conclusion. Recent history is a useful reminder. Biden and his team know well from the Clinton-Trump election of 2016 that a popular landslide may yet prove insufficient in securing the Electoral College. There can be other technical complications as well, as was exemplified by Democrat Al Gore's loss to Republican George Bush Jr in 2000. Although Gore had polled half a million more votes than Bush, the latter got the support of 30 states vis-à-vis Gore's 20. Still, the Electoral College votes were split virtually down the middle: Bush got 271 against Gore's 267 (the victory mark was 270).

A complex legal battle ensued over whether there ought to be a recount in Florida, where the margin of Bush's victory was wafer thin. To this day, many think that in not pushing his legal case for a recount more aggressively, Gore behaved in much too gentlemanly a manner. My personal take on the matter is that Al Gore is one of the greatest Democrats produced in recent times. His dignified acceptance of the legal verdict following a complicated tug of war over electoral laws underlined his commitment to established rules and regulations, which should be the essence of democracy.

When it comes to national power-sharing in a federation, therefore, what matters most is whether and to what extent the rights of constituent states are respected and protected. America's democracy passes the test reasonably well, although there is in recent years a worrying tendency towards White supremacism, concentration of power in office of the President, and a tilt towards plutocracy. There are, of course, other problems too, none more dangerous than the phenomenon of post-truth and the manipulation of social media, trends ably identified by the recent Netflix documentary, *The Social Dilemma.* One may recall that one of Trump's 2016 campaign managers had the audacity to say: 'I have no obligation to be honest with the media'.

Since India is also a federation, albeit the phrase used in the Constitution is 'Union of States', where does it diverge from and converge with the US? Here are some simple comparisons. During the last 73 years (that is, since 1947) India and America have each elected almost the same number of people as their prime minister or president: India 14, America 13. But in the case of India, its biggest state, Uttar Pradesh (UP), which accounts for 16.5 per cent of India's population, has supplied as many as nine of them.

Even Prime Minister Narendra Modi, who has a huge popular base in Gujarat, decided to contest the 2014 and 2019 general elections from Varanasi in UP. His political compulsions were, one, to show his all-India acceptance; and two, to represent the traditionally powerful Indian state. In contrast, America's biggest state, California, accounting for almost 12 per cent of the nation's population, has given them only two presidents: Ronald Reagan and Richard Nixon.

From an obverse perspective, two of America's smallest states, Kansas and Arkansas, each with a less than 1 per cent share of total population, have given two presidents who each completed full eight-year terms: Dwight D. Eisenhower and Bill Clinton, respectively. Now, can one imagine an Indian prime minister from a state whose share in India's population is 1 per cent or less? There are ten such states (out of a total of 28): Arunachal Pradesh, Goa, Himachal Pradesh, Manipur, Meghalaya, Mizoram, Nagaland, Sikkim, Tripura, and Uttarakhand.

Over the years there is a tendency in both the federations towards incremental centralization. The trend is more clearly visible in India, although Americans also often talk about the perils of an Imperial Presidency. The most visible evidence of this centralizing tendency in India is the recent emasculation of Article 370, which has reduced the only Muslim-majority state of Jammu & Kashmir into two non-states (two union territories). The introduction of a one-tax regime for the entire country through the Goods and Services Tax (GST) is yet another example of the same tendency.

Speaking politically, it may be noted that federalism in India got off to a healthy start under the leadership of Jawaharlal Nehru because many state leaders of the early years were themselves powerful figures, having participated in the nationalist movement shoulder to shoulder with Nehru. Stalwarts like B.G. Kher of Bombay (present Maharashtra and Gujarat), B.C. Roy of West Bengal, Sri Krishna Sinha of Bihar, Govind Ballabh Pant of UP, Gopinath Bordoloi of Assam, and many others, accepted Nehru's leadership but did not behave as his minions.

But since the days of Indira Gandhi the picture has changed. Most state leaders now are beholden to the central command and can remain in power so long as they satisfy the latter. Today, under the leadership of Prime Minister Narendra Modi, the tendency is even more visible. In our school days, too, we used to read that state governors were the watchdogs of central interest, but what has changed now is that the governors have become the watchdogs of party interest; party here meaning, of course, the party in power at the Centre. One may mention the recent roles of the Maharashtra and West Bengal governors in this regard.

One last point. Federalism is not an end in itself. Let us not forget that had America strictly followed its federal textbook there would have been no United States today. The American Civil War (1860-5) would have split the nation into two. A couple of decades prior to the event, Alexis de Tocqueville, the French traveller who wrote a magnificent commentary on contemporary America, had said: 'A nation that asks nothing of government but the maintenance of order is already a slave in the depths of its heart; it is a slave of its well-being, ready for the man who will put it in chains.'

What is in danger, therefore, whether it is America or India, is not merely federalism, but the idea of democracy itself. Mark Twain in his characteristic humour had said: 'It is by the goodness of God that in our country we have those three unspeakably precious things: freedom of speech, freedom of conscience, and the prudence never to practise either'.

Essay 5: My Dear America: The Torment of a Disillusioned Fan*

My dear America, shame on you. All democracy-loving people all over the world look up to you for guidance in democracy. You have dashed their faith to the ground, doing so beyond redemption. With a 22 trillion dollar economy, 65 thousand dollar per capita income, 99 per cent literacy, and, over and above, a huge intellectual base that includes as many as 336 Nobel Laureates, nearly thrice the number of the next in line (UK), you could not even conduct an election with dignity!

One would have pardoned you had it been unforeseen. But it was not unforeseen. Everyone across the world, including you yourself, had anticipated that it would end up in violence soon after the results were out. One of your own presidential hopefuls in the early days of the Primaries, Bernie Sanders of Democratic Party, had predicted what could be expected of President Donald Trump if he had an inkling of impending defeat. He would not wait, Sanders foretold, until the final count and would instead announce victory midway and incite his fans to go on a rampage.

Why this embarrassing charade? Do Trump and his fanatic admirers consider the White House their fiefdom which cannot be occupied by anyone else? Even the hysterical enthusiasts of victorious presidential candidate Andrew Jackson two hundred years ago knew that he was not entitled to rule perpetually. Why then

* 'My Dear America', *Dhaka Tribune*, 10 November 2020, https://www.dhakatribune.com/opinion/op-ed/2020/11/10/op-ed-my-dear-america, simultaneously carried as 'My Dear America: The Torment of a Disillusioned Fan', *Newsclick.in*, 6 November 2020, https://www.newsclick.in/My-Dear-America-Torment-Disillusioned-Fan

does this same America, which has proudly conducted peaceful presidential elections and smooth transfers of power from as early as 1789, suddenly finds itself in this cesspool?

I am personally disappointed, and I have my reasons. I was one of the first batch of Indian students to be exposed to American history at the University of Bhagalpur in Bihar in the early 1960s. To the best of my knowledge it was one of a small minority of Indian universities to have introduced American history as an optional course. Later, when I conducted research on America for my doctorate at Jawaharlal Nehru University, I realized it was part of American Cold War propaganda.

Whether or not it was part of CIA activity in India, the course exposed me to America and its history, which in turn informed my understanding of world politics during my future career. The tragic assassination of President John F. Kennedy in 1963 left a deep imprint on me as he appeared to me a young dynamic leader. My interest in America increased further. It remains the first political assassination in my living memory. About Mahatma Gandhi's assassination I had only read in books. It was during the same time that the American Embassy started publishing a monthly newspaper called *The American Reporter*, which was distributed free of cost (though each copy did carry a price sticker).

The magazine carried a regular feature space called: 'Inquiring Reporter'. Readers were invited to contribute answers to the question: 'Which American, living or dead, do you admire the most?' My choice was foreordained. My indisputable hero during those days was Thomas Jefferson. He is known today not so much as the third president of the United States but much more so as the one who drafted America's Declaration of Independence. But what impressed my impressionable mind the most was his commitment to freedom of thought. He wanted these words to be inscribed as his epitaph, inter alia: 'I have sworn on the altar of God eternal hostility against any kind of tyranny over the mind of man.' It was only later that I came to know that Jefferson was, true to his white gentry class, a significant slave owner. Not only that, he also fathered several children with his slave companion Sally Hemming, without emancipating any of them.

There was yet another aspect to my interest in America. From early childhood, the story of Columbus's accidental discovery of America had fascinated me. I dreamt that someday I would go and meet these 'Indians' (in India, the moniker 'Red Indians' remains common) to see whether there was any similarity between us. That dream, however, remained a dream until I visited America for the first time in 1975 to conduct research at the Library of Congress. While in Washington DC, I got in touch with the Bureau of Education in the US State Department to help me fulfil my dream of visiting an Indian Pueblo. I remain ever grateful to the lady officer (I can no longer recall her name) who helped organize my stay for two nights with Louis and Angi in the Yakima Valley Reservation in the state of Washington.

The most memorable event during that visit was my participation in a Yakima Indian get-together. Contrary to my childhood imagination about Indians with colourful costumes and headgears, the people I met were dressed in the most trendy and expensive fashions and extravagantly decked out with jewellery. But what I recall most is the way my farmer host, Mr Louis, dragged me to the podium and loudly declared: 'Here is the real Indian Columbus was looking for.' The assembled crowd greeted the announcement with deafening cheers. My day was made; my childhood dream culminated in this dramatic finale. After my return to India I consulted the American Library in Delhi to know more about American Indians and their tragic history. In due course, I wrote an article on them, which the leading weekly *Sunday* (Calcutta) carried in its 16 April 1978 issue under the title: 'The Other Indians'.

During the final month of my research trip to the United States, I decided to explore the country (thanks to a Greyhound unlimited travel AmeriPass). In those days there used to be so-called 'hospitality centers' in almost every small or big town where Americans could voluntarily register themselves as hosts to young foreigners. The latter were picked up from the local bus or rail station, or airport, taken for a free tour of the town and its neighbourhood, concluding with a lunch or dinner at the host's home. I cannot remember how many American homes I visited this way during that month of crisscrossing the vast United States. It was not the days of Internet otherwise I would have kept in touch with the many lovely American families I met.

Therefore, it pains me when I see the aspects of America I love collapsing in front of my eyes. Americans need not be reminded that their country continues to exercise a massive influence on global norms of orderly life (in many ways this is separate from and does not let the US off the hook for poking its dirty nose in every nook and cranny of the world). If American democracy stumbles, that day is not far when most fledgling democracies in vast parts of the developing world will collapse like the proverbial pack of cards.

As a non-American I have no business to advise Americans but certain things defy anyone's common sense. I am not even arguing that only popular votes should matter and that the Electoral College is anachronistic. I have enough reason to argue (see pp. 182-7) that in modified form it is perhaps the best guarantee for America's federal model. And yet, I cannot believe that such an intelligent nation could be so naïve about setting its electoral house in order. Whoever wins the presidency, the first task on the agenda of Congress should be to elect a bipartisan committee to go threadbare into all that plagues the American election system, debate the report word by word, and pass the final document latest by the year end. Let that be the 2022 New Year's gift to the nation.

CHAPTER 9

South Asia in Perspective: Some Memories, Some Reflections

CHILDHOOD RECOLLECTIONS

I am as old as the decolonization of South Asia. In other words, my personal experience and that of the region are coterminous. It would make sense, therefore, to write this epilogue to this book in a semi-autobiographical mode. Of my childhood memories, one of the most distinct ones is the pile of broken bricks heaped at one corner of the terrace of our two-storeyed Bhagalpur (Bihar) house. We grew up with the knowledge that these brickbats had been kept handy in case our safety was threatened by the potential Muslim rioters. In the background of the sanguinary Partition riots such anxieties were not completely imaginary, although none of our family members were ever exposed to those riots either in undivided or in divided Bengal. In the aftermath of the 1857 anti-British revolt our family had migrated to Bhagalpur from the present-day Hooghly district of West Bengal essentially in search of greener pastures. Since both Bengal and Bihar were then in Calcutta Presidency this movement of our family was not migration in today's definitional sense of the term but it was just a change of residence. In any case, Bhagalpur had not experienced any communal riot in the wake of Partition as some other areas of the two provinces had.

Another story etched in my memory from those days is in a sense a dark comedy. The story is so relevant in the context of contemporary South Asia. I was told by my mother that her husband, who was otherwise not communally minded, was a staunch enthusiast of the Hindu Mahasabha (established in 1915), which was the precursor of the currently triumphant Rashtriya Swayamsevak

Sangh (RSS) that came into being in 1925. The latter gave birth to the Bharatiya Jana Sangh in 1951 which evolved into the Bharatiya Janata Party (BJP) in 1980, the party which has been ruling India since 2014. Because of his ideological mooring my father was animated, even vocally, by the news that Mahatma Gandhi had been assassinated. So much was his elation that the local police, which was then on a drive to round up all those who were sympathetic to Hindu Mahasabha or RSS, had contemplated to pick him up for internment. But for the timely intervention of his Rajput friend and neighbour, Yogendra Singh, who was a member of the District Congress Committee, this extroverted middle class Bengali *bhadralok* would have landed himself in jail. I often shudder to visualize what could have happened to my foodie father in the jail as he could barely survive even for a single day without a sumptuous non-vegetarian meal.

It was in those early years of my life that I had nurtured two dreams, one, to visit an American Indian pueblo just because I used to romantically (though falsely) associate myself with the Red (American) Indians of America, and two, to drive through the Khyber Pass in an open hood jeep to enter into Afghanistan. In subsequent years my first dream was fulfilled as I could spend a couple of nights with a Yakima Valley Indian farming family and enjoy its hospitality (see, pp. 189-90). But my second dream seemed to be permanently shattered by the Soviet invasion of Afghanistan in 1979 and the subsequent civil war that refuses to come to an end. Even after the withdrawal of the United States from the battlefield return of peace remains elusive. Although nothing is predictable in international politics and, who knows, I may still visit Afghanistan via the Khyber Pass route someday but that seems rather unlikely. In the meantime, however, I have tried to compensate for my unfulfilled dream by maintaining an active friendship with my Afghan friend from my JNU days of the early 1970s, who is now settled in America with his Afghan refugee wife. I have visited his family several times.

Barring Afghanistan, however, I have visited all the remaining six South Asian nations a multiple times and whenever I am on those soils I have to constantly alert myself that I am not in some other part of India. The reflexes of the people in all these places are so identical to those of us Indians in various parts of the country that there is nothing un-Indian that can be associated with them. To view it from an opposite perspective they too must not have found in me anything alien either, myself being just another person from somewhere in their own country. The language problem is a reality, leave alone across South Asia which is expected, but also within each South Asian country barring Bangladesh where all speak Bengali (although the tiny community of the Chakmas claims that it is not Bengali-speaking) and Maldives where all speak Divehi, which is closer to Sinhalese. My interactions with cross-sections of people in the region have taught me much more about South Asian consciousness than volumes of academic literature that I have read on South Asian regionalism.

The Partition of India was a massive tragedy, a debilitating one, the trauma of which the region is still struggling to rid itself of. It unfolded in just seven years, from 1940, when the Muslim League passed its Pakistan resolution in its Lahore Session, to 1947, when British India was partitioned into two nations—India and Pakistan. But the Partition could hardly enter into the common man's consciousness at least for another eight-nine years if I can recall certain things from my schooldays in mid-1950s. Although the stories of Hindu-Muslim riots that took place before and after Partition were still in circulation, the geographical ramifications of the vivisection of the Indian nation were hardly understood by the common man. Let me recount our map-drawing experience in our geography class in the school.

I very well remember that the political map of India that we used to draw would invariably include West Pakistan (I cannot remember what used to happen with East Pakistan). The easiest clue to start the exercise was to draw that part of undivided India which constituted the Baluchistan province of West Pakistan. It was something like a horizontal M letter of English, like this: Σ. Indeed India had been divided but for young pupils in Bihar like me (may be in other parts of India as well) it had little meaning. Those friends of ours who hailed from Pakur, a place close to Bihar-East Pakistan border, used to enlighten us about the institution of '*gardaniya* (*gardan* means neck in Hindi) passport'. It connoted the system of illegal yet regular border-crossing of daily agricultural wagers under the nose of the border guards of both countries on the payment of very small bribes. In my later life when I got into more serious academic research on migration I came to know that until the 1965 India-Pakistan war border crossing was so much easier. It was only after that war that border regulations were strictly enforced; not that all illegal crossings stopped but the legal risks and the rates of the bribe became bigger.

It was a common sight in the 1950s to spot Pathans/Afghans routinely roaming on the Indian streets as small hawkers selling dry fruits, used clothes, and doling out petty loans to the needy. The bond between India and Afghanistan is umbilical though the current strategic thinking refuses to recognize that. While Indians with a myopic knowledge of the past, who tend to know only of Khan Abdul Ghaffar Khan, the so-called 'Frontier Gandhi' of NWFP (now called Khyber Pakhtoonkhwa), the man who steadfastly stood for the Gandhian ethos of India's freedom struggle in which there was no room for imagining India in Hindu-Muslim terms,[1] Indians with a deeper sense of history cannot help but recount the fact that the Turko-Afghans, and subsequently the Mughals, who all became a part and parcel of Indian history and to whom India's composite culture owes so much, belonged to the extended Afghanistan-Central Asian region. Zahiruddin Mohammad Babur who laid the foundation of the powerful Mughal dynasty in 1526 had prior to his Indian adventure consolidated his position in Kabul and Kandahar. During the British Indian period, when the imperial interests of Britain and Russia and the national interest of Iran clashed in Afghanistan leading to several wars in the name of the 'great game', they could hardly rupture the social and cultural ties between the Indians and Afghans.

In his famous short story, *Kabuliwala*, Rabindranath Tagore has immortalized the proverbial simplicity of the Afghans. Through the character of Rahmat Ali Tagore has portrayed the innocence of the Pathans coupled with their ruggedness that did not stomach any nonsense when it was a matter of their honour. Rahmat's penchant to return to his motherland to reunite with his little daughter exemplified the pathos of any lonely father in a forlorn land. *Kabuliwala* became the theme of several Indian movies the most famous being the one in Hindi produced by Bimal Roy in 1961. In one of its songs one can feel the reverberation of the wistfulness of these *kabuliwalas* to return to their *watan* (motherland). No wonder that the movie was a hit in Kabul. These three things, that is, an inherent simplicity, the physical ruggedness, and an uncompromising sense of honour, are what Pathans/Pashtuns are made of and this is what the global actors operating in Afghanistan must come to terms with. Lately Americans have learnt it the hard way, which the Russians did earlier. This is the quintessence of the enigma called Afghanistan. Even India could not appreciate this dynamic enough when it supported the 1979 Soviet invasion of Afghanistan in the initial stages of course to realize its mistake soon.

Not directly connected to my own childhood experience, but in the context of 1950s Sri Lanka (then Ceylon), yet another contemporary story may as well be of interest. It was as late as 1955-6 that the Ceylonese people in general did not know that their British masters were no longer in power since February 1948. So much so that the Union Jack (flag of the United Kingdom) continued to flutter in many government offices in smaller towns. Also of interest to recall here is that when Hindi film songs were banned on the All India Radio (AIR) in 1952 they were openly broadcast from Radio Ceylon. It is tragic that the decision in the process deprived so many Indians of what future music historians would call the 'Golden Age' of Hindi film music. It was a boon in disguise though for the Bombay film music. The Radio Ceylon had a powerful transmitter which could cater to the Indian and other audiences in terms of better sound quality. Radio Ceylon's popularity was juxtaposed by AIR's virtual relegation to a nonentity. India realized its mistake but not before 1957. In that year it came out with its Vividh Bharati version of the Radio Ceylon which soon picked up. It succeeded also because in the meantime Sri Lankan (Sinhalese) cultural nationalism had started discouraging anything foreign to be broadcast from the country's soil which prominently included Hindi film songs.

TOWARDS KNOWING SOUTH ASIA

Academically my interest on South Asia as a region was not spontaneous. My first love was American history, maybe my romantic childhood image of American Indians about which I have mentioned above was too deeply etched on my mind. The influence of my favourite teachers in my college days also probably contributed to this choice. Sixties was the decade when the Cold War was quite hot and America was spending millions of dollars (also Indian rupees, thanks to the PL 480 bonanza in the wake of India's food crisis from which India was salvaged by huge wheat imports from America for which payments were allowed to be made in Indian currency) to promote American studies in India. It was against this background that American history as an option was made available to BA (Honours) and MA History students in my alma mater, the University of Bhagalpur (now Tilka Majhi Bhagalpur University). In later years when I did some research on the growth of Area Studies in India I came to know how this introduction of American history in the university course structure was not an academic decision but was engineered by American public diplomacy.

Probably it was for this reason that the Indian Communists, and even some sections of the Congress party, were critical of this development. Some Bihar Legislative Assembly members, mostly belonging to the Communist Party of India (CPI), raised questions about the decision of the University of Bhagalpur to introduce American history at the undergraduate and postgraduate levels. They accused Professor Panchanand Misra, the head of the department of history, as 'a CIA agent'. In 1969, when the annual American History Congress was held in the Banaras Hindu University in Varanasi, immediately after the conclusion of the Indian History Congress, in which the same professor had presided, a large number of leaflets were distributed with the aforesaid accusation that Misra was a 'CIA agent'. The protest, however, petered out in due course and American history continued to be taught in Bhagalpur, which eventually awarded PhD degrees also in the subject. I myself ended up with a PhD degree in American Studies from Delhi's

Jawaharlal Nehru University (JNU) from its School of International Studies.

My migration from American studies to South Asian studies, however, was purely in keeping with my career prospects. From late 1970s onwards South Asian regionalism was mooted as a vehicle of progress for the region. The brain behind this idea was Ziaur Rahman of Bangladesh who floated the idea of South Asian Regional Cooperation (SARC) which was eventually institutionalized as SAARC in 1985 in its first summit in Dhaka in 1985 (see pp. 161-2). It was against this background that I got my first permanent job as an Assistant Director of the Indian Council of Social Science Research (ICSSR) in 1978 to realize before long that I would have to say good bye to my first love, American studies. Since ICSSR essentially catered to the social science research needs of India the maximum that I could keep my academic interest alive with was by researching on Indian politics and its connections with India's foreign policy. It proved to be a foresighted switch.

My official entry into South Asian studies happened when I received the prestigious Humboldt Fellowship of Germany to work on South Asian regionalism as a post-doctoral fellow in the South Asia Institute of the Heidelberg University. Professor Dietmar Rothermund, professor of Indian history in the institute and also its director for long years, and who was my host, has devoted a chapter in his last publication on why he had sponsored my application to the Alexander von Humboldt Foundation for the fellowship. He wrote: 'While working with me at the South Asia Institute, Heidelberg, he concentrated on the prospects of regional cooperation in South Asia. . . . He completed an excellent book *Cooperation and Conflict in South Asia*. It was included in our institute's South Asia series published by Manohar, New Delhi, in 1989' (Dietmar Rothermund, *My Encounters in India*, New Delhi: Primus Books, 2020, pp. 147-8).

Ever since my sojourn to the South Asia Institute in 1985-6 I did not have to look back. Not only that I became a confirmed student of South Asian affairs but also a champion of South Asian regionalism not in the sense the governments wanted it to be but through the eyes of the common man of the region. I think an average South Asian would also love to see it that way—through social bonding for which the biggest hurdle to be crossed is majoritarianism that has become the reality in each of the South Asian nation in some form or the other. In India it finds expression through Hindutva, in Pakistan through Sunni Muslim highhandedness, in Bangladesh through Islamic one-upmanship, in Sri Lanka through Sinhalese chauvinism, and in Afghanistan through Pashtun supremacism. The stories of Nepal and Bhutan are more nuanced but essentially the same. In Nepal though its Nepali nationalism vis-à-vis India's 'big-brotherly' approach appears to be the dominant political narrative, at the subcutaneous level it is the Bahun-Chhetri political dominance which is the overriding reality. In Bhutan it is the case of Ngalong dominance vis-à-vis Sharchops and ethnic Nepalis though it is only the latter about which people talk about. Maldives does not have to worry on this count as it is 100 per cent Sunni Muslim country and if any Maldivian marries a non-Sunni, including Shia Muslim, while abroad s/he is not allowed to return to Maldives.

SOUTH ASIA AS AREA STUDIES

Area Studies as a field of social science research is one of the least discussed themes of higher education in all of South Asia. Though I am not an expert on higher education, I am tempted to write on the subject thanks to the justification I owe to Albert Einstein. In his characteristic humour he had once said: An expert is 'someone who knows more and more about less and less until he knows everything about nothing'. My situation is slightly better. I know something on the subject partly because of my basic grounding in International Relations (IR) research and partly because of my five decades of experience first as a functionary in the ICSSR and then as a faculty in JNU. My stay at the ICSSR had given me an exposure to Indian academic politics, which is as important for understanding the country's higher education priorities as what is promoted in the name of relevance and national interest.

Area Studies as a concept grew in the United States of America in the aftermath of the Second World War. One may argue that even prior to that there were people engaged in research on other countries. For example, many colonial scholars were involved in understanding the so-called native societies. Social and physical anthropologists were interested in Africa because the tribal cultures and tribal physical features interested them. Similarly, the Muslim West Asia and the Hindu India led to serious scholarly pursuits by Western Arabists and Indologists. The contribution of British, German and French scholars in these fields was enormous. It was primarily through their efforts that the Orient was introduced to the Occident. Take, for example, the enormous contribution made by Max Müeller, the German scholar who was in the British imperial service, in translating the Indian classical texts from Sanskrit to English. He made the world aware of 'the wonder that was India', to borrow A.L. Basham's phrase.

Some scholars have argued that the origin of Area Studies lay in 'Orientalism'. According to the celebrated Palestinian-American scholar Edward Said, the 'Orientalism' of the West was essentially meant to promote the interests of the colonial powers through domination and restructuring of the Orient. But let us not enter into this intricate debate here. The dominant view, to which I also subscribe, is that most of the Orientalists pursued their professions purely as academic vocations for the sake of knowledge and curiosity without any ulterior motive. If there was any connection between their efforts and specific state policies it was either coincidental or because the rulers took advantage of the knowledge system, which they did not necessarily create or influence.

In the development of Area Studies in the West, particularly in the United States, the event that played the most catalytic role was the Cold War. Hence the study of the Soviet Union first, and then China, became most important. Keeping this theory and experience in mind one would expect that within South Asia, India and Pakistan would develop their own world class centres of knowledge on Pakistan and India, respectively. But nothing of that sort happened. To put our discussion in perspective my explanation about this Indian neglect may be helpful.

Area Studies had a peculiar beginning in India, where India's immediate neighbours were virtually ignored. For Nehru's India the entire world mattered, in which India's neighbours were at best mere appendices. The Indian Council of World Affairs (ICWA) was established four years prior to India's Independence, in 1943, but it had a global agenda. Even the Asian Relations Conference held from 23 March to 2 April 1947, less than five months prior to Independence, was advertised by Nehru as a larger Asian initiative well beyond India's neighbouring nations, of course Pakistan was a part of India at that time. It was more in keeping with developments in South-East Asia. The Colombo Plan (July 1950) in any case was a Commonwealth initiative that primarily focused against spread of Communism in the South-East Asian region.

In 1955, as an offshoot of ICWA, the first academic institution concentrating on International Relations was launched. Strangely, this specifically devoted school, called Indian School of International Studies (ISIS), conspicuously ignored South Asia, although it had as many as eight departments, namely, International Politics and Organisation (including European Studies), International Law, International Economics, South-East Asian Studies, West Asian Studies, American Studies, Russian Studies and Commonwealth Studies. One may argue that Pakistan (then including Bangladesh) and Sri Lanka (then Ceylon) studies were subsumed in Commonwealth Studies but that is a lame explanation. Besides, a China Studies department and an African Studies department were opened in the University of Delhi. The latter was more due to Nehru's personal interest to help a particular British friend. Hardly any academic justification was supplied otherwise.

Why this academic neglect of South Asia to start with? I have two explanations. One, for Nehru Pakistan was a bad dream which at best be ignored for otherwise it could vitiate the delicate Hindu-Muslim relationship in India, particularly against the background of massive violence and displacement that Partition had caused. Parenthetically, it may be noted that the then Indian government-produced Films Division documentaries ignored Pakistan and Partition altogether. During the first two decades of India's Independence as many as 1,742 such documentaries were produced but none of them talked about Partition, naturally, therefore, about Pakistan (which is a daily recipe now). Their emphasis was on the symbols of modernism—massive developmental projects and public service schemes in the fields of education, health and social welfare. Two, though a foreign policy enthusiast Nehru's emphasis in Indian politics was primarily on development as reflected in his regular letters to the chief ministers (compiled and edited in four fat volumes by G. Parthasarathi).

I want to add here a note which may particularly interest all those in South Asia who think India suffers from a big brotherly attitude to the detriment of regionalism. It refers to the launching of Heidelberg University's South Asia Institute on 23 May 1962. In an article published in *India Quarterly* recently Dietmar Rothermund wrote:

> At the time when the Rourkela plant was built, the shortage of specialised engineers was a pressing problem in India and with German aid one of the new Indian Institutes of Technology was established in Madras (Chennai) in 1959. This period of very active German interest in India also witnessed the establishment of several branches of the Goethe Institute which in India are called Max Müeller Bhavans (MMBs). . . . The South Asia Institute of Heidelberg University, opened in 1962 in the presence of Nehru's sister, Vijayalakshmi Pandit, was another testimony to this German interest in India. Originally it was to be named 'Indo-Asia Institute', but President [S.] Radhakrishnan suggested the name South Asia Institute as he felt that 'Indo-Asia' was reminiscent of 'Greater India' and would be resented by India's neighbours.

It is plausible, therefore, to argue that probably the Nehruvian India's so-called lack of interest in South Asia was also dictated by the consideration that let India assume a low profile in the region lest it would be seen as a big brother, or as a bully.

The neglect of South Asian studies did not start and end with the Nehruvian period. At present there is only one specifically devoted Pakistan Studies centre which is in SIS, JNU. Some universities have toyed with the idea from time to time but no serious thinking has gone into it. But the JNU department is also a one-faculty centre and no significant research can be associated with it. There are some Indian academics who write on Pakistan but most of their publications deal with India-Pakistan relational aspects or in respect of Pakistan as a terrorist threat to India, with particular reference to its activities in Kashmir. Of course, there are some informed journalists and retired intelligence officers who watch Pakistan closely and keep writing for the press and participate in electronic media discussions.

What is discussed earlier about Pakistan is even worse in case of research on other South Asian countries. Leave alone JNU, there are a few scholars in Kolkata who research on Bangladesh and some in Tamil Nadu who do so on Sri Lanka. Because of the East Pakistani/Bangladeshi migrant questions being always domestically important some scholars in India's north-east, most prominently Assam, do work on Bangladesh but their focus is confined to the above issue alone. Nepal is studied more in Bihar, but once again primarily because of the country's Madhesi question. It may be noted that all these concerns have much to do with the respective region's cultural and geographical connections than in response to any considered thought about Area Studies development.

It may be underlined that besides the absence of conceptual clarity about the importance of Area Studies per se there are financial constrains as well. Area Studies research is an expensive proposition because engaged scholars must necessarily visit their countries of choice quite regularly which cannot be substituted by Internet information. An area to be studied needs to be frequented which individual scholars cannot afford to do without public funding. But most of the universities starve for funds to be allocated for field visits, even the so-called 'white elephant' JNU is no exception. It is noticeable that whenever there is an election in India several America's India experts land up to study the situation. How many of India's America experts can afford that luxury of watching an American presidential election. Incidentally it is the USIS, which sometime organizes such trips for Indians and others but their obvious purpose is different. They send only those who have not visited America before, even if that visit was not funded by any US agency. In South Asia only accredited journalists are allowed to cover each other's elections that too not so much in the case of India and Pakistan.

INDIA-PAKISTAN IMBROGLIO, BUT...?

During the past seven decades India and Pakistan have fought three wars (1947, 1965 and 1971), and also one in Kargil in 1999, which was almost like a war which necessitated the good offices of the United States to end the crisis because it could have gone out of hand as both countries had conducted successful nuclear tests in 1998. In 2001-2 also they were close to war when following the Pakistan-sponsored terrorist attacks on Jammu and Kashmir Assembly on 1 October 2001 and on the Indian parliament on 13 December 2001 India had amassed a huge army on the border to show India's determination to retaliate. Once again it was international backdoor diplomacy that helped the temper to cool down. It may be recalled here how General Yahya Khan, that villain of the 1971 Bangladesh liberation war in which Pakistan had to surrender to the India-Mukti Bahini joint command to herald the creation of Bangladesh, was prophetic about this hostile climate.

Just a few days before India's Partition on 15 August 1947, Yahya Khan, then a Major in the British Indian Army taking training at the Quetta Army Staff College, had said to his instructor Colonel S.D. Varma at the 'break-up' party: 'Sir! What are we celebrating? This should be a day of mourning. As a united country, we would have been a strong and powerful nation. Now we will be fighting one another'.[2] He might have messed up the Bangladesh situation of 1971 beyond repair but Yahya Khan was indeed prophetic. It did not even take a hundred days to prove him right. In October 1947 Indian and Pakistani armies were confronting each other in Kashmir—India's first war with Pakistan—just two months after the British left.

Between 1947 and 1965 there was some kind of an equilibrium in the India-Pakistan relationship. Barring the stalemated Kashmir conflict there was no war with Pakistan as such. On the contrary, there were some evidences of thaw as reflected in the coordinated refugee rehabilitation. Although early efforts made in 1949 did not succeed because of serious conflicts of interest between the two countries the Nehru-Liaquat pact of April 1950 succeeded to some extent. It envisaged policies to secure the return of displaced minorities and to protect and return their abandoned properties. In pursuance of these policies Minorities' Boards and Evacuee Property Management Boards were established in both West and East Bengal. In the following decade, on President Ayub Khan's personal invitation to Nehru to see the planning of Islamabad as Pakistan's new capital the latter paid a visit to Pakistan. During those days India also proposed to send Kashmiri leader Sheikh Abdullah to Pakistan as Nehru's emissary to discuss the Kashmir problem. The meeting was scheduled for June 1964 but just a few days prior to that Nehru died and the mission went into the cold storage. Curiously, within less than one year after Nehru's death, Pakistan started its second war on Kashmir in April 1965.

Subsequent deterioration in the India-Pakistan relations is too well known to be recapitulated here but the Mumbai terror attack on 28 November 2008 must be mentioned here as a landmark event. The most visible face among the terrorists was that of Ajmal Kasab who disclosed that the attackers were members of Lashkar-e-Taiba, among others. India was convinced that the attack was masterminded by Pakistan. After initial denial, on 7 January 2009, Pakistan's Information Minister Sherry Rehman officially accepted Ajmal Kasab's nationality as Pakistani. On 12 February 2009, Pakistan's Interior Minister Rehman Malik asserted that parts of the attack had been planned in Pakistan. An Indian trial court on 6 May 2010 sentenced Ajmal Kasab to death on all the 86 charges for which he was convicted. On his appeal against this verdict, the Bombay High Court on 21 February 2011 and the Supreme Court of India on 29 August 2012 upheld his death sentence. Kasab was executed by hanging at Yerwada Jail in Pune on 21 November 2012.

At present, both the states are routinely exchanging fires across the Line of Control (LOC), alleging each other of interfering in each other's internal matters, and taking adversarial positions in most international fora. Activities of Pakistan's jihadist elements on Indian soil constantly concern India, more so in the Kashmir valley. The Pakistan peace dialogue is shelved completely following Prime Minister Modi's determination not to talk till Pakistan desisted from dealing with Kashmiri separatists and engineering terrorist attacks on Indian targets.

While all these issues are discussed quite regularly in India seldom an Indian scholarly writing appears that talk about Pakistan's society and politics. But that does not mean that there is nothing to discuss which is relevant for India's policy making. Ayesha Jalal is right when she says that beyond the proverbial three A's (Allah, Army and America) there is also a fourth 'A'—the *Awam*, that is, the people. Our academic question should be, given the growing anti-Americanism in Pakistan, would the cleavage between the army and *awam* widen? More the United States tries to bail out the army of its entrapment with Islamic militancy more it exposes the army to the militants' wrath which has the potential to enlist larger popular support. Though the US military aid to Pakistan has been traditionally massive the fact is that Pakistan is forced to spend much more in tackling the Islamic militancy than America is willing to spend on that count. 'More than 40,000 terror related casualties were recorded in the decade from 2003 to 2013 while expenditure on security was triple the amount Washington paid Pakistan for military operations in Afghanistan'.[3]

The irony is that America has fattened the army to become its Frankenstein while the army has fattened the Taliban to become its Frankenstein. Now both have become the albatross around the necks of America and Pakistan army which neither is able to shake off. It is not realistic for America to break off ties with Pakistan and lean more heavily on Indian monetary and military help to rebuild Afghanistan. 'Most security experts on the region grudgingly concede that American success in Afghanistan depends on the Pakistani army. *Paradoxically, this army is the main obstacle as well as the key to peace in Afghanistan*'.[4] The recent American exit from Afghanistan is unlikely to make the region more secure. Jalal was perceptive when she wrote:

> One may be tempted to draw the analogy that just like the British left India without settling the question of princely states leading thereby to an unending conflict between India and Pakistan over Kashmir, likewise America's waning interest in Afghanistan that allows the Taliban to once again become the arbiter of Afghanistan's destiny amounts to suggest that the Americans would like to 'avoid losing a skirmish after winning a war'.[5]

These information of course are all available in the public domain. But how does a Pakistani think about India can only be understood by visiting the country and interacting with its common man with an open mind. Such impressions may not be foolproof but so is academic research. I will present here a few nuggets from my diary which may throw some light in way of our perspective building. Let me refer here to my first one-to-one talk with a Pakistani academic. It was in 1989, in Colombo, which evolved into a lasting friendship. He told me how he had met a Hindu for the first time in his life when he was 28, and that too in the United States. Before that he had all kinds of weird notions about Hindus as if they were demons with two horns (exactly his words). My image of a Pakistani was indeed not so bad because we had lived in India alongside Muslims in our day-to-day life and we knew Pakistanis were like us, although they did not like us. Moreover, a large number of Indian Muslims had migrated to Pakistan. Probably more importantly, Pakistani school texts were particularly fashioned to hate Hindus, not so much in India particularly in the early decades (things are fast changing in India too in this regard).

My first visit to Pakistan was in November 1998 as a delegate to the bi-annual convention of the Pakistan India People's Forum for Peace and Democracy (PIPFPD) held in Peshawar. I learnt my first lesson in Pakistan's regionalism, or we may say, federalism, on the breakfast table the morning after my arrival. A group of Bengali students from Kolkata was sharing my table. By eavesdropping I understood that they were just back from their visit to the Khyber Pass, my childhood dream destination (see p. 193). Since my visa did not allow me to go there I tried to know if theirs did. They said that they didn't bother about that and just hired a taxi for a return trip to the Pass. They encouraged me to do the same anytime during the day. But I lacked the necessary courage to violate the rule. At dinner the same day I was introduced to the local Member of National Assembly (MNA), a tall and handsome man in Peshawari suit. Taking advantage of the situation I expressed to him my wish as well my visa problem. His reply was revealing. If my memory allows me to paraphrase it, it was like this: Go anytime. This is Afridi region, who cares for Islamabad. Mention my name, if necessary. Probably what he meant would have worked but I lacked the guts to do anything illegal. That was the end of my dream.

My visit to the International Islamic University in Islamabad sometime in March 2002 was even more revealing. First, the background. I had a scheduled lecture in the American Studies Department of the Quaid-e-Azam University, Islamabad, during the course of which I had mentioned about the inner contradictions of politics in the South Asian nations. After my lecture someone from the audience accosted me with the request if I could address his students as well. He was in the IR faculty of the International Islamic University. He belonged to a post-Partition *muhajir* family from Lucknow which might have made him more nostalgic after listening to my talk which had some references to the post-Partition distress of such families. In response to his request I had to sensitize him to the fact that I was a Hindu and probably his university authorities would not appreciate that. He realized the sensitivity of my concern. He promised that he would get back to me in the evening after getting in touch with the vice-chancellor. He sounded exuberant when he spoke back. The vice-chancellor had agreed provided no girl student was allowed to attend my talk. He had also advised that let the senior and junior classes belonging to his subject be combined to have a larger audience.

The auditorium was packed. Probably it was a rare occasion for them to hear a Hindu professor speak. It was probably even rarer for the students from West Asian Muslim nations who formed a good number in the university. Since the infamous Gujarat communal riots had just taken place in which at least a thousand Muslims had been killed I preempted that most questions could be put in that context. Remembering what Prof. Henry Higgins had done in the Royal Ball in that great Hollywood flick, *My Fair Lady*, I started my lecture with the tragedy itself. Without mincing words I told that just prior to the riots there was the Godhra train massacre in which 59 Hindu pilgrims returning from Ayodhya (where the Ram Temple was to be built) were burned to death. Given the then deteriorating Hindu-Muslim situation in the country it was assumed that the arson was engineered by Muslim extremists. That the event would trigger a Hindu backlash was elementary Indian political science. But what was not political science was that the anti-Muslim riots would continue for so many days. The ruling Narendra Modi government of Gujarat was both slow and lackadaisical in its response which allowed the Hindu rioters to have a field day. Had the government been prompt in taking action casualties would have been much less. I compared the situation with the anti-Tamil riots that had rocked Colombo in July 1983. President Junius Jayewardene was similarly late (allegedly deliberately) in taking action thereby giving the Sinhalese rioters full four days to unleash their anti-Tamil pogrom.[6]

What was most revealing was the lively discussion on the failures of states, both India and Pakistan, on so many fronts, most prominently on the sectarian issues. My lecture, along with the question and answer session, which was to last for 90 minutes continued well into the evening till almost 9 p.m. I have never experienced such a responsive audience. I was forced to accompany them to their student *dhaba* (common man's eateries popular in north India and Pakistan) to share with them their famous *samosas* (local snacks). I realized that given chance South Asian youth can be so constructive and accommodative in their thoughts. Yet another significant experience. Sometime during my talk there was a mild bell which I was told a call for the evening *namaz*. I was almost postponing my talk when my host advised me to carry on. Maximum about 10 to 15 students left (only to return after their prayer) and the remaining did not leave. I thought if this could happen in an Islamic University it must be the same everywhere in Pakistan, another incorrect notion about all Muslims held by non-Muslims almost everywhere that they all read *namaz* five times.

The vibrancy of Pakistani society is noticeable to any visitor. Before I end this section a casual impression I got from average Pakistanis on the Kashmir question may be recorded. In day-to-day conversations Kashmir seldom figures. The type of people I interact will mention about it more in jocular terms. My impression is that they have reconciled themselves to the reality that the present status-quo would continue and it is their day dream to imagine that the entire Jammu and Kashmir would be theirs someday. It is probably the mirror image of India; Indians too dream about getting back the POK someday. The idea that Pakistan is a failed state is also probably stretched too far. One does not come across any such symptom once one lands in Pakistan and moves across places freely. It is good that my impression was vindicated when I heard the German scholar Wolfgang Peter Zingel talking on the theme in his lecture: 'The political economy of a failing (?) state', hosted by the Jamia Millia Islamia, New Delhi, on 26 February 2015.[7] I have not, however, come across a single Indian study addressing the question in a scholarly way though in many seminars in India we hear commentators speaking about it as if it is a self-evident truth.[8]

What I am trying to argue is that this kind of experience about each other is vital for understanding our region which the governments are determined to prevent. Even a strategically harmless topic like personal law debate in South Asia alerts the states not to allow field trips for data collection. My three applications were rejected by Pakistan High Commission in Delhi in this regard (best way of saying 'no' is to sit on the application indefinitely). Ultimately my Lahore-based friend came to my rescue by inviting me for a seminar and helping me get a visa for five additional days. Even that tiny visit was so helpful which allowed me to meet some firebrand women activists and discuss the gender unequal legal situation obtaining in the country from which many women suffered.[9] My one question to all South Asian regimes is to spell out what they gain by preventing academic research on such innocent themes while allowing similar research requests from American or European academics. And then we complain that these Western scholars do better research than us South Asians.

What I have written about Pakistani society is largely true for almost entire South Asia, barring probably Bhutan (except Nepali-majority southern Bhutan) and Maldives (where intellectualism is limited). Since I have not visited Afghanistan I cannot say much first hand. In Bangladesh I was puzzled to see so much of open criticism of the government of Hossain Mohammad Ershad at the height of his dictatorship. Sometime in December 1989, in a public meeting organized by the Bangladesh *Ain Parishad* (Law Council) in which about 600 people were present, I heard one speaker after another attacking the government in harshest Bengali. I returned from the meeting with the impression that if this could happen in an authoritarian regime its days were numbered. Within one year Ershad lost his authority.

INDIA AT THE CROSSROADS

Most South Asian states are beholden to India because of its size, population and economic strength. Pakistan is a notable exception. But so far as an average South Asian is concerned, including Pakistani, he is beholden to India more because of its secularism, federalism and its overall social inclusiveness. Many years ago an eminent Sri Lanka Tamil scholar had told me how important India's secularism was for the region's social equilibrium. If India faltered on this count the entire region would shake, he had cautioned. At that time I did not realize the value of that statement but now I know since India is visibly drifting away from its path in the name of an ascendant Hindutva the *bête noire* of which is India's Muslim community. That it will impact the South Asian social equilibrium before long as four out of eight regional states are Muslim-majority is elementary international relations. There is still time probably to arrest the descent. There are two reasons not to lose hope, one, India's secular constitution, and two, its deeply rooted tradition of coexistence among all kinds of faiths and communities the current downslide notwithstanding.[10]

In India we are living in interesting times. These are titbits collected from my old files. A Deobandi *madrasa*-trained *maulana* coached by an RSS-run training centre makes it to the central civil services exam; a Pakistani rock band, Junoon, performs in Srinagar obviously with Indian visa generally denied to even university professors; Priyanka Gandhi, Rajiv Gandhi's daughter, meets her father's killer in a Chennai jail, a move praised by Asif Zardari, former president of Pakistan, as a fine example of reconciliation; an omnipotent CPM in Bengal gets a beating in rural Nandigram and Singur for being a champion of capitalism and globalization which the party has traditionally abhorred; the Gurjars of Rajasthan, identified under the Other Backward Classes (OBC) list as a Hindu caste, is asking for tribal status (one has heard of tribes metamorphosing into castes but not the other way round); an 'untouchable' BJP wins in the 'out-of-bounds' south India; the same BJP which opposed the India-US nuclear deal and attacked the Congress for signing this 'terrible deal' is now posing to be the greatest pal of America; Pakistani *ghazal* maestro Ghulam Ali plays in the prestigious musical event at Varanasi's Sankat Mochan Temple (Hanuman Temple) in April 2015 and Modi regrets that he could not make it because of his other engagements otherwise he would have loved to, as he is a great fan of the singer; the list is unending. Contrast this with the ban on Indian artistes to perform in Pakistan. Mercifully the internet gives a damn to such government bans anywhere in the world (in China and North Korea there are of course firewalls to prevent free passage of internet signals).

Do all these apparently disconnected headlines point to any bigger picture? Howsoever noisy and tumultuous Indian democracy may appear it is vibrant all the same which is rooted in its history. India's secular tradition is millennia old. It was as early as in 52 CE that St. Thomas had arrived in Kerala (in the extreme south of India) thus marking the beginning of Christianity in the country. Similarly, Islam also came to Kerala well before it came to Sind through Mohammad bin Qasim. Kerala's Muslims are descendants of some of the earliest converts to the religion on the subcontinent. The earliest mosque in the subcontinent is in Kerala. About Sikhism the following passage is enlightening:

> *Guru Granth Sahib* contains 5,894 *shabads* (hymns) that include 938 shabads from non-Sikh saints, sufis, and disciples all across India. These saints, in addition to Punjab, lived in what are today Sindh, Bengal, Uttar Pradesh, Maharashtra, Gujarat, and Rajasthan. In addition to being spread out geographically, they spoke different languages and belonged to different castes. But their message and principles conveyed the unity of society under one God. Some of these saints are: Jaidev from Bengal, Bhagat Sain from Madhya Pradesh, Sheikh Farid, Baba Sundar, Bhagat Ravidas, Balwand and Satta, from Punjab, Trilochan, and Namdev from Maharashtra, Bhagat Dhanna and Raja Pipaji from Rajasthan, Bhagat Ramanand, Kabir, Bhagat Parmanand, Pir Bhikham Shah, and Bhagat Surdas from Uttar Pradesh, and Bhagat Sadhana from Sindh.

Thus, there are many non-Sikhs who worship Guru Nanak spread across Hindu communities in Punjab, Sindha and Kutch. These communities are today spread across the world.[11]

No wonder that religion is so deep-rooted in South Asian politics, which even Mahatma Gandhi had to underline. Here are two quotations form Gandhi and Sir Mohammad Iqbal which would vindicate the point. On 12 May 1920, Gandhi wrote in *Young India*:

> The politician in me has never dominated a single decision of mine, and if I take part in politics, it is only because politics encircle us today like the coil of a snake, from which one cannot go out, no matter how much one tries. In order to wrestle with this snake, I have been experimenting with myself and my friends in politics by introducing religion into politics.

Similarly, Iqbal in his Presidential Address delivered on 29 December 1930 at the All India Muslim League at Allahabad, said: 'One lesson I have learnt from the history of Muslims. At critical moments in their history it is Islam that has saved Muslims and not vice versa.'[12]

Even RSS, leading the Hindutva forces now, tends to realize this the hard way. Lately, it has been trying to woo the Muslims. Mohan Bhagwat says Hindutva minus Muslims has no meaning and the RSS General Secretary Krishna Gopal has said that had Dara Shukoh come to power instead of Aurangzeb the Hindu-Muslim relations would have taken an altogether different shape. The idea is to create a binary between 'good Muslims' and 'bad Muslims'. It is, however, too simplistic to see the power struggle between those two brothers from just the prism of religion which was merely one factor that too not the critical one. Identity formation happened much later, in the mid eighteenth century. Professor Harbans Mukhia, an authority on medieval India, said in an interview to the online portal *Newsclick* on 21 September 2019 that there was a clear line-up of political forces. There were 24 *mansabdars* who were with Dara Shukoh while 21 with Aurangzeb. But the latter included two powerful Rajput *mansabdars*, Jai Singh and Jaswant Singh. The rest is history.

Traditional societies, which include India, have a peculiar relationship with God. I am not too sure whether it is true for the modern societies as well, but quite sure it is so, and in an extended sense it applies to the entire South Asian region at least. Here are two stories to narrate. One was told to me by my ICSSR colleague, Dr. Arun Bali. Once he was travelling by bus near his hometown in Belgaon on the Karnataka-Maharashtra border. There was a scuffle between the conductor and a passenger about the return of change after the purchase of ticket. When the fight was turning violent the driver suddenly stopped the bus near a village temple and made the quarrelling duo to submit to the deity to tell the truth. But in no time the passenger melted into the thin air not to be traced. Evidently the conductor was right. The second story is similarly interesting. In Jogishwar Singh's doctoral thesis (Heidelberg University) he has mentioned about the unwritten God's witness in sanctifying village level loans even in present day Himachal Pradesh.[13]

ELEPHANT IN THE ROOM

South Asia's interstate reality cannot be understood without reference to China though it is not a part of the region as per IR literature. China is now the world's second largest economy and South Asia is one of the poorest regions of the world. China's moneybag, therefore, matters to each of the regional states, more particularly the smaller ones, which are beholden to China to get some of their infrastructure projects financed by it which the Chinese are too willing to oblige. Since India considers these nations to be belonging to its courtyard mutual suspicion and rivalry are inevitable. But the problem is that when India tries to convince its neighbours about China's ulterior motives to tangle them into perpetual debt traps they point out that the same is largely true of India in relation to China. India, which claims to be standing at the gate of the great power club, has made China its biggest trading partner, a position that the United States was holding till recently.

In terms of the respective size of their economies India is way behind China. China's GDP is more than five times that of India, \$15.2 trillion and \$2.6 trillion, respectively. In the IT sector which is going to determine national power in the foreseeable future India is once again no match to China although we have been hearing India emerging as the global IT leader and Bengaluru the IT capital of the world. The reality is quite otherwise. In 2017, of the 10 biggest Internet companies in the world in revenue terms four belonged to China, namely, JD.com and Alibaba, Tencent, WeChat and Baidu. India's Flipkart could manage to figure among the first 25. In 2019, the Baidu search commanded 850 million active mobile users. Such Chinese companies like Huawei, Lenovo, Xiaomi and Tencent have acquired huge global presence.[14]

India-China relations have entered into a difficult phase lately and its reverberations will be felt in the international system and certainly in the South Asian subsystem (see pp. 137-48, 158-9). If not anything, India's image has gone for a toss within the region and all of India's neighbours must be busy recalibrating their equations with both these Asian giants. Without going into the details of this unfolding complication two competing realities may be underlined. On the one hand, India views Pakistan and China as its enemies and is systematically coming closer to America to work out a balance. On the other hand, China considers America as its enemy and competitor for world dominance. China does not consider India to be worthy to be called a competitor. It views India as an impediment to China's territorial ambitions in the region. China has a historical notion about its boundary which India, as the inheritor of the Curzonian notion of imperial India, is not willing to concede. The boundary dispute, therefore, is real and a permanent thorn in the India-China equation.

One can see how much they differ on the point by just analysing the respective lengths of the border that they recognize. For India it is 3,488 km but for China it is merely 2,000 km. Neither the Aksai Chin area of Ladakh which China has occupied during its war with India in 1962 nor the POK, a legacy of the India-Pakistan war over Kashmir in 1947, figure in the Chinese calculations. They are history according to China, but not for India, which is committed to recover them as legitimate territory someday. The border dispute is a permanent pain in the neck for India which the 1993 agreement on maintaining peace and tranquillity, the 1996 agreement on confidence building measures, the 2005 agreement on the political parameters and guiding principles to settle the dispute, and the 2013 agreement on border defecne cooperation have failed to palliate.[15] Ever since China's intrusion into India's territory in the summer of 2020 and continued Chinese occupation of thousands of kilometers of India's land both the nations are engaged in an unending negotiation which India's External Affairs Minister, S. Jaishankar, thinks might carry on for decades.[16] No one knows at the end of the talks, if at all they meaningfully end, what will happen.

In way of perspective building it may be said that India and China have certain basic similarities as well as basic differences. Without understanding them our knowledge about the deeper problem will be incomplete. Whether that will solve the border question is indeed another matter. Both the nations bask in their nostalgic glory of a great past. Also they have their relative superiority complex in relation to their neighbours and, over and above, they think that they are peace loving nations and if they are forced to take arms against any other nation it is primarily because they have been forced to do so.[17] These assumptions had converged in their mutual subscription to the Panchsheel (five virtues) in 1954.

Like the basic similarities, they have their basic differences. First and foremost is that China does not believe in Western style democracy[18] which India does as is reflected in its constitution. India is not only a democracy but its massification had started as early as in 1915 when Mahatma Gandhi, who had an earlier experience of combating Western imperialism in South Africa, made the Indian nationalist movement a people's movement by roping in all social classes through peaceful, legal and non-violent means. In contrast, the Communist Party of China (CCP) which came to power in 1949 through military victory over the Kuomintang (KMT) government, neither believed in making the state inclusive of all social classes nor through peaceful or democratic (Western style) means. Its primary challenge was from the KMT (earlier the Japanese also) which had moved to Taiwan (then Formosa) and, ideologically, all those social forces opposed to communism, which after the unfolding of the Cold War had the support of the United States.

It will be interesting to see how these fundamental differences shape up now that even within India there are forces which do not necessarily subscribe to all that the Constitution of India have steadfastly stood for.

CONCLUSION

South Asia's biggest tragedy is its ignorance about itself. More South Asians know about America or Europe than their own region. The region's middle class, which is fairly large and politically powerful, has seldom visited any South Asian country but a large section of the class has visited the West. The result is that there is monumental ignorance about one another within the region. I have often confronted people in Bangladesh who are surprised that being an Indian how I could speak Bengali so well. Evidently they are not informed enough that the language of India's West Bengal province is Bengali, leave alone that millions of Bengali-speaking Indians are scattered all over India like me who spent first half of his life in Hindi-speaking Bihar and the latter half in the multilingual capital city of Delhi where also Bengalis are in good numbers. Probably the impact of Bollywood movies is so overpowering that they think that only Hindi (actually Hindustani, a mixture of Hindi and Urdu) is spoken in India.

Similarly, I have met Pakistanis who were surprised that I spoke Urdu so well. They do not realize that what I speak is actually Hindi, not Urdu, which has evolved from Hindi.[19] In the socio-political and cultural capital of Sri Lanka Tamils, Jaffna, I have met Tamils who consider their Tamil to be more pristine and perfect than the one spoken in the Indian state of Tamil Nadu, which, according to them has been corrupted by influences from north India. The Gurkhas of north Bengal have their perennial challenge of asserting their separate identity distinct from that of the Nepalis of Nepal, an issue which became central to the Gurkha National Liberation Front (GNLF) movement in the Darjeeling district of West Bengal a few years ago.

After having researched on South Asia for decades, and after having met thousands of people from across the region, one question always haunts me: Who should decide whether South Asian regionalism should work or not, and how. Obviously the political masters decide. Since all the South Asian States are now democratic the logical conclusion should be that these governments have their respective peoples behind what they decide. But has not Gabriel Almond theorized decades ago that very often the government first takes a decision and public opinion supporting that decision is built up subsequently.[20] The phenomenon is not confined to only dictatorships and totalitarian regimes but to democracies equally. Paradoxically it is more so now when the social media is being increasingly manipulated by democratic states and their theoretically autonomous institutions.

The recent, by now famous, Netflix documentary may have focused on the American experience but it can be extrapolated to almost all democratically chosen regimes, including the South Asian. Oxford University's multidisciplinary research study called the *Global Disinformation Order* produced by the Oxford Internet Institute finds alarmingly organized media manipulation in 70 countries. The top seven countries in the list are China, India, Iran, Pakistan, Russia, Saudi Arabia and Venezuela. The study found that in 56 countries there was organized 'computational propaganda campaigns' on the Facebook.[21]

It is the tragedy of human race that whether it is Kautilya or Xun Tsu that they have come out with all kinds of statecraft techniques to organize and ensure societal order through the institution of power but common man is always at the receiving end. Yet in his name all political games are played which he habitually endorses thinking it is in his interest. I am not naive to question this well-established structure. All that I am pleading for is a small intervention that I have suggested above (pp. 165-6). Since the future of South Asian regionalism essentially hinges on India-Pakistan detente let both nations take just one small step. Keeping the second step in mind, that is, free tourist flow, let them make academic exchanges freer than what it is now. They both will fall in the category of public diplomacy in the broader sense. That will probably make it sound more respectable.

NOTES

1. In a recent newspaper article, Ramachandra Guha wrote that while visiting India in 1969, Khan Abdul Ghaffar Khan, popularly known as Badshah Khan, 'scolded us [Indians] for allowing communal violence to smoulder on in violation of the memory of the Father of the Nation. Altogether, Badshah Khan may have been *the bravest Gandhian after Gandhi*' (emphasis added) Remember that unlike other Indian Gandhians he had to live in an undemocratic and militarized Pakistan. See, 'The Twelve Apostles of Gandhi', *Hindustan Times*, 21 September 2019.
2. Shuja Nawaz, *The Battle For Pakistan: The Bitter US Friendship and a Tough Neighborhood* (New Delhi: Penguin, 2009), p. 21.
3. Ayesha Jalal, *The Struggle for Pakistan: A Muslim Homeland and Global Politics* (Cambridge, MA: Harvard University Press, 2014), p. 4.
4. Ibid., p. 5, emphasis added
5. Ibid., p. 386. Interestingly, in a talk delivered at Institute of Social Science in Delhi on 19 November 2019 Sajjad Hussain Kargil, who had fought the Lok Sabha election of 2019 for the Ladakh seat as an independent candidate with the support of both the National Conference and PDF but failed to win, it was possible to conceive that in the abolition of J&K's special status (August 1919) there was a tacit nod from the United States. Could be that India had taken the US into confidence before the move. Given the China-Pakistan strategic tie-up in the region, particularly after the opening of the Karakoram highway, and given the growing U.S. anxiety about the next real strategic contestation between America and China it was possible to argue that the former was thinking of a larger role in the region and in this India was on the same page. It was in this context that one could see the sudden Indian jingoism about taking back the POK expressed at the highest levels of India's External and Defence ministries. Is another great game in the making around post-US Afghanistan?
6. Partha S. Ghosh, *Ethnicity versus Nationalism: The Devolution Discourse in Sri Lanka* (New Delhi: Sage, 2003), pp. 98-101.
7. The lecture was not published, but became the basis for, Wolfgang Peter Zingel, 'Pakistan and its Neighbours: Assessing Economic, Ecological, Social and Political Relations', in Anasua Basu Ray Chaudhury and Vikash Kumar (eds.), *Understanding Transition in South Asia: Economy, Politics and Society—Essays in honor of Professor Partha S. Ghosh* (Gurugram: Academic Foundation Press, 2020), pp. 293-354.
8. In an email to this author, dated 19 December 2020, Wolfgang Peter Zingel wrote: 'Altogether, Pakistan's economy is more robust than generally

expected, although India, long lagging behind Pakistan for most economic and social indicators, could overtake Pakistan in the 1990s (Pakistan's 'lost decade'). In economic terms, Pakistan might be fragile, but it is neither a failing nor, certainly, a failed state. Pakistan's economy to some degree might also be judged as sustainable. Pakistan performs worse, if we look at its social indicators.'

9. Partha S. Ghosh, *Politics of Personal Law in South Asia: Identity, Nationalism and the Uniform Civil Code* (London and New York, 2018), 2nd edn., pp. 142-61.
10. After the war of 1971 there were 93,000 Pakistani POWs in India. India used to send Muslim professors from the Jamia Millia Islamiya (JMI) and Aligarh Muslim University (AMU) to teach them about India's experience with secularism and democracy. One such teacher, Dr. Refaqat Ali Khan of JMI, said to me in a conversation dated 20 July 2013 that it hardly had any impact on them as they were semiliterate. Barring saying 'thank you' they did not open their mouths.
11. Gope Ahuja, 'Nanak's Sindhi Followers: Seeking Access to Kartarpur Sahib', *Economic and Political Weekly* (Mumbai), 54(33), 17 August 2019, p. 36.
12. Both quotations are from Khalid bin Sayeed, *Pakistan: The Formative Phase* (Karachi: Pakistan Publishing House, 1960), p. xiii.
13. Rothermund, *Encounters*, pp. 249-51. For details, Jogishwar Singh, *Banks, Gods and Government: Institutional and Informal Credit Structure in a Remote and Tribal Indian District (Kinnaur, Himachal Pradesh) 1950-1985* (Stuttgart: Steiner, 1989).
14. Ananth Krishnan, *India's China Challenge: A Journey through China's Rise and What it Means for India* (Noida): HarperCollins, 2020), pp. 118-19.
15. Ibid., p. 177.
16. *The Hindu*, New Delhi, 2 December 2020.
17. Alistair Iain Johnston, 'Is Chinese Exceptionalism Undermining China's Foreign Policy Interests?', in Jennifer Rudolph and Michael Szonyi (eds.), *The China Questions: Critical Insights into a Rising Power* (Cambridge, MA: Harvard University Press, 2018), pp. 90-1.
18. Roderick MacFarquhar, 'Does Mao still Matter?', in Rudolph and Szonyi (eds.), ibid., pp. 30-2.
19. Tariq Rahman, *From Hindi to Urdu: A Social and Political History*, New Delhi: Orient BlackSwan, 2011.
20. Gabriel Almond, *The American People and Foreign Policy*, New York, 1950, p. 105.
21. A.S. Panneerselvan, 'Breaking Silos, Regaining Trust', *The Hindu*, 30 September 2019.

Author's Select Publications

Books

The Politics of Personal Law in South Asia: Identity, Nationalism and the Uniform Civil Code, 2nd edn., London/New Delhi: Routledge, 2018.

BJP and the Evolution of Hindu Nationalism: Savarkar to Vajpayee to Modi, New Delhi: Manohar, 2017, Updated Edition of my 1999 book with a changed sub-title.

Migrants, Refugees and the Stateless in South Asia, New Delhi: Sage, 2016.

Ethnicity versus Nationalism: The Devolution Discourse in Sri Lanka, New Delhi: Sage, 2003. Simultaneously published in Sri Lanka by Vijitha Yapa Publications, Colombo.

Cooperation and Conflict in South Asia, New Delhi: Manohar, 1989, rpt. in 1995. South Asian Studies No. 21 of the South Asia Institute, Heidelberg University.

Book Chapters

'Perceptions and Memories: Making Sense of Bangladesh's India Outlook', in *India and South Asia*, ed. Vishal Chandra, New Delhi: IDSA and Pentagon Press, 2015, pp. 59-69.

'South Asia's Response to its Refugee Questions', in *Politics in South Asia: Culture, Rationality and Conceptual Flow*, ed. Siegfried O. Wolf, Jivanta Schoettli, Dominik Frommherz, Kai Fuerstenberg, Marian Gallenkamp, Lion Koenig and Markus Pauli, Heidelberg: Springer, 2015, pp. 101-22.

'Internal-External Security Interface: Case Study of the India-Bangladesh Border', in *Public Security in Federal Systems*, ed. Ajay K. Mehra, New Delhi: Lancer, 2014, pp. 158-81.

'Mapping the Mixed and Massive Human Flows in South Asia: Impact of Women, the Stateless and Other Disadvantaged Groups', in *Unstable Populations, Anxious States: Mixed and Massive Human Flows in South Asia*, ed. Paula Banerjee, Kolkata: Samya, 2013, pp. 18-49.

'From Legalism to Realism in Kashmir: Internationalising the Line of Control', in *State and Foreign Policy in South Asia*, ed. Jivanta Schoettli and Siegfried O. Wolf, New Delhi: Samskriti, 2010, pp. 127- 77. (Originally published in Heidelberg Papers in South Asian and Comparative Politics, Heidelberg University), http://www.sai.uni-heidelberg.de/SAPOL/HPSACP.htm Working Paper No. 7, September 2002.

'Politics of Competing Ethnicity and Violence in India's North East', in *Violent Conflict, Terrorism and Nation-Building: National and International Responses in Sri Lanka and Other South Asian Countries*, ed. K.M. de Silva, Kandy, Sri Lanka: International Centre for Ethnic Studies, 2009, pp. 1-26.

'Country Paper: India', in *Electoral Processes and Governance in South Asia*, ed. Dushyantha Mendis, New Delhi: Sage, 2007, pp. 73-95.

'Identity, Ideology and Conflict', in *Aspects of India's International Relations 1700 to 2000: South Asia and the World*, ed. Jayanta K. Ray, being the Volume X, Part 6 of the *History of Science, Philosophy and Culture in Indian Civilization*, General Editor: D.P. Chattopadhyaya, New Delhi: Centre for Studies in Civilizations, 2007, pp. 127-72.

'Bhutan and India: Partners in Progress', in *Engagement and Development: India's Northeast and Neighbouring Countries*, ed. C. Joshua Thomas, New Delhi: Akansha, 2006, pp. 100-10.

'India in South Asia: Cooperation amidst Tensions', in *India's New Dynamics in Foreign Policy*, ed. Subrata K. Mitra and Bernd Rill, Munich: Hanns Seidel Foundation, 2006, pp. 35-50.

'Population Movements and Interstate Conflicts', in *Peace Studies: An Introduction to the Concept, Scope, and Themes*, ed. Ranabir Samaddar, New Delhi: Sage, 2004, pp. 226-53.

'The Historical and Political Background of the Conflict in Sri Lanka', in *Peace Initiatives towards Reconciliation and Nation Building in Sri Lanka: An International Perspective*, ed. Dagmar Hellmann-Rajanayagam, Kuala Lumpur: The Malaysian Ceylonese Congress, 2002, pp. 69-90.

'Cross-Border Migrations in South Asia and Regional Security', in *Explorations in the History of South Asia: Essays in Honour of Dietmar Rothermund*, ed. Georg Berkemer, Tilmann Frasch, Hermann Kulke and Juergen Luett, New Delhi: Manohar, 2001, pp. 325-36.

'Corruption in India: A Holistic Analysis', in *Principles, Power and Politics*, ed. D.D. Khanna and Gert W. Kueck, New Delhi: Macmillan, 1999, pp. 57-92.

'Bhutan: Ethnicity, Democracy and Nation-Building', in *Democratisation in South Asia: The First Fifty Years*, ed. John M. Richardson and S.W.R. de A. Samarasinghe, Kandy: International Centre for Ethnic Studies, 1998, pp. 213-37.

'Colonial Origins of Sinhala-Tamil Ethnic Conflict', in *Nation-Building in*

South Asia, vol. 2, ed. Ramakant and B.C. Upreti, New Delhi: South Asian Publishers, 1991, pp. 309-29.

'Domestic Constraints to South Asian Regionalism', in *South Asia in Transition: Regional Cooperation, Ethnic Conflict and Political Participation*, ed. Dagmar Bernstorff and Dieter Braun, New Delhi: Manohar, 1991, pp.1-24.

JOURNAL ARTICLES

'The Citizenship Amendment Act, 2019: Politics of Citizenship in India', *BEI* [Bangladesh Enterprise Institute] *Journal* (Dhaka), 3(1&2), January-July 2020, pp. 39-52.

'"Nehruvian" Cinema and Politics', *IIC Quarterly* (New Delhi), 46(2), Autumn 2019, pp. 90-9.

'Changing Frontiers: Making Deeper Sense of India-Bangladesh Relations', *South Asia Research* (New Delhi), 31(3), November 2011, pp. 195-211.

'The Elephant in the War: India and the Afghan-Pakistan Link', *Canadian Foreign Policy Journal* (Ottawa), 17(1), March 2011, pp. 50-61, co-author: Jorge Heine.

'Islamic Extremism in South Asia', *International Journal Law, Crime and Justice* (Amsterdam) (formerly, *International Journal of the Sociology of Law* [Oxford]), 36(4), 2008, pp. 286-97.

'Conservative Ascendancy in Bangladesh', *South Asian Survey*, New Delhi, 12(2), July-December 2005, pp. 247-65.

'Globalization, Hegemony and Conflict in South Asia: An Indian Perspective', *Sandhan*, Journal of the Centre for Studies in Civilizations, New Delhi, 4(1), January-June 2004, pp. 1-50.

'The Muslims, South Asia and the United States: A Post-Nine Eleven Analysis', *South Asian Survey*, New Delhi, 10(1), January-June 2003, pp. 101-23.

'Positive Discrimination in India: A Political Analysis', *Ethnic Studies Report*, Kandy, Sri Lanka, 15(2), July 1997, pp. 135-88.

'Language Policy and National Integration: The Indian Experience', *Ethnic Studies Report*, Kandy, Sri Lanka, 14(1), January 1996, pp. 49-72.

'Foreign Policy and Electoral Politics in India: Inconsequential Connection', *Asian Survey* (Berkeley), 34(9), September 1994, pp. 807-17.

'Bangladesh at the Crossroads: Religion and Politics', *Asian Survey* (Berkeley), 32(7), July 1993, pp. 697-710.

'Bhutan: Ethnicity, Democracy and Nation-Building', *Ethnic Studies Report* (Kandy), 10(2), July 1992, pp. 48-56.

'Terrorism and SAARC', *India Quarterly*, New Delhi, 43(2), 1987, pp. 121-37.

'Domestic Support for Mrs. Gandhi's Afghan Policy: Soviet Factor in Indian Politics', *Asian Survey* (Berkeley), 23(3), 1983, pp. 261-79. Co-author: Rajaram Panda.

'Domestic Sources of India's Policy of Non-Alignment', *India Quarterly*, New Delhi, 36(3-4), 1978, pp. 348-62.

ARTICLES IN OPINION MAGAZINES

'Kashmir: An Alternative Perspective', *Mainstream*, New Delhi, 33(35), 3 August 1996, pp. 11-17.

'Science versus Superstition: Reflections on the Milk Miracle', *Mainstream*, New Delhi, 33(45), 30 September 1995, pp. 5-6.

'Ram Temple Controversy: Time for Dispassionate Introspection', *Mainstream* New Delhi, 29(4), 17 November 1990, pp. 9-13.

'Kashmir Tangle and Indo-Pak Relations: Some Suggestions', *Mainstream*, New Delhi, 28(34, 35) 16, 23 June 1990, pp. 15-17 and 33-5, respectively. (In two parts.)

'Afghan Imbroglio: Solution on Whose Term?', *Mainstream* (New Delhi), 28(27), 28 April 1990, pp. 11-13.

'Afghan Accord: An Analysis', *Mainstream*, New Delhi, 26(34), 4 June 1988, pp. 20-1.

'Kashmir Politics: Some Reflections', *Mainstream*, New Delhi, 21(45), 9 July 1983, pp. 31-3 (co-author: Indra Ghosh).

'Uncertainty in Bangladesh', *Mainstream*, New Delhi, 20(30), 27 March 1982, pp. 15-16.

'Limits of Diplomacy', *Mainstream*, New Delhi, 19(52), 29 August 1981, pp. 28-30.

Index